REA

American Child

American Childhoods

JOSEPH E. ILLICK

PENN

University of Pennsylvania Press

Philadelphia

10 9 8 7 6 5 4 3 2 1

Published by
University of Pennsylvania Press
Philadelphia, Pennsylvania 19104-4011

Library of Congress Cataloging-in-Publication Data

Illick, Joseph E.
    American childhoods / Joseph E. Illick.
        p. cm.
    Includes bibliographical references (p.) and index.
    ISBN 0-8122-3659-9 (cloth : alk. paper)—ISBN 0-8122-1807-8 (pbk. : alk. paper)
    1. Children—United States—History. 2. Children—United States—Social conditions.
I. Title.

HQ792.U5 I45 2002
305.23′0973—dc21

                                                                        2001054095

For Joe, Katie, and Clara; Maia and Sarah.
And in memory of Gayle.

Contents

Preface

There is no single comprehensive text on American childhood. While materials exist for writing such a history, the matter of structuring the grand narrative remains challenging. The term "American" suggests unity, and surely at any point in time the national environment has confronted all children with common issues. But ethnic, racial, class, and regional (not to mention gender) differences have led to a diversity of experiences during childhood, and thus we must approach the topic as American childhoods.

I have attempted to capture this diversity in this structure of this book, while also recognizing the changes childhood has undergone over time. The narrative thus proceeds chronologically while focusing on particular social groups. I first address childhood among the resident American Indians, the first European immigrants, and the imported African slaves. (I begin these narratives in the seventeenth century. Since significant cultural traits, most notably among the American Indians, persisted for centuries, I follow these stories toward the present.) I then look at the newly emergent middle and working classes of the nineteenth century in the context of an industrializing society. Finally, I contrast the disparate childhoods of suburban, urban, and rural America in the context of a modern, consumption-based society.

Despite the varieties of childhood, as we enter the third millennium it appears that Americans are agreed on the primary goal of child rearing: forging an independent and competent adult from a dependent, naive child. Doesn't every good parent today want to raise autonomous progeny? However modern we are, some bit of the past always creeps into the present. Seventeenth-century Puritans, for example, were intent on breaking the will of the infant, an aim that reappears in the child-rearing literature of the religious right today. Certainly one virtue of studying the past is that it helps explain the present. (Another virtue: As we view the varieties of past childhoods, we may work up more empathy toward, or at least tolerance of, the diversity that exists today. We may even become less accepting of the poverty in which a quarter of the nation's young are living.)

Even if Mom and Dad wish to promote Junior's autonomy, they face limits. Public policy is only one of several forces outside the home (the media would have to be cited as another)—forces neither neutral nor impersonal but representing special interests—which are apt to diminish the power of parents, especially those lower in the class structure.

Undaunted, many parents wrestle with the issue of how children should be prepared for adulthood. No longer do we send seven-year-olds into the workforce, though the inclination of some parents to subject their youngsters to intensive academic toil reminds us that such an approach has not been laid to rest. It also makes us wonder whether there was ever a time of carefree childhood.

All of these items—parental practices in the past, ethnic rivalries, social forces outside the household—bear on the matter of childhood autonomy, an issue that logically arises in a modern democracy. It is of concern not solely to historians and political scientists but to psychologists as well. Freud confronted it and, later in his career, was able to muster some optimism about it. Of course, the behaviorists, given their devotion to environmental determinism, never doubted that parents could create the conditions for it—if they so desired. Erik Erikson, whose early training took place in Vienna, features autonomy as the positive counterweight to shame and doubt in the second of his eight stages in human development. And no one in the field of psychology has paid it more attention than the Scottish psychiatrist John Bowlby, who defected from orthodox psychoanalytic theory to a perspective he labeled attachment theory, the major tenet of which is that consistent attachment to a caregiver promotes autonomy.

The consideration of autonomy when dealing with childhood is appropriate in a nation which has put so much emphasis on individual freedom. Needless to say, all parents limit the liberty of children to some degree but would disagree about what manner of restraint on behavior should be exercised and for how long. Some cultures in the American past (and present) have valued independence more than others, and some cultures have possessed a surer sense than others of how to nurture it.

Yet even assuming a certain parental desire and competency with respect to fostering autonomy in youngsters, there have always been social barriers to its realization, obstacles related to gender, status and class, race and ethnicity. No one writing about American childhoods can reckon without these factors.

All of us have been children, and many of us have raised or are raising children. We cannot doubt how difficult it is to understand this stage of life, how elusive its complexities are. We try, as historians, to capture the world of the young, governed by our prejudices and hampered by the meager sources available to us. Children have left almost no records of their childhoods, so the reconstruction of the subjective experience of being a child must depend on other factors (including our own imaginations, supplemented by the psychological theories discussed above). I have hazarded thoughts about this hard-to-discover inner life, but I have tended more to discuss the circumstances that surrounded children, that created their outer life, as it were.

I have described the expressed attitudes of adults toward childhood as well as their behavior toward children, often separate matters. This evidence exists in far greater abundance than records about what children thought. Some of this evidence is inferential, as for example the correlation between high child mortality rates and adults' apparent repression of feeling toward children—or the relationship between the need for labor and children's early entrance (by our twenty-first-century standards) into the workforce. Such inferences—that parents are apt to love less the child who is more easily lost, that survival has dictated the toil of the very young—are closely related to the conditions that shaped the development of children, demographic (for example, a predominantly young population in the seventeenth and eighteenth centuries), geographic, economic (especially the class position of the child), ethnic, and gender. In other words, I am concerned throughout this book with the place of children within the whole of American society.

The subject is enormous indeed, and scholars have honestly disagreed about aspects of it. In order to present a manageable volume, I have not pursued every line of inquiry but, rather, have often referred to major studies that will enable the reader to push further in chosen directions.

Part I
Early America

American Indian Childhood

Chuka was born in Oraibi, reportedly the oldest continuously inhabited town in North America, in 1890, just before the Anglos descended on his isolated Hopi mesa. While his mother was pregnant—originally with twins, melded into one child by the medicine man—she took all precautions, such as avoiding serpent images so as not to turn her fetus into a water snake. His father took care to injure no animal, thus protecting the life of the unborn. At delivery the infant's navel cord was cut with an arrow to make him a good hunter; he was bathed in yucca suds and rubbed with juniper ashes. After his ears were pierced, he was wrapped in a blanket and placed in a bent-branch cradle padded with cedar bark, with an ear of corn on either side. An aunt simulated a house for him by applying finely ground cornmeal to the four walls of the room. Then his mother began nursing him.

Twenty days of carefully followed rituals culminated in the naming ceremony. Women from his father's side washed the room, bathed mother and child, and named the young one ("Chuka" means mud, a mix of sand and clay, to signify that although he had been born into his mother's Sun Clan, he was also part of his father's Sand Clan). At dawn, the baby was carried to the edge of the mesa and presented to the Sun god.

His first three or four months were spent flat on his back, wrapped tightly and shrouded, in the cradle, where he was fed on demand—not only milk but food chewed by the admiring relatives. He urinated any time, anywhere, but was held outside the door when he defecated. His playmates were dogs, cats, his brother, and his sister, who carried him on her back in the manner of his mother when she ground corn or went to the spring. He fondled his penis, as did his siblings and visiting adults. When he became aware of his parents' lovemaking, he was moved to another room to sleep.

Because he had been twins in the womb, and antelopes are usually born twins, he was considered special and his doings were referred to as antelope ways, especially his extraordinary climbing skills. These powers did not protect him from illness or accident, but blind old Tuvenga of the Greasewood Clan was always able to intervene with a cure. Chuka and his friends ran naked around the mesa unless warned that the newly arrived missionaries were visiting. These intruders preached that the local gods were no good, but their warnings did not end such tribal ceremonies as snake gathering. (Chuka "believed the snakes were spirit gods who brought rain and would never harm anyone with a kind heart.") Nor did those warnings prevent his grandfather from putting pinon sap on Chuka's forehead to protect him from the evil spirits that invaded Oraibi in December.

He tagged after his elders, mimicking their working and eating habits, their ways of conserving water and finding fuel, and was on his way to becoming a healer. At the age of nine, however, Chuka was sent to the new missionary school at the foot of the mesa next to the trading post, where his hair was cut and he was given a suit and renamed Max. From that point forward he lived in conflict between cultures, but he never abandoned the Hopi life.[1]

The earliest immigrants to America were *Homo sapiens* who hiked across the treeless plain—now the Bering Strait—that connected Siberia to Alaska, a distance of less than 60 miles. They came during the late Ice Age (Wisconsin glaciation) when sea levels were several hundred feet lower than they are today. Twenty thousand years ago, the harsh weather conditions and limited food supply dictated that only small bands of constantly mobile hunters, on the trail of mammoth, bison, reindeer, and musk ox, could survive. These were the original American Indians.[2]

Beginning about 15,000 years ago, the Earth's climate began to warm, melting the ice sheets that blocked the southern migration of the Indians.[3] It was only then that the Indians could move into the diverse environments of North America, a continent with greater climatic variation than any other except Asia, not to mention North America's variegated geology and topography, soils and vegetation.

It is customary to divide the Indians of North American into culture areas, each of which includes nations that, in response to the regional environment, adopted substantially the same ways of life.[4] In the course of their migrations some hunters, fishers, and foragers also became farmers. The most important agricultural innovation was the domestication of maize about 3,000 years ago. The cultivation of this soil-depleting crop led nomads to settle.

The importance of farming varied with the growing season of the settlement area. It was the dominant activity on the eastern part of the continent in the culture areas of the Northeast (from the Atlantic to the Great Lakes and from lower Canada to Illinois and North Carolina) and the Southeast (from the Atlantic to the Mississippi River). Hunting predominated elsewhere, save for some coastal areas where fishing prevailed and parts of the dry Southwest where gathering was more important. By the time the Europeans arrived (though they would not have noticed), the natives had achieved a substantial harmony between the local ecology and human subsistence.

Where farming was more intensive, settlement was more sedentary. Yet even in the farming areas, though men aided women in clearing the land, it was the women and children who did the agricultural labor—cultivating, weeding, and harvesting corn, beans, and squash; hunting and picking wild berries, fruits, and nuts—while men (and sometimes younger women) were on the hunt in the spring, early summer, and fall. The villages with their bark-covered houses were fully occupied for only part of the year. In the hunting regions, where the game was larger and journeys after it longer, the Indians remained nomadic. These native economies, seemingly primitive, supported a population of 5 to 10 million in what is now the United States and Canada.[5]

When the Europeans arrived, their demographic impact was immediate and tremendous. Indian populations were decimated by diseases such as smallpox, diphtheria, scarlet fever, and yellow fever against which they had no immunity.[6] Native lifestyles must have changed in response to such a holocaust, but we are so dependent on *post*colonization descriptions by the immigrants for our knowledge of the ways of the natives that we cannot be sure of the nature of those changes.

Our initial focus is on the natives of the culture areas in North America first affected by the European presence, those of the Northeast and Southeast, people sometimes simply referred to as the Eastern Woodland Indians.[7] True, they spoke different languages (Muskogean in the Southeast; Iroquois in the eastern Great Lakes, St. Lawrence valley, and Upper South; Siouan also in the Upper South; and Algonquian elsewhere). Places of residence varied in size from several thousand inhabitants to a few score of souls. Politically, organization ranged from democratic and libertarian to hierarchical and authoritarian.[8]

But there were also similarities, including those regarding child rearing.[9] A pregnant woman was regarded with awe. Thought to have unusual spiritual power for good or for ill, she was best avoided—though not, it seems, if she were unmarried. Then, at least among the Huron, each of her several lovers would come to her and claim the child was his. Were she married and still nursing, she might well elect for an abortion so that she could focus her attention on the infant in her arms.[10] In either case, the importance of the child was evident.

The male missionaries and traders who visited the Indians gave testimony to the prospective mother's good health during pregnancy and her painless delivery, sometimes with medicinal aid. Not that they were there to witness the birth, since the native woman either went off by herself to have her child or gave birth in the presence of her tribeswomen. But these men usually observed that the mother reentered normal life immediately.[11]

The newborn child was immediately prepared for the world. Among the Huron, according to the Jesuit priest Gabriel Sagard, the mother "pierces the ears of the child with an awl or a fish-bone and puts in the quill of feather or something else to keep the hole open, and afterwards suspends to it wampum beads or other trifles, and also hangs them around the child's neck.... There are some also who even make them swallow grease or oil as soon as they are born."[12] Most Indians immersed children at birth, the water temperature notwithstanding; some circumcised them.[13]

Sagard, noting that children played naked in the snow as well as in the hottest sun, concluded that "they become so inured to pain and toil that when they have grown up and are old and white-haired they remain always strong and vigorous, and feel hardly any discomfort or indisposition." This conditioning, he thought, even accounted for the women maintaining strength through pregnancy, giving birth easily, and recovering immediately.[14]

In reality, there was a 50 percent child mortality rate due to the rigors of Indian life, not to mention recurrent smallpox epidemics as a result of contact with Europeans. Children were born at approximately four-year intervals due to protracted breast-feeding, prohibitions on sexual relations while nursing, abortions, and even infanticide. All these factors stabilized the size of the population. Families were small by European standards; three or four children appears to have been the average.[15]

It was common to name a child at birth, possibly from a supply of names available to the clan, or in response to an event of the day or the appearance of the child, or after an animate or inanimate object (eagle, the wind). Among the Powhatans it is thought there was a secret as well as a known name. Amonute, given the pet name of Pocahontas (little wanton) by her father, only later revealed her real name, Matoaka. Boys took on nicknames that captured their exploits, which probably put pressure on them for further achievements. The Jesuit Barthelmy Vimont claimed that Huron males changed names as they moved through life stages, to combat illness and in response to dreams. (Most Huron believed they had two souls, one of which remained with the body unless it was reborn as a child, explaining why some children resembled their dead ancestors.) Finally, the name of a recently deceased person would be passed on to another member of the tribe so the appelation was not lost.[16]

European observers, hardened to infant mortality, were impressed by

1. The attachment between parent and child among American Indians is shown by this wooden figurine of a mother carrying her child, discovered in Ohio and dating from c. 400 BCE to 400 CE. Reprinted by permission of the Milwaukee Public Museum.

the fondness shown toward and good care taken of Indian children by their mothers.[17] This quality was nowhere better demonstrated than in the feeding of the infant. For, as the priest Chrestien Le Clercq observed, "It is a thing unheard of that they should give them out to be nursed.... By this conduct they reproach the lack of feeling of those [French] mothers who abandon these little innocents to the care of nurses.... Our poor Indian mothers have so much affection for their children that they do not rate the quality of nurse any lower than that of mother."[18]

Sagard applauded the women who gave their young "the very same meat that they take themselves, after chewing it well, and so by degrees they bring them up. If the mother happens to die before the child is weaned the father takes water in which Indian corn has been thoroughly boiled and fills his mouth with it, then putting the child's mouth against his own makes it take and swallow the liquor." Men could be solicitous in other ways as well. Charlevoix told of a father who, seeing his daughter pick up a dead mouse to eat it, took it from her and began carressing it "in order to appease the genius of the mice, that they may not torment my child after she has eaten it." He then returned the mouse to her.[19]

While Europeans may have quarreled with some Indian practices, such as bathing and exposing the infant in the coldest weather, breast-feeding impressed them. (Charlevoix, however, condemned as "barbarous" the custom—he knew not how widespread—of putting to death young children whose mothers died before they were weaned or even burying them alive with their mothers.) Nursing went on for several years.[20]

During this time the child stayed close to its mother, usually transported on a cradleboard. The explorer Mark Catesby described it as "a flat board about two feet long and one broad, to which they brace the child close, cutting a hole against the child's breech for its excrements to pass through; a leather strap is tied from one corner of the board to the other, whereby the mother slings her child on her back, with the child's back towards hers; at other times they hang them against the walls of their houses, or to the boughs of trees." Fur trader Nicholas Perrot observed glass and porcelain ornaments on the board and, if a male child, a bow attached.[21]

Robert Beverley, a Virginian, observed that after the infant's "Bones begin to harden, the Joynts to knit, and the Limbs grow strong," the child was allowed to crawl, at which time the board was abandoned and the child was carried "at their [the mothers'] backs in Summer, taking one Leg of the Child under their Arm, and the counter-Arm of the Child in their hand over their Shoulder; the other Leg hanging down, and the Child all the while holding fast with its other Hand; but in

Winter they carry them in the hollow of their Match-Coat at their back, leaving nothing but the Child's Head out."[22]

The young Indian's world changed dramatically at approximately three years. "Nothing can exceed the care which mothers take of their children whilst in the cradle," remarked Charlevoix, "but from the moment they have weaned them, they abandon them entirely to themselves; not out of hard heartedness or indifference, for they never lose but with their life the affection they have for them; but from a persuasion that nature ought to be suffered to act upon them, and that they ought not to be confined in any way."[23] Of course, it's impossible to abandon a three-year-old to his or her own resources; the child would not survive.

But it was possible to nurture the child's freedom. Charlevoix again: "The children of the Indians after leaving off the use of the cradle, are under no sort of confinement, and as soon as they are able to crawl about on hands and feet, are suffered to go stark naked where-ever they have a mind, through woods, water, mire and snow; which gives them strength and agility, and fortifies them against the injuries of the air and weather.... In the summer time they run the moment they get up to the next river or lake, where they remain a great part of the day playing."[24] The Old World commentator was startled by a childhood so different from what he had known, characterized as his was by enforced restraint and modesty (Chapter 2).

Most notably, the negative side of parental control was largely absent. For example, when French explorers and priests encountered the Huron, nothing shocked then more than the absence of physical punishment as a means to discipline Indian children. Europeans remarked on the fact that the young were not struck by their parents. "The greatest punishment ... in chastising their children, is by throwing a little water in their face," commented Charlevoix from Missouri while living among the Potawatomie and Miami. From the Southeast, however, came reports of Creek parents occasionally scratching disobedient children and, along with the Chickasaws, allowing young ones to be beaten by someone outside the household.[25] Nevertheless, corporal punishment was much the exception rather than the rule. Youngsters were apparently free to ignore anything that did not please them.

Still, young children must have remained under the watchful eyes of their parents and, probably, the entire village community.[26] The aim of American Indian parents was to train male hunter-warriors, who would be required to act individualistically yet always conform to the demands of a communal, conservative, homogeneous society. Females were instructed as planter-gatherers, who must possess wilderness survival skills as keen as those of the males. Children were expected to adopt the clearly defined gender roles expected of them. Sagard noted:

The usual and daily practice of the young boys is none other than drawing the bow and shooting the arrow.... they learn to throw the prong with which they spear fish.... But if a mother asks her son to go for water or wood or do some similar household service, he will reply to her that this is a girl's work and will do none of it.... so also the little girls, whenever they begin to put one foot in front of the other, have a little stick put into their hands to train them and teach them early to pound corn, and when they are grown somewhat they also play various little games with their companions, and in the course of these small frolics they are trained to perform trifling and petty household duties."[27]

Scantily clad in winter, boys hardened their bodies as they did their minds; their elders expected self-control and absence of "womanly" emotion. Their thoughts were to be focused on places seen and words spoken.[28] Surely the example of parents, especially warrior-fathers, forsaking corporal punishment must have contributed to children, especially sons, exercising restraint.

Seventeenth- and eighteenth-century Europeans explained the absence of corporal punishment from Native American practice as a consequence of the fear that a child so humiliated would commit suicide or, recalling the act in adulthood, would seek revenge on his or her

2. As they played, American Indian boys were also trained to be hunters and warriors. This idealized portrait by the Flemish engraver Theodore de Bry was based on the paintings of a French artist who had traveled in the New World. Theodore de Bry, *Grandes et petits voyages* (1598–1634).

parents.[29] Contemporary historians have found other motives. George Pettitt cites as the "chief inhibition ... the fact that pain per se cannot be used as a fear-producing, coercive force in a social milieu which places a premium upon ability to stand pain and suffering without flinching." Furthermore, he suggests that children must feel protected from punishment by their families, that children are specially linked to the spiritual world and as such receive kindness and respect, and that the patience and stoicism fostered by life in the cradleboard makes an Indian child "amenable to an early training, so strongly marked by indulgence."[30]

Since we have plenty of evidence from the Europeans themselves that children were being guided by their elders, we must take the European amazement at Indian permissiveness as an indication that Europeans were far more overtly coercive with children. "Fathers and mothers neglect nothing, in order to inspire their children with certain principles of honour," observed Charlevoix of the Miami and Potawatami, adding that "in this consists all the education that is given them," an observation which seemed to imply that more was needed. Charlevoix concluded with an expression of surprise: "It would seem that a childhood so ill instructed, should be followed by a very dissolute and turbulent state of youth; but ... the Indians are naturally quiet and betimes masters of themselves, and are likewise more under the guidance of reason than other men."[31]

The development of self-restraint and stoicism, initiated in childhood, was closely linked to the cultivation of autonomy, highly prized in adulthood. Historian James Axtell writes, "For the individual, a major goal was to be in control of oneself and one's destiny.... Those people who enjoyed the greatest autonomy ranked highest in Indian eyes.... Those who enjoyed power were expected to limit its exercise so as not to impinge upon others." Power was invisibly gained and lost; while it could not be guaranteed that the powerful would disregard the powerless, it was best to avoid others (who *might* hold power) for fear of antagonizing.[32] In this way, self-restraint, the presentation of a stoical exterior, was linked to autonomy.

Furthermore, the absence of corporal punishment—by its very nonpresence—promoted autonomy. There is no doubt in the contemporary psychological literature that the presence of such punishment erodes autonomy.[33]

Education of the young was primarily but not only imparted by the *example* of elders. John Heckewelder, himself a missionary, in addition credited the didactic skills of the mother and father, as well as the message they conveyed. Parents prepared children "for future happiness, by impressing upon their tender minds, that they are indebted for their existence to a great, good and benevolent Spirit, who not only has given them life, but has ordained them for certain great purposes." These purposes were best explained by the elders of the tribe, who must be respected. The parents, "seconded by the whole community," proceeded to make their young "sensible of the distinction between good and evil," instructing them practically rather than theoretically.[34]

A related but different means of instruction was storytelling. This oral literature was entertaining but, more important, conveyed cultural beliefs and practices. Often the leading characters of legend and myth were children or youths, making clear that the young were targets of these stories.[35]

The test of childhood training would be in adulthood; the transit from the one stage of life to the other was well defined. For girls there were sometimes rituals surrounding the onset of menstruation. The French trader and army officer Pierre Liette observed of the Illinois nations: "When it is their first time, they make themselves cabins in the wilderness at a distance of more than ten arpents [c. one-half mile] from the village, and all their relatives tell them to abstain from eating and drinking as long as they are in this condition, telling that they see the Devil [manitou], and that when he has spoken to them they are everlastingly fortunate and achieve the gift of great power for the future."[36]

For boys, whose passage through puberty was less biologically evident, there were more elaborate ceremonies: the huskinaw and the vision quest. Both involved isolation as well as sensory deprivation and stimulation; the purpose was to begin life on a new course, though without forfeiting the training of childhood, or to locate through visions the spirits that dominated the young person's life. Sometimes the tribal adults gave to the young man a new name, the meaning of which might shame, exalt, or even assign a personality to the recipient.

The huskinaw varied in detail from tribe to tribe, but its general characteristics were captured in Robert Beverley's description from Virginia: "The Choicest and briskest young men of the Town ... are chosen out by the Rulers to be *Huskanawed.* ... the principal part of the business is to carry them into the Woods, and there keep them under confinement, and destitute of all Society, for several months; giving them no other sustenance, but the Infusion, or Decoction of some Poisonous Intoxicating Roots: by virtue of which Physick, and by the severity of the discipline, which they undergo, they become stark staring Mad: In which raving condition they are kept eighteen or twenty days.... they perfectly lose the remembrance of all former things, even of their Parents, their Treasure, and their Language.... thus they unlive their former lives, and commence Men, by forgetting that they have ever been boys."[37]

The vision quest could also be generally characterized, as it was by the Moravian John Heckewelder, who was sympathetic toward the natives but skeptical of this particular practice. "When a boy is to be thus *initiated*, he is put under an alternative course of physic and fasting ... until his mind becomes sufficiently bewildered, so that he sees or fancies that he sees visions, and has extraordinary dreams.... Then he has interviews with the Mannitto or with spirits.... His fate in this life is laid entirely open before him.... The boy, imaging all that happened to him while under perturbation, to have been real, sets out in the world with lofty notions of himself, and animated with courage for the most desparate undertakings."[38]

Less skeptical, the historian George Pettitt concluded two centuries later that the vision quest and consequent acquisition of a guardian spirit was intended "to produce an independent, self-confident, and self-reliant personality, buoyed up by an inner conviction of his ability to meet any and all situations."[39] If confidence was instilled by memories of parents whose support was ever present in childhood, the guardian spirit could be pictured as the ongoing representation of those parents.

And so the line between childhood and adulthood was clearly drawn. All American Indians, even a boy who survived the amnesia allegedly brought on by the huskinaw, would draw upon the lessons instilled in the early years to govern the behavior of the later ones. Sex after puberty was considered normal. Marriage partners might be tentatively chosen by parents, and a young man could be expected to consult the parents of his intended. Yet there was no coercion when it came to marrying and deciding whether to remain wed.[40]

The experience of childhood among the sixteenth-century Pueblo Indians of southwestern North America, whose culture dated back centuries to the by-then-extinct Anasazi, was both similar to and different from that of their distant cousins on the Atlantic coast. Like the Eastern Woodland Indians, the Pueblo Indians led lives governed by ritual. The umbilical cord of the newborn was buried inside the house (female) or in a cornfield (male), making clear the sexual division of space and labor. The boy's penis was sprinkled with water, while the girl's vulva was covered with a seed-filled gourd, just as in the natural/adult world clouds/men poured their rain on seeds/women, causing them to germinate. On the fourth day, the medicine man presented the infant to the rising sun, named it, gave it an ear of corn (representing the Corn Mothers, who gave life) and, if a male, a flint arrowhead (to create thunder and lightning). A female remained attached to her place of birth, while a male moved houses, living with his mother as a boy and moving at adolescence into a kiva to learn male lore.

Gender was not the only social division (but one in which women were the more powerful in a horticultural society); age also mattered. Children were immediately indebted to their parents, who had had to pay the medicine man, and there continued a dyadic relationship between givers and receivers that was ordinarily between seniors and juniors. None were more powerful than the katsina, or ancestral dead; all adolescents were initiated into the katsina cult, learning what dire punishment awaited those who did not respect generational reciprocity. With menstruation, girls entered womanhood through initiation into clan-based groups. Boys had to kill an enemy before they could be inducted into the warrior fellowship through a physical ordeal reminiscent of the Eastern Woodland Indian huskinaw.[41]

With the Spanish conquest and the imposition of Christianity in the seventeenth century, Pueblo Indian society was fundamentally altered. The Franciscan priests set about their goal of conversion by upsetting the age relationship, turning sons from their natural to their spiritual fathers, beginning with baptism. Parents were humiliated (by casting adults in the roles of devils in religious dramas) and fathers emasculated (by violating the gender division of labor), while children were courted with gifts (the Franciscans playing upon the Indian belief that favors must be reciprocated). Livestock and lessons in animal husbandry not only yielded baptisms and pious lives but undermined the authority of the Indian hunt chiefs. The friars also offered Indian youth the nurturing benefits associated with mothers. Only those Indians who strongly resisted Christianity, among them the Hopi, remained matrilineal societies.[42]

The Hopi managed to remain remote from European American— first Spanish, then English—culture into the mid-twentieth century. The cradleboard remained, as did long-term nursing on demand. Mainstream medicine was rejected (and infant mortality was high); punishment (and then by the maternal uncle) was notably absent, while rewards persisted; children grew up always in the presence of others. Girls were taught domestic skills by mothers. But boys learned farming from their fathers; some games remained that were reminiscent of the warrior past. Initiation rites continued, though not as celebration of puberty.[43] Children were forced to go to school, but they handled education through "surface accommodation," since their elders had successfully erected a "communal wall" around them.[44] Thus, the Hopi maintained a strong cultural link with the past.[45] The same would certainly have to be said of the Chippewas.[46]

In 1937 the German psychoanalyst Erik Erikson, recently arrived in the United States, accompanied an anthropologist colleague from Yale to visit the Dakota Sioux. He was struck by the catastrophes that had

3. Europeans remarked on the use of the cradleboard when they first encountered American Indians. The continuity between past and present in American Indian life is evident in this photograph of a Hopi mother and child, taken by anthropologist Edward S. Curtis in 1921. Library of Congress.

befallen these native Americans—loss of the buffalo, the defeat at Wounded Knee, loss of their cattle—and the government's "imposing and humane" response. (Although Erikson does not mention it, the secretary of the interior and the head of the Bureau of Indian Affairs at this time were more informed and empathic than such officials had or have been before or since.) In conversations with the "heavy-hearted" native Americans, as well as with educators and social workers of Indian and European background, he probed for the issues of contemporary Sioux childhood.[47]

Erikson was astonished to find that "Indian children could live for years without open rebellion or any signs of inner conflict between two standards [the traditional training of their childhoods and the demands of European American society as encountered in school] which were incomparably farther apart than are those of any two generations or two classes in our own culture."[48] Students were apathetic or passively resistant. Erikson concluded that a white conscience would never be implanted in the Indian child while he/she was brought up the old way, that is, indulged as an individualist, unlike the white child whose

4. The Hopi environment in which Chuka grew up would have been familiar to his distant ancestors. Photograph by Edward S. Curtis. Library of Congress.

impulses were regulated in early life. The Indian child viewed the world as "dangerous and hostile."[49]

That cosmos was on the brink of change. World War II proved disruptive to American Indians: Men joined the armed services, and women took defense jobs. City living was nontraditional, as was some of the work done by rural women in the absence of manpower. But disruption also heightened cultural awareness and even a return to practices long abandoned. Average annual income tripled during the war, but the returning veterans were worldly and had problems adjusting.[50]

After the war the government began implementing its so-called termination policy of doing away with tribal governments and the trust protection of Indian territories while granting land to individual Indians who would now pay taxes and obey the laws of the states they inhabited. As a corollary to termination, Indians were encouraged to relocate in cities, and by 1958 about 100,000 had done so, most without federal assistance.[51]

Relocation was a failed attempt at assimilation; it resulted in continuing ghettoization and poverty. The deplorable living conditions of American Indians described by anthropologist Lewis Merriam in 1928, though they may have been temporarily improved due to the rising income in World War II, were confirmed by reports from the states of California and Michigan in 1966 and 1972, as well as the Census of 1990. Perhaps the most serious problem of all was confronted when the Indian Health Service was created in 1954. Though underfunded, IHS has addressed itself to the endemic (and epidemic) matter of fetal alcohol syndrome. Why Indians were and are particularly vulnerable to alcohol abuse is unclear, but they were killed by it at five times the rate of other Americans in the 1990s.[52]

Alcoholism and suicide, poverty and unemployment—these realities more closely describe the life context of Indians than any other group in the United States today. The "environment of evolutionary adaptedness" defined by Bowlby has been long lost. Although the federal government has been paying more attention to the needs of Indian children as evidenced by such legislation as the Indian Education Act (1972), the Indian Self-Determination and Education Assistance Act (1975), the Indian Health Care Improvement Act (1976), the Tribally Controlled Community College Assistance Act (1978), and the Indian Child Welfare Act (1978)[53]—and there is no denying the impact of this attention—nevertheless, the situation is far worse for Indian children today than it was in the past.

2.
European American Childhood

Richard Mather was born in the village of Lowton, England, in 1596, the son of a yeoman who, though not wealthy, assigned his son to a schoolmaster rather than putting him directly to work. Young Richard studied Latin and Greek, the latter through reading the New Testament, and at 15 became a schoolmaster himself. Three years later he underwent the agony and exhilaration of a conversion experience, influenced by Jesus' admonition that "Except a man be born again, he cannot see the Kingdom of God." He also attended Oxford, though for only a year, departing to take holy orders despite his nonconformist views—he was a Puritan. In 1635 he left England for Massachusetts Bay with his wife, Katherine, and children.

In 1639, already a highly regarded minister in Dorchester, he became the father of Increase Mather. Increase's mother taught him to read as a small boy, and his father instructed him in Latin and Greek. The lad entered Harvard when he was 12, but his frail constitution caused him to leave after six months and study with a private tutor until he returned to the college as a senior in 1656. Already he had undergone conversion, a process initially inspired by his mother—she told him of her desire that God should give him grace—and precipitated by his serious illness. His mother's deathbed wish was that he should become a minister. Full of dread and self-abasement, he finally determined that he had indeed received God's grace, and he gave his life to Christ.

Increase was the youngest of Richard's six sons. The first of Increase's nine children, Cotton (whose maternal grandfather, John Cotton, was the outstanding Puritan divine of Massachusetts's first generation), was born in 1663. Cotton prayed as soon as he could talk, and he was able to read and write before he began school, where he thrived on the classics under a tutor before entering Harvard at 12. His religious zeal—he reproved his playmates for their wicked deeds and began fasting at 14, a facet of his lifelong habit of denial in the service of the spirit—and his intellectual fervor—he ultimately published over 400 works—belied his inability to guide the Bay Colony, in the manner of his grandfathers and father, as it lurched from Puritanism to Yankeedom.

Despite an early speech impediment, he decided on the ministry, delivering his first public sermon at 17 in Dorchester and joining Increase at Boston's Second Church, where he remained with his identity linked to his father; even the threat of Increase's absence produced such anxiety that the impediment would usually reappear. At 23 he married the first of three wives, who produced 15 children, 6 of whom died young and only 2 of whom survived him. In 1699 he published *A Family Well-Ordered, or an Essay to Render Parents and Children Happy in One Another,* in which he depicted the model parent as intrusive and persistent, never missing an opportunity to teach, yet compassionate, "so tempered with kindness, and meekness, and loving tenderness" that their children would fear them only "with delight."

His principles were put to the test by his first son to survive infancy, Increase, born in 1699, whose undisciplined ways, dissolute manner, and death at sea were the source of disappointment and anguish. Indeed, just as Cotton found it difficult to separate from his own father, so he often overidentified with his own children and always had trouble respecting their autonomy. He did have the satisfaction of seeing his youngest son, Samuel (born 1706), graduate from Harvard and enter the clergy in the manner of previous Mathers.[1]

The Europeans who settled along the Atlantic seaboard in the seventeenth century were mostly English, immigrants from a society where their small world centered upon home. "Time was," writes Peter Laslett of preindustrial England, "when the whole of life went forward in the family, in a circle of loved, familiar faces, known and fondled objects, all to human size." The term "family" connoted the independent nuclear unit of dominant father, subordinate wife/mother, and submissive children; it might also include apprentices and servants. Seventeenth-century England was not, Laslett reminds us, a "paradise or golden age of equality, tolerance or loving kindness." Most people were exploited and oppressed; the nation was controlled by a small minority of the literate, wealthy and powerful, a situation mirrored on the familial level: "[I]f a family is a circle of affection, it can also be a scene of hatred. The worst tyrants among human beings, the murderers and the villains, are jealous husbands and resentful wives, possessive parents and deprived children. In the traditional patriarchal society of Europe, where practically everyone lived out his whole life within the family, often within one family only, tension like this must have been incessant and unrelieved, incapable of release except in crisis."[2]

Immigrants to America came from the hamlets and villages that housed three-quarters of the English and were typically a few hundred in size, provincial cities and market towns whose populations numbered in the thousands, and London, a metropolis of 200,000 in 1600 that almost tripled in size (and contained 10 percent of the national population) during the seventeenth century as rural residents became urban. Although most of the country's restless population remained within half a day's walk of home, Bernard Bailyn observes that the "peopling of British North America was an extension outward and an expansion in scale of domestic mobility."[3]

These early immigrants, even if recently citified, carried the cultural baggage of rural England, "the knots of households originally set by the first colonizers and run by their successors after a thousand years and more." The peculiarity of each village was a function of its origins (e.g., Celt or Saxon), its economic assets in addition to agriculture (e.g., mining, weaving), and the nature of its farming (open-field or enclosed). A shared characteristic was a strong sense of community and, if there were no gentry resident, the dominance of the yeomen, with complementary public participation by husbandmen, tradesmen, and even laborers (but not paupers). Each plot was worked by the man, his wife, and their children, but the community members toiled together during the summerlong harvest. All were Christian literalists, holding the same moral view of the world and coming together for every gathering in the church or meeting house, not in the pub.[4]

Traditional societies have lower life expectancies than industrial ones, yielding younger populations. Almost half of the early seventeenth-century English were children, typically distributed at 6.4 per family.[5] Unfortunately, this is about the extent of information demographic historians convey about the young; hence, it is necessary to turn to literary sources—the records of the upper strata of society—to get a view of child rearing.

Pregnancy was not regarded with awe in England as it was in native America; it was seen as a burden. Women were warned to avoid rigorous exercise, bad smells, salted meats, and corsets (though a swathe for the belly was advised). They were subject to dieting, blood letting, and reminders that good coloring was the promise of a boy while "a pale, heavy, and swarthy countenance,... [a] face spotted with red" was predictive of a girl. Not surprisingly, there were astrological forecasts and magical attempts to control conception and the sex of the fetus.[6]

No English women on record walked into the wilderness to deliver stoically in solitude. Rather, approaching the event in the knowledge that she and her offspring would be fortunate to survive, she worried as she climbed into her bed and submitted to a midwife and the women who would restrain her during labor. Only occasionally was a surgeon summoned to perform with his tools, and then the prospects were hardly reassuring. Although no figures exist regarding the death of mothers in childbirth, child mortality ranged from 12.6 to 15.8 percent in early seventeenth-century England.[7]

The rituals of the newborn began with shaping the head, if ill-formed, and wrapping it. The ears, eyes, nose, and mouth were to be cleansed, as well as the body with fresh butter, oil of roses, or oil of nuts, and the stomach was to be purged of its "clammy Phlegm" with sugared wine. The body, like the head, was to be swaddled "to give his little Body a streight Figure, which is most decent and convenient for a Man, and to accustom him to keep upon the Feet, for else he would go down upon all four, as most other Animals do."[8] This was more confining than a cradleboard, which allowed its American Indian occupant freedom from the waist up.

Tied into her cradle, the English infant spent the first month on her back, then on her left or right side with her head raised so the "excrements" might flow more easily out of her brain. Her room was to be neither too hot nor too cold, too dark nor too light, and at least until three or four years she was to be encouraged to sleep more than wake.[9] The initial steps in firm parental control were thus taken.

Whether or not to nurse the child was a controversial issue. Advice givers inveighed against wet nurses, yet listed their necessary qualifications. The color, taste, and texture of her milk must be tested, but more important was the quality of the person, since it was well known that character was transmitted through that milk (therefore, never employ a redheaded, i.e., fiery-tempered, nurse). The risk was evident: Children died under the care of negligent nurses.[10]

A sick mother might have no choice but to hire a nurse, nor would a wife, if her husband viewed the baby as an obstacle to intercourse and protested its presence in the bedroom.[11] (Wet-nursing occurred among Americans Indians only if a mother died; alive, she would not be deprived of that strongly valued proximity to her child.) The consequence of this practice is evident in a tale that began appearing in conduct books in the late sixteenth century. A child allegedly told his mother: "You bore me but nine months in your womb, but my nurse kept me with her teats the space of two years.... As soon as I was born you deprived me of your company, and banished me your presence; but she graciously received me." The child's anger should not disguise the fact that in this case the nanny appears to have become an adequate attachment figure who, if not dismissed too early, could nurture the child with his parents as ancillary figures. But it should be added that at least one seventeenth-century observer remarked: "In those dayes, fathers were not acquainted with their children."[12]

The absence of parents during infancy was not a portent of relinquished control over children. Toddlers were encouraged, indeed virtually forced, to walk through the use of contraptions with wheels or leading strings attached to their clothing. Parents pushed the young to mental precocity as well. Unlike American Indians who permitted children to find their own ways, English elders coerced. "Indulgence is the very *engine* of the Devill," warned one.[13]

Examples of permissiveness exist, but they are rare. Moralists condemned it. John Donne observed with pride, "Children Kneel to ask blessing of parents in England, and where else." Parents were cautioned against undermining their own authority "by being too fond of your children and too familiar with them at sometimes at least, and not keeping constantly your due distance: such fondness and familiarity breed contempt and irreverency in children." Roger North demonstrated how, for those parents who could not resist, the tendency to be lenient could serve authority: "Great use may be made of that fondness which disposeth parents to gratifie children's litle craving appetites, by doing it with an adjunct of precept, as a reward of obedience and vertue, such as they are capabale of, and at the same time being kind, and tender in Gratifiing them. This makes yong Creatures thinck that their will is not enough, without other means, to obtein their desires, and knowing that, they will Conforme, which breeds an habit of order in them that lasts to the end. The Contrary is seen, when fondness makes parents Indulg all things to children."[14]

Corporal punishment was pervasive, administered to girls as well as boys by either parent. A daughter observed about angering her father: "I expected no less than to have been shut up in a dark room for a week or a fortnight together and to have dined or supped upon birchen rods." About a mother's attitude toward her children it was recorded: "She loved them dearly without fondness; was careful to give them Nurture as well as Nourishment, not sparing the Rod when there was just occasion." Outsiders also administered punishment. Wrote one doting grandmother to her son about her grandson, "Let me beg of you and his mother that nobody whip him but Mr. Parrye," his tutor. In the classroom, beating was the accepted way of maintaining order and ensuring learning; a schoolmaster was typically depicted with a birch rod in his hand.[15]

The English took book learning seriously. In the seventeenth century the educational complex began at petty schools (basic literacy) and moved on to free schools (mathematics, English composition, and rhetoric), grammar schools (free school curriculum plus classical linguistics and English grammar), universities, and Inns of Court. There were only two counties in the kingdom where there was not a grammar school, offering the possibility of free tuition, within 12 miles of any family. For those children not sent to school, there was apprenticeship or servitude. The practice of putting children out of the house was attributed by one foreign observer to the "want of affection in the English."[16]

That judgment seems harsh. Evidence exists, for example, that the English were paying much more attention than previously to identifying and combating disease in children. Child advice manuals showed less interest in magic and religious fatalism, more in rational analysis. As children became more likely to survive illness, adults probably found it easier to become emotionally invested in them—and, conversely, becoming more affectionate, parents no doubt searched more diligently for cures.[17]

The scholar and physician John Locke embodied this new attitude better than anyone. He was analytically modern regarding pregnancy and childbirth, disapproved of swaddling, encouraged crawling, and admonished parents to strengthen the self-sufficiency of the child by distinguishing between "the wants of fancy and the wants of nature," being neither indulgent nor punitive. His advocacy of hardening children (feet in cold water, open air, minimal clothing—"the body may be made to bear almost anything") bore similarity to the American Indian regime, as did his recommendation of a simple diet (though he opposed permissive feeding and favored "going to stool regularly" to be accomplished by enforced sitting). The rod was to be avoided, as were rewards. "If you can get into children a love of credit, and an apprehension of shame and disgrace you have put into 'em the true principle." He recognized the limits of rules, the virtue of play, and the importance of parental example. Indeed, to put his plan into effect, parents would need to spend considerable time with their children, a revolution which did not take place in seventeenth-century England.[18]

Meanwhile, thoughts of family and child rearing were playing an important part in shaping the English movement to America. Captain John Smith challenged fathers to send their children to Virginia, where they might build estates greater than in England. But he did not want to divide families, and so he suggested sending only "such as with free conscience may be spared" and "fatherlesse children." William Bradford justified the Pilgrim movement to New England by observing that parents, now in exile in Holland, were obliged to become the too heavy taskmasters of their children, who were sometimes "drawn away by evil examples into extravagent and dangerous courses" by Dutch youth.[19]

The imagery of the departing settlers was also that of the family, as illustrated by the words of the Massachusetts Bay Company members: "[We] esteem it our honor to call the Church of England, from whence we rise, our dear mother; and cannot part from our native country, where she specially resideth, without much sadness of heart and many tears in our eyes, ever acknowledging that such hope and part as we have obtained in the common salvation, we have received in her bosom and sucked it from her breasts. We leave it not therefore as loathing that milk wherewith we were nourished there; but blessing God for the parentage and education.[20]

At the beginning there were two distinct English settlements in America, one around the waterways of Chesapeake Bay, the other amidst the rocks, rills, and templed hills of New England. The village culture of the parent country, and more specifically East Anglia where most New Englanders originated, was closely reproduced in Boston and environs. In the Chesapeake, settlement was spread out through the country, much in the way that people lived in the south and west of England, which supplied most colonists to Virginia.[21]

Initially peopled by young, unmarried males in search of wealth, Virginia had a terrible time getting established, while the small nuclear families who reached Massachusetts prospered. The 20,000 immigrants to New England naturally increased to 100,000 by 1700 as freedom from indenture, a balanced sex ratio, a healthy climate, and plentiful food encouraged early marriage, a high birthrate, and a low mortality rate. In the Chesapeake, the population was sustained only by continuing migration from England (and of Africans from the West Indies) due to features exactly the opposite of New England. The large, stable nuclear family of the North stood in stark contrast to the constantly reforming household (due to the high mortality rate) of the South, which might contain a mixture of "orphans, half-brothers, stepbrothers and stepsisters, and wards running a gamut of ages. The father figure in the house might well be an uncle or a brother, the mother figure an aunt, elder sister, or simply the father's 'now-wife'."[22]

The patriarchy of England and New England could not be immediately replicated in the Chesapeake, since early parent death (fathers in the first generation in Andover, Massachusetts, often lived into their eighties, while in Maryland men typically perished in their early forties) and consequent reformation of the household meant that parental control could not easily be exercised. However, family stability did exist for Chesapeake children due to a permanent network of relatives and quasi-relatives.[23]

Because Chesapeake society in the seventeenth century was largely populated by male immigrant servants who were not free to marry until they had served their terms and who died early in the disease environment, families were significantly smaller than in New England. Not only were there fewer children per nuclear unit, but there were lots more orphans. Children without any parents were assigned to new families.[24]

Although an expectant mother in either New England or the Chesapeake was accorded deference and protection due to her condition, pregnancy was seen neither as a time of special power (as among some American Indians) nor as a burden (as among some English). Childbirth, which took place in the home and was attended by a midwife and other women but no males, was painful and dangerous. One birth in thirty saw the death of the mother, explaining the shorter life expectancy of women than men. After delivery, unlike the American Indian example, the new mother spent days in bed and remained at home for weeks.[25]

A first child was most likely to be given the name of his or her same-sex parent, while the sibling following a deceased child was apt to inherit the name of the one who died. Naming appears to have been a way of drawing the newborn into the family network. It also might testify to conditions of birth (hence, Oceanus Hopkins, delivered on the *Mayflower*), parental expectations (Samuel Sewall named his son Joseph, "in hopes of the accomplishment of the Prophecy, Ezek. 37th"), or outright invention (Rich Grace, More Mercy).[26]

Infants were treated similarly in both regions, with the very significant exception of the attention paid to the religious life of the Puritan child from the baptism that immediately followed birth to the formal catechizing, at home or in church, that lasted until his sixteenth birthday.[27] Probably the neonate was swaddled in the English manner for the practical purpose of keeping it warm and because of a concern for its being prepared to stand and walk upright.[28] Swaddling would have lasted for about three months, whereas breast-feeding continued through the first year (when it ceased, conception became easier and probably occurred within the next several months). Until the baby walked, it was carried in the arms of one of its parents.[29] Demographic historian Robert V. Wells has observed that "today children have a better chance to celebrate their sixtieth birthdays than many babies born before 1800 had of living to the age of one!"[30] The most common causes of death stemmed from infant feeding problems made more fatal by the inability to deal with dehydration accompanying vomiting and diarrhea ("the flux") due to gastrointestinal illnesses.[31]

In the Chesapeake it appears that an infant could command parental attention during its initial two or three years, after which it was considered a self-sufficient child—and was likely to have lost one or both of its birth parents. Children and adolescents who have lost a father, mother, or both are more than ordinarily susceptible to psychiatric disorder, often involving suicide or psychotic depression.[32] It is doubtful that the familial stability allegedly provided by "relatives and quasi-relatives" could compensate for parental loss. Probably any contemporary psychoanalyst or psychiatrist would take strong exception to the Rutmans' observation that for the children of the Chesapeake, "death was a singing watchman in their world, teaching them from an early age that life was transitory," since it implies that the young easily adapted to the circumstance of loss.[33]

The trauma of parental loss in the Chesapeake was paralleled in New England by the drama of breaking the child's will, that is, the systematic

5. Baby Mary Freake's stiff posture on her mother's lap suggests either that she was wearing a corset under her bodice or that the unknown Massachusetts artist who painted her c. 1670 wished to depict her as capable of standing as an adult. *Mrs. Freake and Baby Mary.* Worcester Art Museum, Worcester, Massachusetts, gift of Mr. and Mrs. Albert W. Rice.

suppression by parents (more likely, the father) of the child's early attempts at self-assertion during that period which unsympathetic adults today have labeled the "terrible twos."[34] Such children were the potential victims of caretakers who could be considered "physically present but 'emotionally' absent."[35] Roger Williams argued that the extreme affection of Indian parents for their young made "their children sawcie, bold, and undutiful," while Cotton Mather depicted the natives as "lying wretches ... lazy wretches ... out of measure indulgent toward their children; there is no family government among them."[36]

Breaking the will, of course, involved the mental manipulation of the child, a recent addition to the parental armory justified by the concept of infant depravity; willfulness connoted sinfulness from which children must be protected. A far more common means of controlling children was the use of corporal punishment, about which the rule was to stop short of maiming the young one.[37] Life did have its lighter side, however. Puritans recognized that younger children should be allowed to play when "their bodies are to weak too labour, and their minds are too shallow to study," as the cleric John Cotton observed.[38]

Since distinctions were seldom made on the basis of age—young and old engaged in activities together, work or play, though the latter was suspect in New England—Cotton's pronouncement may stand as an early recognition of the distinctiveness of childhood. What would later be regarded as a plaything was in the seventeenth century quite possibly interpreted quite differently; a doll in the hands of a witch was dangerous, while the coral in a baby's silver rattle was not only a teething device but, it was believed, also warded off disease. Not until the mid-eighteenth century did playthings appear in portraits of American children.[39]

Clothing, however, was worn discriminately. At the age of seven or eight, boys no longer wore skirts but were put into breeches, marking their entrance to manhood as well as into the workforce. Girls at this age remained skirted, symbolizing their continuing (indeed, lifelong) subordination to males; they also were initiated into chores appropriate to their gender. But if children were dressed as miniature adults, they were not regarded as such; elders were discussed differently than children in diaries and journals, the law distinguished between young and old, and children were accorded only limited religious participation, though they were baptized, taken to church, and catechized.[40]

Church membership customarily was not granted until young adulthood (as the result of a conversion experience), but by the middle of the seventeenth century elders were anxiously concerned for the salvation of youth and the future of the church. Hence they not only attempted to heighten the spiritual awareness of young people but made arrangements (contrary to prior rules) for them to enter at least halfway into the body of communicants.[41]

Older children were also specially designated through the frequent practice of sending them out of their own homes to begin their working lives. It is a matter of controversy whether this "putting out" system, widespread at least in New England, was primarily for the purpose of apprenticeship or to relieve household tensions. It has been suggested that Puritan parents felt themselves in danger of being too loving and lax toward their children or, a rather different motive, were fearful of household conflict (an explanation based on the observation that

6. Eight-year-old David Mason, recently breeched, stands beside his younger sisters, Joanna and Abigail. All three were portrayed in adult costume by an anonymous Massachusetts painter. *The Mason Children: David, Joanna, and Abigail*, attributed to the Freake-Gibb Painter, 1670, oil on canvass, 39½ in. × 42½ in. The Fine Arts Museums of San Francisco, gift of Mr. and Mrs. John D. Rockefeller 3d to the Fine Arts Museums of San Francisco, 1979.7.3.

children were not farmed out until puberty, just when friction might occur).[42] It also seems possible that houses became too crowded. In Rhode Island and New York during the eighteenth century, for example, 70 percent of the white inhabitants lived in half the households.[43]

Apprenticeship was directed at older children, and so was education. Masters, like fathers, were required to educate as well as to feed and clothe their charges (and like fathers they had paramount rights to the custody and control of children in their households). Among the Puritans, reading was considered a necessary complement of childhood, since it provided access to the Scriptures. Families were expected to carry the burden of education in early New England, although as early as 1645 a grammar school was founded in the town of Dorchester. Educating and catechizing were one and the same, begun as soon as the child could comprehend and absorb.[44]

Such issues as spirituality, leaving the home, and education, focused as they were on youth, raise the question as to whether, as separate as childhood was from adulthood, there may have been a transitional stage between them. Although it is a matter of debate, there is persuasive evidence that by the late seventeenth century a youth culture existed, distinct from the adult world.[45] Whereas American Indian youths underwent trials to qualify as members of adult society, European Americans of the same age appear to have increasingly resisted the world of their parents, perhaps due to the repression of early childhood.

The eighteenth century was characterized by the growth of population and wealth in the English colonies in America. In the Chesapeake, this amounted to the expansion of the tobacco economy as well as a soaring number of African slaves and non-English settlers. Furthermore, the family was no longer shattered by frequent death as it had been in the seventeenth century; it could now assume a patriarchal structure. In New England, the mercantile economy grew along with commercial seaports. As the population continued to increase naturally, land became a relatively limited commodity with consequent pressures on the family to provide for members of the rising generations, a situation which posed a challenge to patriarchy.

Between the Chesapeake and New England, there emerged a thriving group of middle colonies—New York, Pennsylvania, New Jersey, Delaware—where commerce and agriculture flourished, as did the population, much of it Dutch, German, and Scotch Irish. South of the Chesapeake but lagging behind it in growth were the Carolinas and Georgia, largely English with some Germans and Scotch Irish in the backcountry.

In general, child rearing in eighteenth-century America showed a continuity with the past and new developments reflecting the changed

circumstances of Americans.[46] Those colonists remaining deeply influenced by religion, who can be labeled evangelicals, persisted in
believing that children were depraved and in attempting to break their
wills. But a new secularism, often associated with the Enlightenment
as well as the emerging world of commerce, enabled other mothers
and fathers, more moderate than the evangelicals, to deal in a gentler
way with their young, expecting responsibility without demanding submission. Yet a third group of parents, genteel in their circumstances,
remained partly rooted in the distant past; though they believed in personal autonomy for themselves, they were unable to concede it to their
progeny. They indulged their children not to nurture them but because
they were indifferent to them. Their remoteness may explain their per-
severance in the time-honored practice of beating, a punishment often
administered by servants rather than themselves.[47]

Such styles of parenting can be assigned to geographical regions and
economic classes, as well as to specific types of families. The evangelical
method was most typical of isolated rural areas and the ever-expanding
frontier where poorer people lived in nuclear families dominated by
the only two adults present. Recent immigrants from Germany and
Northern Ireland can be placed in this category, though not in every
instance. The children of the Moravians who settled Bethlehem, Pennsylvania, for example, spent 15 to 20 months being nursed by mothers
(who lived separately from fathers), after which time they lived in nurseries with other toddlers and were supervised by single women. At four
or five they were moved to sex- and age-segregated living units.[48]

The more secular (or moderate) style was apt to be found in somewhat affluent farming villages and commercial towns where the community, especially family relatives who played influential roles in the
lives of children, diffused the authority of the parents. In this category,
for example, would be the Quakers who emigrated to Pennsylvania from
northwestern Britain, where their leaders had "demanded that parents
suppress all impulse in child rearing and accept it as a loving responsibility requiring full vigilance and total self-control." Probably no parents
paid their children more attention than the Quakers. Believing that
their progeny lived somewhere between Adam's sin and Christ's seed,
they rejected Puritan predestination and embraced an environmental
perspective; it was up to them to make sure that their children saw the
Light. Admonished to intervene vigorously but never impulsively, always
tenderly so as not to provoke the tender souls to wrath, Quaker parents
were constantly restrained by reason and moderation. They reminded
their children of godly duties by outfitting them in plain attire and
cautioning them to spend more time praying than playing.[49]

Quaker fathers tended to be generous in the disposition of land to their children, thus forsaking inheritance as a tool of control. In eighteenth-century New England, the pressure of population on the land led younger sons in search of a living to emigrate to newly opened western areas or eastern seaports, in either case residing beyond the reach of the household of origin. Parental power in New England was also dissipated when, in an attempt to bolster church membership, adults put pressure on the young to have conversion experiences, an action which ultimately augmented youths' potency by encouraging them to become decision makers.[50]

The third or genteel style could be found in those places where prosperity was based on land and slaveholding. Here the extended family, now stabilized by lengthened life expectancy, was dominated by a patriarch (just as the power of the father was declining in moderate families), while children were often tended to by servants. Genteel childhood was qualitatively different from other childhoods in that the progeny of planters had power over other human beings—and they knew it.[51]

The growing wealth of eighteenth-century Americans, or at least some moderate and most genteel households, allowed for a longer childhood and, in the face of declining infant mortality, perhaps a greater investment of emotion in children. As childhood lengthened, the family became more complex by way of accommodation and more stable with lengthened life expectancy.[52] Finally, if there was an adolescent *culture* in seventeenth-century New England, there were *actual adolescents*, that is, young people regarded as neither adults nor children, in the eighteenth century.[53] Young Benjamin Franklin, who spent his early teen years searching for a career, was one of them.

Among the evangelicals, who viewed the years of youth as the time for religious rebirth—which is to say, the time for suppression of the self—adolescence was a time when personal autonomy could only be interpreted as sinful, a denial of God's sovereignty. The young person was admonished to return to the selflessness of early childhood. Yet the effort to produce conversion experiences in youth had the ironic effect of endowing the young with more power.[54] The rise in premarital pregnancy in the eighteenth century was another indication of adolescents gone astray.[55]

Among the genteel, personal autonomy was also suppressed as the indulgence shown toward the very young was abandoned when dealing with youth. Girls were socialized into their subordinate roles as women, and boys were coached to be dependent upon their fathers for their very identity.[56] Thus, the consequences of an evangelical or genteel rearing were similar, even though parents differed in the ways they had distanced themselves from their children.[57]

Only among the moderates, who accepted the self as worthy of love, respect, and nurture, do adolescence and autonomy appear to have traveled together. Quite literally, since moderate youth was most apt to be mobile and, therefore, well served by autonomy. Examples would include Franklin's break from his family in Boston and subsequent journey to Philadelphia, as well as John Adams' leave-taking of the farm in Quincy, his residence at Harvard, and his training in law at Worcester.

Josiah Franklin, described by his son as a man whose "great excellence lay in a sound understanding and solid judgment," employed Benjamin to assist him as a tallow chandler but, noticing that the boy was unhappy, escorted him through Boston to observe various tradesmen at work until father and son settled on printing as a career. If the elder Franklin made a mistake, it was in having Benjamin apprentice to his older brother, James, who proved too much a taskmaster. The independent-minded Benjamin resolved the sibling conflict by escaping Boston for Philadelphia.[58]

The parents of John Adams, Susannah and John, taught their son to read early and put him in school, even allowing him to change from one master to another at his request, and certainly encouraging him to enter Harvard. "Although my Fathers general Expectation was that I should be a Divine," the younger John later remembered, "I knew him possessed of so much Candor and moderation, that it would not be difficult to remove any objections he might make to my pursuit of Physick or Law or any other reasonable Course."[59] Like Josiah Franklin, John Adams the elder was a reasonable man.

Of course, the revolutionaries of 1776 were recruited not only from moderate households. Historian Philip Greven has observed that the issues of power and authority raised at that time provoked three distinctive responses. Evangelicals saw the mother country and the father-king as symbols of their powerful parents who must be resisted. Moderates, whose childhood experience was not so extreme, could accept limited authority but knew liberty had to be defended. The genteel remembered authority as distant but indulgent, awesome and respectable; power was neither dangerous nor necessarily in conflict with liberty.[60]

The differences among European American households in the colonial period could be exaggerated. They shared some fundamental characteristics from the perspective of the family cycle. The first stage of this cycle was marriage itself (women in their early twenties, men in their mid-twenties), followed by the arrival of a child about a year and a half later, an experience that then recurred every 24 to 36 months for two decades. Typically the last child departed the home 40 years after the arrival of the first, yet marriages lasted only 30 years before one partner's death. Younger children were apt to lose one or both parents. Earlier-born children had younger and more vigorous parents; later borns had parents whose attention was distracted by their older siblings, who were inclined to be healthier than they.[61]

Health, or illness and death, was a matter beyond the control of eighteenth-century Americans. Epidemics, such as smallpox, diphtheria, and yellow fever were most feared, though inoculation for smallpox was accepted before 1800. But intestinal disorders, infections, and lung diseases claimed more victims, with devastating impact on small children. The scattered nature of the population not only served as a natural quarantine but also preserved the ill from damaging medical care, though doctors were in fact searching for ways to improve health care, including gathering statistics on the effectiveness of cures. Nevertheless, religion, folk healers, and/or common sense were the recourse of parents whose children fell ill.[62]

Finally, all households shared the point of view that, in one way or another, children must be controlled. The War for Independence may have reflected some loosening of (or, at least, the desire to loosen) the reins of household authority, but the campaign against English tyranny did not improve the lot of native Americans or African Americans under the yoke of European Americans. Most European Americans were in some way contemptuous of Indians[63] and African Americans, viewing them as uncivilized (perhaps childish in the manner of their own youngsters) and therefore undeserving of the autonomy the European Americans were seeking for themselves.

For most Americans, life changed little with the onset of the nineteenth century. Virtually all of them lived in communities of fewer than 2,500 people in 1800. Four-fifths were farmers, and agricultural produce was consumed locally except in the South where cotton was produced for an international market. Rural isolation was and for a long while would remain the American way of life, celebrated by the well-traveled Thomas Jefferson when he spoke glowingly of the agrarian republic. As president, Jefferson doubled the size of the nation, an act consistent with his faith in the yeoman farmers who would populate the West, where, not incidentally, his dedication to the democratic credo was justified by the widening of the franchise.

Alexis de Tocqueville, drawn from his native France to the New World political and social experiment in the 1830s, observed the triumph of equality over aristocracy throughout the fabric of American life, including the family. True, he conceded, during the child's earliest years the father exercises "the domestic dictatorship which his sons' weakness makes necessary.... But as soon as the young American begins to approach the man's estate, the reins of filial obedience are daily slackened.... In America there is in truth no adolescence. At the close of boyhood he is a man and begins to trace out his own path." And this occurs without struggle, since parent and child agree on the inevitability of the latter's independence.[64]

Despite the universal sweep of Tocqueville's observations, he captured some Americans more accurately than others. His description best fit the moderates who lived in the farming villages and commercial towns on the eastern seaboard, while it did not truly grasp the situation of the westward-bound evangelicals—or, for that matter, of the genteel southern folk.

Those Americans who moved to the western frontier saw—and employed—children as workers who contributed to the family economy, much in the manner that youngsters had been perceived and used on the Atlantic seaboard in the seventeenth century. Frontier families were patriarchal: Primary authority was vested in the father, who directed the family economy, and females were regarded as inferior to males. The economic interdependence of the family was assumed, even to the point of suspecting emotional family ties. Religious institutions reinforced this ideology. Only as time passed and the community became settled was the patriarchal structure threatened.[65]

Such was the case when New Englanders moved to upstate New York, for example, and the situation remained the same as Americans marched across the continent. On the Illinois prairie during the earliest phase of settlement, family characteristics were a repetition of those witnessed generations earlier in the East.[66] And these conditions prevailed as settlers pushed further westward. Woman were constantly pregnant, the child mortality rate was high, and surviving youngsters were expected to work hard, usually at gender-defined jobs. "It was instilled in us that *work was necessary,*" a woman remembered of her childhood on the Texas frontier. "Everybody worked; it was part of life, for there was no life without it." Parents themselves were too busy to devote time to controlling the lives of their offspring, beyond issuing labor assignments. But children did have emotional needs, to which mothers paid far more attention than fathers. The latter were resented for their exclusive attention to the work regime.[67]

In the South, too, mothers played the predominant role in child rearing, at least regarding infants. Fathers devoted little routine time to children, though their authority became apparent around the age of four. Boys, especially, were subject to patriarchal power and were regularly put to the test of manliness, as they had been in the previous century. Premium value was assigned to honor, in contrast to the importance placed on godly conscience by the evangelical pioneers. Shame rather than guilt was the agency of discipline, though of course corporal punishment was ever-present.[68]

In the North, traditional values regarding child rearing survived. Until the mid-twentieth century, almost all farms were family farms, and they relied primarily on family members for labor and management.[70] Early nineteenth-century childhood, in other words, was developing regional characteristics in the Northeast, South, and West, as well as between urban and rural areas within those regions. As we shall see in Chapter 4, the middle class in the towns and cities of the Northeast during the nineteenth century led the way in a new approach to child rearing.

7. In nineteenth-century Nebraska, as in seventeenth-century Virginia or Massachusetts, girls and boys toiled at daily chores. Reprinted by permission of the Nebraska State Historical Society.

African American Childhood

Frederick Douglass was born in 1818 in Talbot County, Eastern Shore, Maryland, and there he spent his early years in the cabin of his grandparents, Betsy (slave) and Isaac Baily (free), along with cousins and an infant uncle. His mother lived nearby, though he did not see her during those years (later they were together several times) and was never deeply attached to her, a situation he blamed on slavery. His father, whom he may never have met, was white. "Slavery has no use for fathers or families," he later reflected, but he claimed to have had a carefree and happy childhood with his grandmother, an intelligent woman who was physically powerful and skilled in fishing and farming.

She introduced six-year-old Frederick to his siblings at Wye House, a 12-mile-distant plantation managed by her master, Aaron Anthony (rumored to have been the boy's father), for the wealthy and prestigious Lloyd family. She then slipped away, to the distress of her grandson, who never again fully trusted anyone. At Wye House, the very bright and impressionable lad experienced the indignities and cruelties of slavery, as well as the resentment of fellow slaves, especially an auntie who bristled when Lucretia Anthony Auld—daughter of Aaron and wife of Thomas (also rumored to be Frederick's father)—fed and cared for the boy. Lucretia took Frederick to Baltimore, to live with Sophia and Hugh Auld, Thomas's brother and sister-in-law.

"I saw what I had never seen before; it was a white face beaming with the most kindly emotions; it was the face of my new mistress, Sophia Auld." So Frederick wrote of his new circumstances. "I had been treated as a *pig* on the plantation; in this new house, I was treated as a *child*." About a year later Aaron Anthony died without a will, and the boy, now part of an estate to be divided among Lucretia and her two brothers, was sent back to the place where he had been born. Again he was rescued by Thomas Auld and returned to Baltimore, where Sophia taught him to read, a subversive act which aroused her husband's wrath. But it was too late. As Frederick wandered the city, and especially the docks, he improved his reading, not to mention his listening, heard the word "abolition," talked with indentured and free laborers, and got religion.

The Aulds recognized the rebellion brewing in his mind and, perhaps to protect the 15-year-old, shipped him to the run-down port of St. Michaels, back on the Eastern Shore. But Thomas Auld would not allow Frederick to have a Sabbath school for other boys—shades of Nat Turner! Rather, Auld hired him to Edward Covey, a pious "nigger-breaker" who owned a farm nearby. Six months of beatings led the adolescent to fight back to a draw, an act for which he was not punished. In St. Michaels for the slack winter season, he organized youths again, this time for an escape. When it failed, Auld sent him back to Baltimore to be hired out as a skilled laborer. It was from this city, disguised as a seaman, that Frederick Douglass traveled by ferry, train, and steamer to Philadelphia and freedom.[1]

Most of the Africans brought to North America had come from west and west-central Africa. In the seventeenth century they arrived by way of the West Indies, while in the eighteenth century the vast majority came directly from Africa. Along the 3,500 miles of coastline from Senegal to Angola and its interior, there is considerable variation in climate, vegetation, and, consequently, ways of living. In this enormous area several hundred languages and myriad social customs flourished.

Nevertheless, there were elements of continuity within this vast region, linking its inhabitants to one another. The primary mode of identification for the African was the family and its descent groups. In west Africa, descent passed through the male, in west-central and central Africa, through the female. In either case, polygyny, the practice of a man possessing several wives or concubines, was a frequent if not universal practice.

Most Africans lived in small villages, although there were also large trading centers. Local economies were pastoral or agricultural, not based on hunting and gathering. Slavery among African peoples existed as an institution tied to the kinship system, with slaves employed as outsiders within the family but deprived of the protection that derived from belonging to the kinship group. Most slaves were women; enslavement of children and removal far from home was also a frequent practice. But the system in Africa, integrated as it was with kin and community, hardly resembled the North American chattel system, in which each slave was an individual commodity, legally salable.[2]

It was impossible to carry intact African customs of childbirth and child rearing to America, yet certain ones did survive in the New World, a fact largely unacknowledged until the middle of the twentieth century.[3] Childbirth in Africa was a women's affair, and not until the mother had spent six days lying with her child on a mat was a priest admitted to bathe (for the first time) and name the child, the name having been

selected by the child's father in communication with spirits he encountered in a dream or while possessed. Childbirth in America drew to
some extent on African folk beliefs, represented in such behavior as
placing iron under the bed at parturition to ease birth pains and using
cobwebs to stem hemorrhaging, as well as disposal of the placenta and
treatment of the navel cord.[4]

The African practice of naming a child for the day, month, or season
of his or her birth, as well as using the African rather than English des-
ignation, was evident among American blacks, slave and free. Often
naming was delayed until it was reasonably certain the newborn would
survive, since the necronymic pattern typical of European families, that
is, bestowing the name of a deceased child on one newly born, was
rejected in favor of recognizing the individual identity of the child.
Finally, names were chosen to honor kin, showing the importance of
the extended family.[5]

In west Africa, women nursed their children for two to three years and
abstained from sexual intercourse until weaning was complete, yielding
a birth interval of three to four years.[6] Across the Atlantic in the eighteenth century, when the slave population began to reproduce itself
naturally in North America, nursing lasted a year or less, a situation
probably brought about by the requirement that a mother return to
work within a month of delivering. Indeed, immediately after delivery
she was expected to do her own cooking and cleaning, activities that
probably contributed to the high infant mortality rate.[7] She had either
to take her infant into the fields or return to the slave quarters several
times a day to feed it. (In Africa it was common practice for mothers to
carry infants on their backs while they worked.)[8]

The relationship between work and infant survival, however, begins
not after delivery but in the earliest months of pregnancy, at which time
diet and the effects of disease are also critical factors. There is certainly
evidence that many planters took the well-being of mother and child
seriously. It is much less clear whether they understood the importance of
early work release, even in times of illness. (Indeed, one slave mother
related her work situation to her son's retardation.) Of course, many
European Americans remained fatalistic about child death, black or
white.[9]

The death rate among black infants was exceptionally high compared
with that of their white counterparts, a fact attributed to nutritional
liabilities, crib death, and poor postnatal care, as well as to neonatal
tetanus, infanticide, worms, and overt sickle cell disease.[10] Once weaned,
babes were under the care of children, usually siblings, only a few years
older than themselves. (Babysitting chores ended at seven or eight.)
This child care practice had roots in Africa. Among the Tiv of central

Nigeria, for example, a six-month-old is assigned to an older sibling, usu-ally of the same sex, who takes on the role of protector and accompanies the child everywhere.[11]

Anthropologists who have studied the Mandinka of Senegal argue that child caregivers not only "manage and shape the behavior" of their younger siblings but may also "facilitate the elaboration of certain val-ues, attitudes, and beliefs that are subsequently critical elements of adult social behavior." These child caregivers are part of the village social struc-ture and are able to articulate their responsibility.[12] But in America these caretakers were unsupervised unless an aged nonworker was available, and there appears to have been no village social structure to regulate their activities. While it is hard to believe that such care was trustworthy and easy to agree with the observer who sees child neglect as "insepara-ble from slavery and its work demands," some historians have judged that plantation nurseries resembled contemporary day care centers.[13]

But the basic psychological point is that for the African American child, the mother was frequently inaccessible (at least on the planta-tion—there were, of course, other living situations), having to return to work soon after she delivered.[14] One former slave explicitly recalled his "want of parental care and attention," noting that his parents were simply unable to tend him during the day.[15] It is not clear whether inac-cessibility in itself raises fear in a child—or whether fear is aroused either by the distress an infant feels in the absence of someone who will soothe and feed it or by the greater intensity of response when an infant undergoes fear-inducing experiences (e.g., the presence of a stranger, a loud noise) alone. But separation inevitably engenders fear, although being left with a familiar companion/caretaker in a recognized place, as was the case with the young African American child, would mitigate the situation.[16]

Psychologist Lester Alston believes that the issue for the slave child was not bonding and attachment but satellization, the process which "permits children to develop sources of status and self-esteem around two years of age, once the 'inflated sense of self-worth' and the omnipo-tence of infancy are ended." In his view, owners were too powerful and parents too subjugated for slave children to look anywhere but toward the owner for status and self-esteem. Thus, a child could have developed an early autonomy, only to have it undermined during the satellization period.[17] Quite to the contrary, Wilma King asserts that slave parents were able to show their children "how to forge a balance between social courtesies to whites and their own self-esteem," while Marie Jenkins Schwartz argues that slave parents were always strong enough to negoti-ate with owners and taught their children through the example of their refusal to follow orders from owners. However, these two historians agree that parents had precious little time for their children.[18] It seems unlikely that fathers and mothers would have been able to instruct the young in lessons of self-esteem unless they were demonstrably powerful and/or the owner was weak and ineffectual.

In the Chesapeake in the eighteenth century, mothers usually were not separated by sale from their small children and so could expect to see them in the evenings; on large plantations, over half the fathers might also be present. Other fathers and older working children were

8. Slave children had to care for themselves and each other, since their parents were constantly at work. Reprinted by permission of the Valentine Museum/Richmond History Center, Richmond, Virginia.

likely to reside on nearby farms. With the emergence of a native-born slave population, a kinship network appeared, similar to that which existed in west Africa, allowing most children to live in the presence of familiars. A less positive scenario is that while planters valued the nuclear family—it was, after all, the unit of food and clothing distribution, the reproductive unit, and it served to attach potential runaways to the plantation—African Americans valued the whole extended family, which was seldom kept intact. The grim picture shows that the slave family, extended or nuclear, was always vulnerable and that most fathers did not live with their children.[19]

It would be only speculative to assert that children had, and at what age they had, the matter of their futures in mind. To some historians it appears that they played games which stemmed from their dawning recognition of their enslaved condition: "whipping" and "auction" perhaps provided ways of acting out so as to neutralize the real events. This interpretation is challenged by the observation that whipping games, for example, are universal. Certainly slave children saw their parents (but not their white peers) beaten, and their parents in turn beat them—whether because this was traditional practice or to prepare them for their adults lives. This violence must have assaulted any sense of autonomy they were developing.[20]

On the other hand, that black and white children played together on the plantation, usually boys with boys and girls with girls, probably made the future seem less portentous. Their games were influenced by the African past and the European American present. Nineteenth-century children, black and white, everywhere played the same games, though slave children transformed to their own uses the European games they learned from their white playmates. And white children, more than any other persons, taught their black peers how to read. Finally, white masters frequently petted black children, much in the patriarchal manner that they dealt with their own young.[21]

But the treatment, both positive and negative, was inconsistent. Meals, for example, were served to slave children in troughs, as if they were animals. The diet for children was exceedingly poor (meat was typically absent from their meals), as evidenced by the delayed growth of young slaves, at or below the rate of children of corresponding ages in the poorest populations of developing countries today. Diet did not improve until they entered the workforce, that is, until it was profitable to feed them well, after which time they showed remarkable powers of catching up in size.[22]

African American children were not usually required to do more than light work until the age of 10 or 12, when the harsh field life began.[23] This new situation marked the movement from childhood into adulthood. Sometimes it was accompanied by sale away from family.[24] Their parents, or at least their mothers, had trained them to be submissive workers, conforming (at least in appearance) to the demands of house mistresses, drivers, and owners who felt free to interfere in the child-rearing process. In Africa, children were taught their future tasks by imitating their parents of the same sex. African American parents did not have the luxury of teaching by example, and unlike European American parents they did not have firm control of their children.

The movement from childhood to adulthood in Africa was accomplished not by going to work or by separation from family but by initiation rites, much in the manner of American Indians.[25] The dramatic change in behavior and even in attachments must have had profound psychological meaning for the African American adolescent, perhaps intensifying early childhood fears of loss, a situation which served the interest of the slaveholder if only by investing the alternative to the hard labor of slavery—escape—with terror. If separation from family

9. During slavery, black children not only played with white children, as this woodcut from the 1840s shows, but sometimes learned to read from them. Library of Congress.

accompanied the new work regime, it would serve as an obstacle to the normal socialization of a young person. Simultaneously, the search of the newly separated adolescent for attachment probably reinforced the kinship system. It may also have contributed to the high rate of mental illness among slaves, a matter that has received little historical attention.[26]

The Emancipation Proclamation and the Thirteenth Amendment were intended to free African Americans from slavery. And, indeed, the institution disappeared—though immediately former slaveholders and other whites, as well, attempted to apprentice black children, even taking them from their parents who, the whites alleged, were unable to support them.[27] Yet black Southerners remained prisoners within a society controlled at every level by whites whose racial attitudes were unaltered by military defeat and proclamations of liberty. To them, blacks were inferior and must act appropriately. Until well into the twentieth century, the best African American parents could hope to do for their children was acquaint them with the demands of white domination and teach them the acquiescent behavior necessary for survival without sacrificing completely their sense of self-worth, their racial pride, and their hope.[28]

Parents could not, however, prepare children for the first humiliating racial insult. Even having white playmates was no insurance against it; indeed, under these circumstances it could be all the more hurtful. Robert Russa Morton never forgot the day when an eagerly awaited white playmate arrived home from prep school: not only was Robert's effusive greeting met with coldness but his childhood friend refused to shake hands; Robert was profoundly affected. And such insults were reified by continuing harassment—"The white children I knew grew meaner as they grew older," one black woman recalled—until a reservoir of resentment and vindictiveness built up.[29]

Yet in no way could the flood gates containing these feelings be released on whites. Rather, black children had to master the mechanisms of control, even appear happy with their subordinate condition. Not surprisingly, young blacks became surreptitious students of their white enemies—the classroom of experience for African Americans whose schools were underfunded or nonexistent. (Blacks with white assistance had set up some public and private schools, but the poverty of the freed slaves and the resistance of Southern whites meant that funding was never close to adequate.)[30]

This was not a world parents could explain to children, much less justify except as the will of the Lord. Booker T. Washington, queried about "what sometimes seem hopelessly discouraging conditions," reminded his questioners "of the wilderness through which and out of which, a good Providence has already led us."[31] Indeed, because they too were the victims of white oppression, parents might well vent their anger and frustration on their offspring. Richard Wright described his boyhood in a household filled with sanctimony and violence; he was alternately preached to and beaten. Nor could whiteness be kept out of the black community, as skin hues, facial features, and hair texture created distinctions and hence divisions among African Americans.[32]

Despite these conflicts, the black family, both rural and urban, was a strong institution. Against great odds, African Americans had sought to cement slave marriages and families, simultaneously showing deep concern over their children's futures.[33] Herbert Gutman observes that in 1880 "between 66 percent and 75 percent of black children under the age of six everywhere lived with a mother and a father," while the so-called matrifocal family hardly existed. Between 1880 and 1900, however, the nuclear household declined in importance while the numbers of augmented and extended households increased. And intrafamily problems, ranging from desertion to intergenrational battles, existed. Yet long marriages remained common, as did the attachment of parent to child.[34]

Family cohesiveness, however, only hints at child-rearing practices within the household, though we can suppose continuity between the late nineteenth and the mid-twentieth century, about which we do have evidence. Illegitimate births were common before first marriages; mother and child almost always remained in the grandparental household, which served as a secure social setting for the child or children until the mother made a stable marriage. The first child was the most fondled and stimulated and often became the most self-confident and capable, illegitimate or not.

The greatest life pleasure of adults was found in relations with their young children. Hence, the infant's environment was fully human, virtually without baby furniture; it was held or carried most of the time, and even when bedded it was frequently accompanied. When the mother cradled it in her arms or held it in her lap, she also caressed it while her eyes explored its face. In the crowded household there were always others who wanted their turn, so that the infant was awake most of the day and slept a long night in its parents' bed. The giving and demanding of food was also an interactive routine. Bladder and bowel functions were quickly responded to, and training began early. Play most usually revolved around the pretense that the baby was aggressive, that it would bite and fight, and the mother in response was both indulgent and disciplinary but always involved.

With the revolution of walking, expectations changed. The former lap-baby, now knee-baby, was expected to use the chamber pot or excrete outside, but otherwise it could freely explore so long as it caused its mother no trouble. She began disciplining with a light switch, often playfully. The child world expanded to include the children's gang, whose members ranged from 15 months to a nurse-girl or boy of at least six, reminiscent of child care under slavery. But the mother remained engaged, enjoying the toddler's newfound independence. Thus the

10. The African American family, which existed under slavery, grew in strength after Emancipation. This five-generation family was photographed on a South Carolina plantation. Library of Congress.

basis was laid for a healthy self-esteem, which made it possible for the parents to change their focus to the next sibling in line while expecting the almost three-year-old to transfer his allegiance to the children's gang, the core of which was the children of one family with some neighborhood hangers-on.

With these playmates the child ran, climbed, gossiped, seldom fought, and rarely saw toys. At 9 a boy might leave the group to range farther afield with his male age mates, unless he was the nurse, in which case he might remain until 14. Girls stayed on into adolescence, subdued and resigned, a mood foreshadowing the course of an adulthood lacking social status or material security but promising the pleasure of producing children. For girls and boys, the insular world of the black family was far safer than venturing into the larger society.[35]

African American childhood in the eighteenth and nineteenth centuries was profoundly affected by the social context of slavery and its aftermath. That context was accompanied by an ideology, a perception of the black minority, held by many white Americans. It was enunciated by George Wallace, a segregationist when he began his four terms (elected in 1962, 1970, 1974, 1982) as governor of Alabama, who reportedly gave barracks lectures during World War II defending his white supremacy position: "I don't hate them. The colored are fine in their place. But they're just like children and it's not something that's going to change. It's written in stone."[36] It did change, and Wallace recanted. Nevertheless, the idea of African Americans as children has had a history in America dating from the mid-nineteenth century.

Historian Thomas Webber argues that the planter class aimed to have slaves internalize values which would make them conscious of their own inferiority, "overflowing with awe, respect, and childlike affection for the planter and his family," happily aware of the rules of slave behavior, and convinced that slavery was not only right but the best of all possible worlds. Slaves were kept ignorant of the outside world and the written word, denied privacy, forbidden to recall their African past, and refused the very privileges that defined their white counterparts as adults.[37]

While Webber argues that most of the values, attitudes, and understandings taught by white masters were not accepted by black slaves, he concedes that one must look deep into the slave literature to reach this conclusion. In other words, even if slaves were not convinced by their masters, they had to disguise their true beliefs. How long this masquerade persisted, whether it still goes on, is a matter of debate.[38] But whichever side of the issue is taken, it seems that African Americans *eventually* fulfilled the expectations of European Americans who wanted to perceive them as perpetual children.

This was not the initial European perception of the African. Of course, blacks were subordinated in early American life, and probably they were believed to be inferior, although it was seldom argued before the 1830s that their inferiority was permanent.[39] However, the Abolitionist attack on slavery led to the Southern white defense that blacks were inherently suited to the institution and unfit for freedom, that they were in fact happy only under the guidance of white masters. While white servitude had naturally disintegrated, permanent black slavery was compatible with liberty and equality, as well as the biological inferiority of the African—by the 1840s, scientific evidence was marshaled to show that blacks constituted a separate species of person.

This sort of thinking could even be used by antislavery thinkers, such as the Unitarian pastor in New York who, on determining that the Negro's "nature is singularly childlike, affectionate, docile, and patient," concluded that it was un-Christian to oppress such a person. Indeed, were Negro characteristics not Christian virtues? Most white Northerners could not shake their racism, however, and when Republicans embraced the idea of Negro franchise after the Civil War, it was not as a consequence of believing in racial equality but, rather, the result of political expediency.[40]

White leaders in the postwar South adopted a paternalistic attitude toward blacks, expecting that these recently born citizens would turn as children to their political fathers. And, unsurprisingly, there were slaves who remained loyal to their former masters—and there were previous owners who insisted on retaining young blacks until they reached twenty-one.[41]

These leaders simply assumed segregation and, in fact, were essentially racist. As Darwinism became popular, they—and most others of European stock—accepted it as a newer justification for hierarchical assumptions. This was, in fact, a more benign point of view than another late nineteenth-century opinion: that blacks had degenerated since being freed from slavery.[42] The African-American-as-child was, at best, a permanent foster member of the American family.

This statement was graphically illustrated in D. W. Griffith's film *The Birth of a Nation* (1915), based on Negrophobe Thomas Dixon's novel *The Clansmen* (1905), in which book the African American is described as "half child, half animal." Griffith, whose father had fought for the Confederacy and later lost the family fortune, looked back fondly to a paternalistic South where all black slaves acted as children and, after the war, all freed blacks (save for a few "old faithful") behaved like animals, most notably the predatory males, until put in their place by the Ku Klux Klan.

This enormously popular movie, characterized by President Woodrow Wilson as "writing history with lightning," set the stage for the many films in which blacks, or rather black men, performed as inferiors, their characteristic depiction until World War II.[43] It was the stereotype promulgated even by whites who considered themselves friends of the African American, such as the prominent Atlantan who wrote in 1906: "The Negro race is a child race. We are a strong race, their guardians." In Walter Hines Page's novel *The Southerner* (1909), a character observes: "The Negro is a child in civilization.... Let us train him.... Let us teach him to do productive work, teach him to be a help, to support himself, to do useful things, to be a man, to build up his family life."[44]

The use of the male pronoun in this last passage, the admonition "to be a man," points to the assumption implicit in the white discussion of blacks since the word "child" had been introduced before the Civil War: not the African American but the African American *male* was the subject. This focus might be attributed to the exclusivity of male suffrage in defining an American citizen or to the fact that almost always men created the image of black-as-child (the important exception was *Uncle Tom's Cabin*).[45]

But deeper feelings also contributed to the focus on the male. The child/animal dichotomy suggests that a savage who is feared must be domesticated into a child who is either permanently immature (the Negrophobe viewpoint) or educable (the Negrophile perspective). And the dichotomy was perpetuated into the twentieth century. Donald Bogle titles his "interpretive history of blacks in American films" *Toms, Coons, Mulattoes, Mammies, and Bucks.* Toms are, of course, faithful and submissive, while coons are lazy and unreliable, but both exhibit childlike characteristics in contrast to the undesirable, animallike bucks.[46]

But the mammies and mullatoes? Both are women, the former portrayed as dark, fat, and competent, the latter light, curvaceous, and sexy. One raises boys, the other tempts men—the madonna and the whore. Historian Catherine Clinton asserts that the mammy is almost absent from the documents of antebellum America; she "was created by white Southerners to redeem the relationship between black women and white men ... a counterpoint to the octoroon concubine, the light-skinned product of a 'white man's lust' who was habitually victimized by slaveowners' sexual appetites."[47] Probably Clinton is guessing about the motive, but she is correct in pointing to the post–Civil War emergence of fond Southern white memories of the mammy as child rearer and household organizer.[48]

Indeed, it is undeniable that Southern white children in the prewar years were cared for by black women, just as white children had black playmates. Historian Eugene Genovese, who is convinced of the *real* presence of the mammy, captures both her strength and her weakness:

"More than any other slave, she had absorbed the paternalist ethos and accepted her place in a system of reciprocal obligations defined from above." Strong because she operated resourcefully and responsibly within the system, she was weak because she could not pass her power to other blacks without making them even more dependent.[49] She was domesticated, though hardly made childlike, from the beginning and, hence, even more reassuring than a tom or a coon. Unlike the mulatto, she was neither a reminder of interracial sex nor a prod to the libido. That the most famous rendition of her character came from a white man in blackface—Al Jolson singing "My Mammy"—adds a bitter irony to the perspective.[50]

A turning point in the understanding of black male character came in 1941 when anthropologist Melville Herskovits published *The Myth of the Negro Past*. Herskovits accused scholars and policy makers of basing their work on myths that supported racial prejudice, the first one of which was "Negroes are naturally of a childlike character." Pointing to the sophistication of an African worldview, he concluded that "such maladjustments to the American scene as characterize Negro life are to be ascribed largely to the social and economic handicaps these folks have suffered, rather than to any inability to cope with the realities of life."[51]

World War II was a turning point in race relations in the United States, not because of white academic writing (American historians in the late 1950s were still fighting about whether the slave was actually a Sambo)[52] but because the determined action of African Americans, oftentimes lawyers, and the official response as seen in the desegregation of the armed forces in Korea and the *Brown v. Topeka Board of Education* decision of the Supreme Court.[53]

The courage demonstrated by African Americans during the ensuing civil rights struggle surprised most white Americans, as indeed it should have. The long and concerted effort to marginalise blacks and rationalize such treatment on the basis of their being essentially simple, weak, and vulnerable was confounded by their willingness to confront their enemies at lunch counters, schools, and courthouses, to create public demonstrations where sometimes their very lives were at stake. Ironically, in view of the perception of blacks as childlike, black youths played a leading role in the sit-in and voter registration movements, while both black children and youths desegregated the schools. What could have happened in their upbringing to encourage them to act so independently of white expectations?

It was a question all thoughtful Americans asked. Robert Coles, a white child psychiatrist from Boston, traveled to the South—"a region that considers them not merely children but (as Negroes) the children of children"—to find out, though he had to confess that it was "difficult to discover what prompted the initiative taken by these young people. A common charge is that they are 'brought out' by conspiring adults. Often it is quite the contrary; nervous parents have been afraid to allow their children's participation in the initially tense months of school desegregation, let alone the more volatile uncertainties of street demonstrations." Yet again and again, as he visited black families (and white as well), first in New Orleans and then Atlanta, he learned that black parents unfailingly prepared their children to survive in the intimidating white world.[54]

Ruby was one of the four little Negro girls who entered two white (and almost empty) elementary schools in New Orleans in 1960 to the accompaniment of mobs, threats of violence, television publicity and international attention, and intervening federal marshals. Coles had been studying stress in children created by severe physical illness and found that he could communicate better with young children through drawings than by talking. Ruby, six years old, never used the colors brown or black except to denote ground, and she consistently drew whites as larger and more lifelike than Negroes—until she realistically portrayed her maternal grandfather, who "has a farm that's his and no one else's." Although Ruby claimed to be happy living in New Orleans, she also wished for a farm, and her mother assured her the family could always stay with grandpa, who "can lick anyone and his brother together." (Ruby's father, who received a Purple Heart in Korea for risking his life to rescue a white soldier, was currently jobless—due to Ruby's school situation—and depressed.)[55]

Although temporarily suffering an eating problem, apparently brought on by a mob member who every day shouted she would poison and choke the child to death, Ruby was a healthy survivor. So were many other black children subjected to stress as a result of their roles in the racial struggle. Coles searched for an explanation. Yes, parents prepared their children, but they emphasized endurance (which certainly embraced nonviolence), not protest. The children wondered why they should face tyranny rather than danger; their parents were compromised by endurance. Yet even their peers were astonished. A white seventeen-year-old girl asked Coles: "Where did they ever learn to behave like that?" His answer (not to her) was that, compared with their age mates, "many of the youths taking part in racial demonstrations are better integrated psychologically as well as racially. They act out of deep moral convictions.... But for many of both groups [demonstrators and hecklers] the differences are less psychological than social or cultural."[56] History has the answer. This was not the first generation of African Americans to want freedom, nor the first generation of European Americans to resist granting it. But encouraged by federal action in the armed services and in the courts, not to mention the attention showered on these steps forward and their consequences on television, these black youths were able to act on beliefs long and deeply held.

11. Ruby's drawings revealed her changing thoughts about herself, her family, and her white schoolmates in the 1950s (*upper left,* white girl by Ruby, age 6; *upper right,* Ruby by Ruby, age 6; *lower left,* Ruby's grandfather; *lower right,* Ruby by Ruby, age 7). At this time, unlike the era of slavery, black and white children were not playmates. Figures 1, 2, 3, and 5 from *Children of Crisis: A Study in Courage and Fear,* volume I, by Robert Coles. Copyright © 1964, 1965, 1966, 1967 by Robert Coles. By permission of Little, Brown and Company (Inc.).

Part II
Industrial America

Urban Middle-Class Childhood

Thomas Mellon was born in northern Ireland in 1813 and, five years later, accompanied his parents to America, where they settled in western Pennsylvania and began tilling the land. Young Thomas was farming full-time by the age of 12, but reading Benjamin Franklin's autobiography two years later turned him in another direction: "Here was Franklin, poorer than myself, who by industry, thrift and frugality had become learned and wise, and elevated to wealth and fame." Thomas had already visited Pittsburgh, where, a neighbor observed, he would see more in a day than in a lifetime at his home in Poverty Point. And he did. "The whole scene was new to me, and impressed me with an idea of wealth and magnificence that I had before no conception of." His father expected him to continue farming, though he was allowed three or four months of school in the winter. When he was 17, his father offered him land of his own where, he realized, he could spend his lifetime "making an honest, frugal, living by hard labor, but little more.... All my air castles and bright fancies of acquiring knowledge or wealth or distinction were wrecked and ruined." Instead, he entered college, then studied law and became a major player in Pittsburgh industry and banking.[1]

Mellon's life captured the transition from early agricultural society to a form of social organization more closely resembling our present urban way of life, often referred to as "modernization." This process has been viewed from the perspectives of personality and social character, technology and the economy, and demography.[2] One way of looking at the change does not preclude another. Indeed, there is substantial agreement as to what happened.

Beginning at the personal level, it is apparent that seventeenth-century English emigrants to the New World were seeking freedom from traditional authority and demonstrating an openness to new experience, two modern attitudes. Also modern in tone was the American settlers' proclivity for altering the natural and social environment, as well as their talent for ambitiously pushing themselves forward as Thomas Mellon was later to do. By the eighteenth century it appeared as though the religion of the founders was endangered by reason and secular education, traits associated with the Enlightenment—and with Benjamin Franklin. Members of the avant-garde in America actively took charge of their lives rather than passively accepting an assigned lot, driven by an inner force that cried out for self-expression and independence. Most European Americans struggled with the issues, though they arrived at divergent solutions (see Chapter 2 on the evangelicals, moderates, and genteel) and, quite logically, attached themselves to the War for Independence in different ways.

The late eighteenth century witnessed not only a political revolution but a demographic one as some Americans began practicing birth control and limiting family size (including longer times between births and ceasing to give birth at a young age) to improve economic opportunities for themselves and their offspring.[3] This occurred before major cityward migration (and immigration) took place.

Finally, the flurry of commercial activity in the seventeenth century, which grew into a storm in the eighteenth and established a financial basis for the industrial revolution in the nineteenth, provided clear evidence of modern development. The ideological basis was present as well, in the openness to novelty, dedication to reason, and willingness to alter the environment—all attitudes intimately related to the technological change fundamental to industrialization. (By industrialization is meant the creation of new sources of energy and power which transcended human strength, substituted mechanical device for human skill, and drew upon and altered natural resources.)

Industrialization was central to modernization. Energy and power were concentrated in one place, the factory, which needed a labor force, which in turn led to the concentration of population in the industrial city. Urbanization fed upon and fostered internal migration and immigration from abroad. An educational system was established to inform and socialize the children of the new city dwellers. And a centralized bureaucratic government emerged that first nurtured and later attempted to control industry and its social offshoots.

Industrialization took place quickly in the United States. When the nation was created, 95 percent of its inhabitants lived on farms or in villages. (And in 1800 the median age of the American population, typical of a traditional society, was 16; it was twice that 150 years later.)[4] During the nineteenth century these traditional communities were transformed into an urban, industrial culture. The movement began in the Northeast, where commercial seaports—Boston, New York, Philadelphia—were already established. By the 1880s the largest sector of the economy was industrial; by 1920 most Americans lived in urban areas of more that 2,500 people.

The impact of modernization was profound. Movement to the city signified not simply a shift from farm work to factory labor but the transformation of a way of life. Rural America was governed by nature. A day was framed by the rising and setting of the sun. Human existence found its analogy in the passing of the seasons, beginning with the birth of spring and maturing into the death of winter. And life was lived in a community of familiar faces. In contrast, industrial America was timed not by nature but by the clock. Work had previously been accomplished within a small, personal world where there was hardly a distinction between employer and employee. Now labor became a commodity, wages the connection between anonymous worker and manager, and efficiency the goal of production.

The mass society that was emerging operated on new principles. Natural rhythms were absent from the city, as was a sense of community. Government was less local, more centralized; although it was democratic (if one were an adult white male), it appeared remote. Contributing to the feeling of anonymity was the rapid growth of the population, including a large foreign component that was apparently unaffected by the idea of birth control. (Contraception itself was an intrusion on the natural rhythms of rural life.) Mass public education was also mechanized, with compulsory attendance (eventually), uniformity of course offerings, measurement of results, and—most important for a consideration of changes in childhood—age grading.

Ranking was not a novel concept. In the hierarchically structured traditional society, status had of course been critically important. Position was based on religious standing, on family, on landholding, but, given the limited resources, not much on monetary wealth. In the new age of production, where wealth abounded and multiplied, society was not really status-ridden. Rather, it was class-divided, and class was determined by income. Mobility was not only geographical but occupational and, hence, class-directed. Parents who were aware and ambitious could, should, and surely would try to imbue their children with traits most likely to succeed.

Middle-class parents had the resources to do so, while working-class parents did not. The latter were too busy trying to survive, and their children were expected to contribute to this effort by holding jobs. These youngsters might be fortunate enough to absorb a few years of public schooling, which was not compulsory until the turn of the twentieth century. Their life chances were clearly different from those of middle-class children.

In the urban middle class the father/mother/child triad was dynamically changing as America entered the nineteenth century. In the patriarchal family of the seventeenth and eighteenth centuries, the father was theoretically and actually king; because of his real and continual presence on the premises, he directed the activities of the home, including the raising of children. His wife bore and nursed the infant; that was expected and considered natural. But while she played other roles, always subordinate to her husband, he was the final authority for the young. His mode of governing, as we have seen in Chapter 2, varied from the genteel to the moderate to the evangelical household.

But changes were taking place in the late eighteenth century. In those regions where population growth exceeded the resources of land to support male offspring, younger sons wandered off to the seaport cities in search of employment or to the West in quest of land, thereby weakening the power of their fathers over them. Patriarchalism was in gentle decline, but motherhood was on the ascendant. The American Revolution and the creation of the new nation caused commentators to reflect on the importance of women insofar as they were responsible for raising public-spirited sons. Beyond narrowly political considerations, books printed in England and works written in America stressed the positive qualities of the maternal role.[5]

But as critical as the altered roles of parents was the changing perception of the child. In portraits painted after 1770, childhood was depicted as distinctly different from adulthood. Furthermore, childhood had become a longer stage, both in art and in life, and developed its own visual vocabulary (clothing, toys, behavior) in paintings and, presumably, in reality.[6] Finally, children were now being described as born into the world with minds as blank slates, therefore totally malleable, not to say innocent and vulnerable. A mother's sacred duty was to protect and rightly shape them, a task that had always been hers in their earliest years but previously went unheralded when infancy seemed less important. By the end of the nineteenth century, business success was being explained by the principle of self-help; its literature glorified, more than any other factor, the presence of a mother who molded her son's character.[7]

Life in the city reified these trends. Father journeyed to a job that occupied him the day long, rendering him even less dominant at home. His urbanized wife, alone in the household, assumed major responsibility for child rearing—and was soon being depicted as specially endowed to care for the young, being more virtuous than her male counterpart. (This, at any rate, was the propaganda of preachers who faced increasingly female congregations.) An ideology that reflected these changes was evident in an unprecedented number of advice books on family management issued in the 1830s, just as the urban middle class was establishing itself. Such manuals aided former rural folk in their acculturation to city life, especially in the upbringing of bourgeois children.[8]

This literature was true to reality as it demoted father from his previous position of eminence, though he was sometimes viewed as the authority of last resort, at least in principle. But even in principle the father's power was slipping. During the seventeenth and eighteenth centuries colonial courts, under the sway of English common law, granted

12. Motherhood assumed more importance in the nineteenth century, in fiction as well as in fact, a trend accentuated by the frequent absence of the father from urban family life. Louisa May Alcott, *Little Women* (Boston, 1868), frontispiece.

him full power (and the mother only reverence and respect) over children. An orphan, legally speaking, was a child whose father had died. In the nineteenth century this thinking changed with an altered view of the child, which supposed that children had interests of their own, interests better served by a nurturing mother than a less sensitive father. Divorce was infrequent, but in a custody dispute the mother was likely to be awarded the child. At the death of a father, far more likely to occur than divorce, the mother was increasingly likely to be granted guardianship even if her spouse willed it otherwise.[9]

Fathers did not suddenly disappear, nor did a more gentle discipline sweep all households. In 1831 Francis Wayland, fourth president of Brown University, proudly explained how he starved his willful infant son into submission. Even Bronson Alcott, father of the author Louisa May, though an enemy of Wayland's Calvinistic idea of infant depravity, expected of his daughters conscientious self-control, not to mention affection and reason, at an early age. What made him a nineteenth-century parent was that he applauded the will for its role in the triumph of the child's higher nature over baser instincts.[10]

The new advice literature correctly assumed that mother would be bringing up the now-smaller brood. There is no doubt that husbands and wives were deliberately limiting the size of their families, with mothers bearing children frequently in the first years of marriage, then slowing down or ceasing to reproduce. "Voluntary motherhood" was based on considerations of physical and mental health, as well as a desire for greater independence on the part of women (presumably a consequence of *their* childhoods), and men cooperated, though male goals seem to have been primarily economic. In the seventeenth century a married woman typically produced 7.4 children, while in the late eighteenth she bore 6.4, in the early nineteenth 4.9, and in the late nineteenth 2.8. In 1933, when fertility was temporarily at the end of its decline, it stood at about 30 percent of the 1800 figure. Fewer children, of course, meant that parents could devote more attention to each child.[11]

Childbirth had been the riskiest of business in early America. After 1770, male physicians entered a field which had been the province of midwives and neighborhood women. These men made the procedure safer, though at the expense of the women attendants. What had been a community event among women became secluded (though not without husbands agonizing about doctors being in intimate contact with their wives), just as family life was becoming a more private matter.[12] Housing improved during the nineteenth century, in terms of not only construction, heating, and plumbing but also space, granting more privacy to inhabitants and specialized room use.[13]

Family privacy was directly related to the new concept of childhood innocence and vulnerability. Mass society was novel, it was strange, and especially to homebound mothers who could only imagine its dangers, it was frightening. The unknown "others" out there in the city created uncertainty, worry, and fear. These feelings could be and probably were projected onto children, those innocent and vulnerable beings threatened by the urban environment. Indeed, if parents were nostalgic for their own rural childhoods, there would be yet more reason to see innocence, simplicity, and happiness in their children. Home was a sanctuary, a place where childhood could be nurtured.[14]

In this haven, especially given the new focus on early childhood, a mother's job was crucial. She must feed the newborn for its and her own good health. To put the infant out to nurse had long been condemned on religious grounds, and by the turn of the nineteenth century it was denounced on medical grounds as well. Swaddling had been abandoned by the 1770s as an infringement on the infant's freedom to develop, as had any artificial means of hastening a baby's walking.[15] More attention than ever was devoted to the very young.

Although children were not put out to nurse, middle-class mothers often had domestic help, and they worried about the effect servants might have upon children, not only physically (exposing them to the elements, drugging them) but mentally (filling them with fears or superstitions, failing to impart appropriate morals). Yet there was no doubt that domestics could and did have a positive influence, simply by aiding a stressed mother but also by providing companionship, reassurance (sleeping in the same room with infants), and even friendship. Edith Wharton, reflecting on her nurse Hannah Doyle, wrote: "I pity all children who have not had a Doyley—a nurse who has always been there, who is as established as the sky and as warm as the sun, who understands everything."[16]

Perhaps not so much in the first year but certainly as early as possible, a mother, with or without a servant, was expected to implement the primary principle of family government, the obedience of the child. The religious justification for obedience was that parents symbolized the authority of God, and some advice givers echoed their evangelical forebearers: "Children are brought into existence and placed in families, not to follow their own wayward inclinations, but to look up to their parents for guidance; not to teach but to be taught; not to govern but to be governed."[17] There was, however, a more secular and utilitarian justification for obedience. It led to self-control. What was initially parental censure of inappropriate behavior—and, of course, the child's learned acceptance of parental command—would ultimately lead to rational *self*-restraint, that is, the child would come to understand the parent's reasonability. Needless to say, parental example was also essential to success in raising the young.

This, then, was a mother's responsibility. In the implementation of it she was more delicate with her charges than her husband had been, less inclined to corporal punishment, more apt to rule through affection and example.[18] She put internal direction of the child ahead of external control. Rather than ridiculing or shaming those under her command, she would build with the malleable material in her hands a conscience, there to house guilt. Shame receded with the rural community that had vitalized it. In the anonymity of the city, each individual had to police him/herself. But given the fact that boys were expected to move out into the tempting world while girls would remain in the home, it was more important that sons rather than daughters know the meaning of guilt.

Sigmund Freud, who was a product of urban bourgeois culture, traced guilt directly to the Oedipus complex. A little boy, probably between the ages of four and six, desired his mother and thus was forced to contemplate eliminating his father, whom he loved. Hence guilt. Freud fared less well in assigning a similar complex to little girls, and for good reason. In the frequently father-absent middle-class urban households, boys were a set-up for the Oedipus complex; girls were not. (Recall from Chapter 2 how rural Southern boys, being inculcated with a sense of honor by their fathers at this time, were different from Northern middle-class boys learning guilt from their mothers.)[19]

The consequences of a mother-dominated upbringing must be measured by the psychological yardstick used to assess them. From an attachment point of view, for example, the pervasive presence of mother, unencumbered by the many children who would have claimed her attention at an earlier time, should have contributed to feelings of autonomy in the child. And the urban middle-class focus on *self*-control should have further fostered autonomy. But simultaneously, at least for boys, it appears to have introduced conflict between initiative (the world of the business-occupied father) and guilt (the lessons of the child-rearing mother). This conflict may have later inhibited the young man attempting to make his way in the world, not only in a career but in romance.[20]

Fear as a parental tool was notable for its absence. "A more sentimentalized view of motherhood meant a reduction in the use of fear in favor of more gentle, time-consuming persuasions," according to historians Peter N. Stearns and Timothy Haggerty. For the first time, parents were warned to avoid using fear to discipline children, although nothing was said about how to deal with fears that children manifest. It was advised that boys should courageously face and master fear, unlike their sisters, who were sheltered from it (hence the word "sissy" for fearful males).[21]

An outside observer would not have guessed these differences by looking at sisters and brothers together. All infants wore long gowns, usually white (pink and blue sex identifications were pre–World War II creations), until they were six to nine months old, when they were attired in ankle-length dresses. At about three years they donned half-length petticoats and pantaloons, the mid-nineteenth century being the first time girls had ever worn pants of any description. Giving girls the same freedom of movement as boys raised objections; during the later nineteenth century pantaloons became frillier and shorter until they finally became underwear. That children between the ages of three and

13. Children in the urban middle class were dressed alike, thus distinguishing childhood from adulthood, but boys and girls had different toys, as this rendering by an unidentified artist c. 1840 shows. Brother, not sister, would ride a horse with whip in hand. *The Hobby Horse*, gift of Edgar William and Bernice Chrysler Garbisch, Photograph © 2001 Board of Trustees, National Gallery of Art, Washington.

seven dressed alike and wore the same hairstyles reinforced the idea that childhood was a separate stage of life, a point of view taken up by romantic writers who endowed that stage with a special spirituality: Innocence and joy were more to be desired than age and wisdom.[22]

Yet Victorian parents could view children androgynously only so long as they were sure the nature and destiny of either gender was unalterable. If costume was a symbol of asexual innocence, toys pointed girls and boys toward their separate roles in adult society. Lads received more gifts, usually related to sports or military endeavor. Despite the decline of corporal punishment, a favorite was the pony whip, surely a badge of authority. Girls typically were given dolls or doll-related toys, often too delicate to be played with.[23] Recalling her late nineteenth-century childhood, Zona Gale wrote, "They [boys] were always producing something from their pockets and examining it, with their heads together, or manufacturing something or burying something, or disputing about something unguessed and alluring. Their whole world was filled with doing, doing, doing, whereas ours was made wholly of watching things get done."[24]

By the mid-nineteenth century the differences between male and female were considered so vast that child-advice books were often aimed solely at one gender or the other. The sexes were thought to be divided by powerful emotions, none more potent than anger: Sweet little girls must repress it totally, in preparation for their role of family maintenance; nasty-tempered boys must master it without losing it. Anger was offensive to parents but a virtue in the worlds of sports, business, and politics. Boys were to conquer fear, girls to be sheltered from it. Jealousy was endemic among girls, far less evident among boys. These emotional distinctions could be overridden by romantic love, which both girls and boys imbibed from their mothers.[25]

Not only the interior world of emotion but the exterior world of play reflected gender distinctions. Toys are the implements which, when they survive, tell us that play (a process) and games (the process with rules) existed. To learn about children, adults (notably anthropologists) studied these activities, beginning in the 1880s.[26] Manufacturers, every bit as smart as anthropologists, began producing toys in large numbers after the Civil War. Drawing on the standards of the hardware trade, toy makers used a simple construction, appealed to the parents who would understand and buy the product, and recognized that toys were used by children to mimic adult—that is, gender-divided—roles. Toys were featured in department stores that were being built in cities in the 1870s, and they were available as well by mail order, since most Americans were still living on farms. Toys were the topics of persuasive advertising that signaled a mass-market revolution in merchandizing, and by the early twentieth century retailers were beginning to recognize the value of making a pitch directly to children through magazines.[27]

The entrepreneurial spirit was not alone responsible for toys. Urban middle-class parents were empathic toward children's play. The home, once a workplace, now catered to leisure. Smaller families meant fewer siblings; toys substituted for playmates—and, in the absence of real labor, helped train children in work values such as competition. Toys in the increasingly private home provided an alternative to street play, aiding parents in isolating and thus training the child. But toys also catered to children's fantasies. And toys were gifts, the agents by which wages were transformed into family sentiment radically different from the world of work.[28]

Boys had to cross the bridge in the other direction, from the family to the marketplace, from childhood to the self-made manhood of nineteenth-century America. Accorded a freedom that girls lacked, boys burst outdoors at age six, roughhousing in ways forbidden at home, yet learning at the same time to contain their emotions. Companionship, not intimacy, was the aim, with no room for weaklings or crybabies. The popularization of sports, especially baseball and football, could only reify these values. The "ultimate value was independence."[29]

A boy could not shake himself free of the guilt imposed by his mother; indeed, he added to his psychic repertory the shame he felt when he could not fulfill the expectations of his pals—and he lived in that divided world the rest of his life. In his youth when he had left his family, he confessed to homesickness and compensated by creating or joining clubs, the best known being the YMCA, which replicated family and honored friendship. Mother and sisters were not forgotten, and in his mid teens, the time of puberty in the nineteenth century, he developed an almost obsessive interest in girls—from afar. Meanwhile, he drew close to his chums, demonstrative toward them both verbally and physically, yet saving his sexual self for marriage, anxious though he was about being drawn back into the women's sphere, the home.[30]

The augmented concern with rearing boys and girls signified an interest in children's well-being that carried into the field of health. Although physicians harmed as much as helped patients until the late nineteenth century, hygiene and medical care for children received more notice than ever before. The first scientific treatise on child health appeared in 1825, while at the same time doctors began publishing on diseases of children. The first two hospitals which treated children exclusively were established in the 1850s, though at that time mortality statistics indicated no improvement for children since 1790. Not until the 1880s was infant mortality steadily decreasing in New York City, a phenomenon related to recognition of the salutary effect of milk—

and its pasteurization, since it was the discoveries of Pasteur, Koch, and Lister which provided the evidence that germs caused infectious disease. (The understanding of germ theory did not lead physicians immediately to change their treatment of infectious diseases, which had to await the development of sulfa drugs and penicillin in the mid-twentieth century, but such measures as sanitation, vaccination, and the identification of infant mortality as a public health problem helped prevent disease.)[31]

It was also in the 1880s that the American Pediatric Society was founded by Jacob Jacobi, who proclaimed that the "pathology and therapeutics of infancy and childhood do not mean the very same things in adults[;] they mean more than merely reduced ages and doses." Only a few years earlier, Elizabeth Blackwell had attempted to rouse parents in taking the initiative on children's diseases; now she and others were calling for the sex education of children.[32]

In these years, good health and life expectancy increased significantly. (White males were expected to reach 40 in 1850, slightly over 48 in 1900, 56.3 by 1920.) Deaths from infectious diseases, especially among young people, were on the decline due to preventative measures, such as the establishment of state and city health boards. Midcentury reformers focused on hygiene and health issues. Disease fell into the category of a natural process which could be controlled rather than a religious scourge brought on by God. Businessmen and politicians saw that investment in public health was profitable. The lives of children seemed progressively secure, which *may* have allowed their parents to invest more emotion in relationships—the point is debatable.[33]

The middle-class child not only received serious medical attention but became the subject of social celebration. By midcentury, birthdays were being commemorated, and in a novel way: Only kids were invited to the parties. While holidays in the seventeenth and eighteenth centuries were community affairs for adults, in the nineteenth century celebrations moved into the private home and centered around children.

Christmas, for example, was totally altered. In Europe before the settlement of America, there was a long holiday season from the Feast of St. Nicholas (December 6) through the Feast of St. Stephen (December 25) to the Feast of the Magi (January 6), with parades, bonfires, feasting, drinking, and dancing. Such celebration fell victim to the austerity of the Protestant Reformation, especially in its rejection of saints. There was no Christmas in colonial America. But it was revived, almost invented, in the nineteenth century by literary persons, the most notorious of whom was Charles Dickens. *A Christmas Carol* (1843) created an event that had never existed, celebrating the family and particularly its children. Its message of family unity, benevolence, and brotherhood was deeply appealing during the Civil War. Christmas became a children's holiday, with a tree and stockings to be filled with toys and sweets; no youngster was to be denied. Parents who felt guilty about forsaking handmade toys for manufactured ones made Santa Claus the mediator of gifts, thus ameliorating the guilt.[34]

Stories for and about children reaffirmed the centrality of the young. For boys, there were the Horatio Alger books, tales of adventure in which the protagonist set his sights on achievement in the world and eventually prevailed without losing his moral sights. In *Bound to Rise* (1873), Harry Walton left his boyhood farm for opportunity in the city, dangerous though it was, and succeeded without sacrificing his traditional ideals. Girls could learn from reading Martha Finley's *Elsie Dinsmore* (1867), the heroine of which was dogmatically bound to her religious beliefs and, showing the superiority of the innocent world of the child to the compromising cosmos of the adult, redeemed her elders. In *Little Women* (1869), Beth was similar to Elsie, whereas her three sisters tended to have trouble overcoming their faults on their way to building their respective characters. In all three books, children were exemplary.[35]

Further proof that young people, and especially those in the urban middle class, were the subjects of special attention existed in the field of education. Despite the seriousness with which schooling was taken in seventeenth-century England, formal education was not a high priority in colonial America or in any traditional society. The Puritans, however, had only one foot in tradition; the other was moving into a modern sort of self-awareness. Reading the Scriptures was fundamental to an individual's

14. When children became the focus of the middle-class home, holidays became *their* days, as this 1894 lithograph of a birthday party illustrates. Courtesy of Strong Museum, Rochester, New York © 2001.

finding and maintaining a personal (rather than only a social) relationship with God. Many Puritans were university men. In 1647 the General Court of Massachusetts required towns of a certain size to establish and support what amounted to a system of free public education. Outside New England, the state did little for education. Parents taught children, and masters instructed apprentices, at least in theory.[36]

The tempo picked up in the eighteenth century. The academy movement, under the baton of the worldly Benjamin Franklin, was responsible for preparing young men in subjects such as science, math, history, and modern languages that led to careers in the trades and professions other than the ministry. Franklin also played a major role in founding the University of Pennsylvania, one of a number of colleges established during the Great Awakening of the 1740s which, despite their religious origins, offered decidedly secular instruction. The creation of the new republic stimulated thought about the kind of citizens needed to sustain a democracy, thus forging an ideological connection between healthy self-governance and popular education, though in fact there existed no uniform system of education but a varying mix of private and public (often one in the same) institutions.[37]

In American cities in the late eighteenth and early nineteenth centuries, the wealthy hired tutors or sent children to boarding school while members of the middle class (that is, anyone able to pay tuition) sent their young to academies or independent pay schools which might or might not receive state funding. There was a considerable variety to choose from, girls as well as boys attended, and additionally there were charity schools for the poor.[38]

The diversity of choice in the city was not reflected in the country. The typical farm community or small town schoolhouse was a dilapidated one-room structure, overcrowded in the winter (after harvest and before planting), irregularly attended by pupils—boys *and* girls—from 4 to 14 (though only a small minority of teenagers went to school during the nineteenth century) who were expected to be silent except when reciting what they had memorized from the books usually brought from home. Seated uncomfortably on high backless benches where they must maintain balance or fall to the floor, they had to behave or be beaten. Obedience, as at home, was the watchword, but its accomplishment was rougher. The teachers were watched and often controlled by the parents, in whose households they lodged in rotation.[39]

At this point the government, under the influence of a new generation of educational reformers (to be distinguished from Thomas Jefferson and his contemporaries), stepped in to change the situation. They called for state intervention in the very years, 1830 to 1860, when urbanization, industrialization, and immigration were altering the American social landscape, and they succeeded where their predecessors had failed, probably because education was perceived as an appropriate response to larger changes.[40] Capitalism, most vigorous in the northeastern United States and especially in the cities, not only placed a premium on literacy and numeracy but, given its centralizing force (e.g., in creating larger and larger markets), it weakened rural isolation and hostility to state funding for education, thus aiding reformers.

The reformers also wanted to alter classroom content, much in the manner that writers of child-rearing manuals sought to change discipline in the home: by substituting internal controls for corporal punishment. (Indeed, women were replacing men as school teachers—they were less expensive and allegedly superior instructors of the young—just as wives were taking over the roles of their husbands as rearers of the young.) Reformers further insisted that the authority of teachers could not be compromised by parents.[41] Work was being taken out of the home by industrialization, and now the school was to be the final word in instruction. The family, which in earlier centuries had been the primary economic, educational, and emotional unit in its residents' lives, was diminished and mutated by these losses; its major function became an emotional or nurturing one. Meanwhile, schools were assigned a mission they could seldom fulfill.

Of course, both parent and teacher believed in the control of the child, the importance of obedience. Both subscribed to moral discipline. And it is certainly true that just as parents, mothers anyway, feared the city and its strangers, educational reformers were disturbed by the developments implicit in modernization and saw a high correlation between personal morality and social order. The properly instructed student would be a good citizen.

Although the public (or common) school movement from 1830 to 1860 was responsible for creating statewide systems of education, and probably half the population under 20 now attended school, it was in the city—where there was a notable shift from private to public schooling—that novel conditions, particularly density of population, called for novel solutions. Schools were graded with regard to age (and toddlers were excluded), the curriculum was standardized, a corps of supervisory personnel oversaw the school operation, and teacher training gained attention.[42] What had existed in the rural district schools—where attendance may have been higher than in the city but was limited to the winter months—in a prior generation seemed lackadaisical by comparison. Historian Priscilla Clement observes: "Classrooms were scenes of military-like drill and were staffed by teachers who commonly attributed 'intellectual failure' to 'moral laxity.'"[43]

Developing along with the common schools, indeed sometimes paving the way for them and often influencing them, were Sunday schools. Begun in England and reaching the United States in the 1780s, Sunday schools offered reading and writing to children, especially African American children, who worked on weekdays. (The early Sunday schools were criticized for usurping the family's nurturing function, although most of the scholars were drawn from the working class and the teachers were of middle-class origin.) With the Bible frequently the text and ministers often the sponsors, the Sunday school became an institution focused on the development of piety; it also broadened its constituency from working-class children to the young of all classes. The original publications of the American Sunday-School Union, founded in 1824, were designed to give instruction in reading, as were the similarly moralistic McGuffey readers, which first appeared in 1836 and were widely used in the common schools.[44]

The school was hardly alone in moving from a heterogeneous agency to an age-graded, specialized operation. Birth control diminished the size of families; intervals between children at first became longer, though by the end of the century children were being born closer together in age. Social groups were altered in the same direction. Whereas in the

15. The urban classroom, in contrast to the one-room schoolhouse, was typified by order and discipline. Students of the same age studied standardized textbooks under the stern eye of a trained teacher. This photograph was taken c. 1899 in Washington, D.C. Library of Congress.

early nineteenth century the term "young people" referred to youths in their teens and early twenties, who were generally free of adult supervision since it was assumed the older would look after the younger, increasingly age peers formed social groups.[45]

Similarly, the workforce had featured a mixture of ages. Farm boys of seven or eight toiled with men (who controlled the work situation), though they might attend school in the winter. Trade or construction labor was also available on a seasonal basis, as was domestic service or industrial employment for girls. Because toil was so pervasive, it was not a sign of independence; wages were typically turned over to parents until the youth reached 21. Few jobs were so technical in nature that a long education or apprenticeship was required. At first this worked to the young person's advantage. In the early nineteenth century, commercial and industrial opportunities made it possible for youth to shed the dependency typical of farmwork and take on adult (or potentially adult) jobs. But with increasing industrialization, toil became more specialized, and professions emerged for which training was considered necessary. By the late nineteenth century, the school was becoming an institution that certified students for work.[46] Up to this time, boys had seldom attended high school, which was a new addition to public education mainly serving girls. However, as the nation's economic system became more complex and the range of available work kept pace, parents were hard put to provide their children useful information about careers, leaving a void for high schools—and, as it turned out, colleges—to fill. While this situation detached young people from the home (though parents did not encourage youths to strike out for themselves), it did not render them more independent. Instead, from 1890 to 1920, institutions began to be developed which since then have delayed youth in its achievement of adult status.[47]

These institutions could be found within colleges and high schools, as well as in Protestant churches. In the colleges fraternities, athletics, and debating societies, formerly run by students, increasingly came under faculty and administration control. The curriculum still reflected traditional values, but it was no secret that business favored the collegian over the young man who received his education in the shop or the plant. A college education had acquired cash value. High schools emulated the social as well as the academic practices of colleges, and in extending control over extracurricular life they did even more to undermine student autonomy. Simultaneously, the young people's movements that already existed in the churches were greatly expanded, and in the course of this growth every effort was made to take over the spare-time activities of youth. Women, such as those who sparked the temperance movement, were frequently the agents of control, although the YMCA, the leading youth organization of the nineteenth century, was created by men.[48]

During most of the nineteenth century, youth had been characterized by semidependence, which meant total subordination at some times and complete freedom at others. The environment of young people was casual and unstructured; in contrast, children were being regulated in the home and beyond. (The school reforms of midcentury affected mainly 6- to 13-year-olds.) Surely the extension of control from children to youth—what might be considered a lengthening of childhood—owed some of its energy to the success of these measures with younger children, even if the ostensible reason for the extension was that the years around puberty must be guarded. Fear of the "dangerous classes," the young people from laboring backgrounds, led some moralists to designate them as inferior to middle-class youth. It was in this context—romantic views of childhood and fears of modern living—that the concept of adolescence arose. Many religiously inclined psychologists speculated and wrote about adolescence as a turbulent stage of life, implying that young persons at this stage of life needed control.[49]

Foremost among them was G. Stanley Hall, a psychologist and university president long engaged in child research, of which his two-volume study of adolescence was the crowning achievement. Describing this stage of life as a "new birth" that ushered in a period of "storm and stress" characterized by emotional opposites (selfishness and altruism, bravado and a sense of unworthiness), Hall saw its essential cause as biological. Sexuality was of critical interest to him, an area where the young person must establish a balance between freedom and control by sublimating sexual feelings into religious and other intellectual or creative activity. His depiction of the adolescent struggle was, in a sense, a veiled narrative of the late nineteenth-century thinker whose faith was being undermined by modern science in a world where rural America was superceded by a new urban, industrial society. Yet at the same time adolescents were undeniably a social group at the turn of the century, and Hall's portrait of their world was the first systematic study of its kind.[50]

In the sphere of fiction, older childhood was portrayed in the late nineteenth and early twentieth centuries as "a time of serious and often painful preparation for life." Girls were allowed to be independent—restless and willful—but in achieving adulthood they had to adapt themselves to more modest social expectations. Boys, less imaginative than determined, acted courageously but were expected to become modest team players.[51] Without using the word "adolescence," writers identified the process—not surprising, since fiction accurately mirrored reality, or at least half of it. Girls enjoyed freedom until puberty, when, as one of them remarked, she lost her "happy-go-lucky, carefree childhood" during her thirteenth year. Boys were given more latitude for the time being, but they were pushed by their parents toward organizations that encouraged the strenuous life within a framework of subordination. That they continued to resist these efforts was evident in the turnover rate for the Boy Scouts.[52]

Another explanation of this surge toward control may lie in psychologist Elizabeth M. R. Lomax's observation that "a major change occurred in the middle of the nineteenth century, when the child changed from an issue for discussion to an object of scientific observation." G. Stanley Hall played a major role in this work by initiating the child study movement, which featured a two-pronged approach to youngsters from birth through adolescence: Parents were encouraged to keep logs of their children's behaviors, while experts were to circulate questionnaires on aspects of child thought and activity.[53] Hall's aim—"to base education on a scientific study of child development"—arose in the wake of the kindergarten movement. By the turn of the century his attention had fastened on secondary education and adolescence at a time when high schools were growing exponentially.[54]

Schools created by middle-class Americans might be expected to reflect bourgeois values and experience: The home was a haven from society; order and discipline were the reigning virtues in socializing the newly prized child. But unlike households, schools could not be sanctuaries, since the intent (certainly in high schools) was to attract all social classes. Schools could, however, be places of order and discipline. This would not be an easy achievement in high schools if adolescents were the turbulent creatures described by Hall, yet that was the rationale for taking charge. It is clear that control was an important issue. But given American frugality when it came to funding education, order and discipline would have to be achieved in heavily populated classrooms, usually by undereducated teachers.

Under these circumstances the individual child was not likely to be appreciated, especially if the school was perceived as a way of keeping kids off the streets.[55] Nor was there agreement on what the individual child needed. The theoreticians of the kindergarten, Europeans such as J. H. Pestalozzi and Friedrich Froebel, spoke of the education of the whole child.[56] The tradition of American moralism stated that education should build character, not foster individuality. Educator John Dewey, addressing what he saw as a conflict between liberty (for creativity) and order, in 1900 condemned the suffocating regimen, the enforced passivity, the mass-audience approach of the typical classroom and called for an ideal school as an enlargement of the ideal home: "The life of the child becomes the all-controlling aim." Psychologist Arnold Gesell, once a student of G. Stanley Hall's, argued in 1912: "Nature endowed the six-year-old with an impulse to investigate, pry into and discover. Some primary schools are veritable tombs of deadened curiosity and initiative."[57]

But it was in elementary schools that most students were enrolled (20.4 million in 1920, compared with 2.4 million in secondary schools, attending an average of 162 days a year). Characterized by testing and the consequent categorization of students, a practice running counter to the ideals of Dewey and Gesell, schools focused on reading, arithmetic, language, spelling, penmanship, and geography. "We went to school for facts and got them," recalled Henry Seidel Canby. Students sat still and silent. Corporal punishment was on the decline, at least officially, but the atmosphere was repressive.[58]

While high schools were as stifling as primary schools, they ran into an issue the lower grades did not need to face: the nature of the curriculum. The issue was whether the secondary school could remain a democratic institution and yet send students in different directions, toward college or toward work. In fact, immigrants entered in proportionately smaller numbers than natives; more girls were enrolled than boys; and the middle class had a richer curriculum and graduated more students than the laboring class.[59] In other words, some social inequities were reproduced in the schools, though not the relegation of females to second-class citizenship, but the promise of American society was there as well, judged by the astonishing rise in high school enrollment from 1890 to 1930.

If schools simulated society in some ways, they contributed to changing it in others, most notably by age grading students. Nowhere was this more apparent than in the high school. Despite class, ethnic, and gender differences, the isolation of peers together at a time in the student's life when identity was in process of formation led to group conformity and homogenization of thought; by providing mutual reassurance through mutuality of interests, it also eased the way from childhood to adulthood. True, some reformers applauded peer bonding because they saw it as a way of weaning immigrant youngsters from their foreign parents. But the reformers' aim was Americanization. The unintended consequence was in planting the seed of youth culture, which when it bloomed yielded neither the order nor the discipline adults wished for.[60]

The children of the urban middle class were the beneficiaries of maternal attention, guaranteed by a smaller sibling population. This situation provided a good beginning for autonomy, which was also nurtured by the abandonment of swaddling and the easing of corporal punishment. The construction of internal controls, the instrument of obedience in the malleable child, also favored individual independence, though boys profited more than girls. The young received more attention than ever before, both in the home—where, for example, the celebration of birthdays and holidays was focused on children—and in society—where children figured importantly in literature, in health concerns and scientific studies, and in education. Yet middle-class adults were fearful of the rapidly urbanizing society in which they lived and, seeking to protect their progeny, devised institutions which emphasized control rather than autonomy. Ironically, it was age grading—a method of regulating if not dominating children—in schools (a process which was reflected in the family, social functions, and the workplace) that paved the way for the recognition of a later stage of childhood, adolescence, a stage which soon developed a culture of its own to rival the world of the parents. In this regard, young people ultimately achieved an independence of the older generation that was unintended.

Urban Working-Class Childhood

Johanna Marie Carle was born during the autumn of 1798 to Hannah and Peter Carle, Dutch immigrants who had settled in Philadelphia three years previous. Peter was a day laborer who walked a mile every morning to the wharves along the Delaware River, his first place to seek work. Hannah remained in their small rented home, cooking for boarders taken in when times were bad. One out of every four or five children in the city died during infancy, and Johanna was among them, expiring at thirteen months of worms. Her funeral cost a week's wages.

Philadelphia was the wealthiest of the late eighteenth-century pre-industrial cities along the Atlantic coast. It was supported by commerce and populated by merchants and skilled and unskilled workers. At the time of the American Revolution, it was the second largest city in the British Empire, boasting 40,000 inhabitants. Despite high levels of mortality—smallpox was the major killer until the yellow fever epidemics of the 1790s—the population multiplied due to German, Scotch Irish, Irish, and (after the Revolutionary War) French newcomers, as well as migrants from the countryside.

Philadelphia's great wealth, derived primarily from commerce but abetted by shipbuilding and housing construction, was unequally distributed from the outset. In 1800 there was a bigger gap between rich and poor than ever before, with the middle class enjoying mixed success. Inhabitants of the port city had access to a variety of foods, yet laboring families existed on flour, cornmeal, and rice, plus whatever they could raise themselves. The yellow fever epidemics killed four times as many members of the lower as the upper class, and the poor were twice as likely to die of tuberculosis.

Although home construction flourished, workers were usually tenants or boarders. As the forests around the city were felled, heating costs rose. Add in the price of clothing and it is easy to see why working-class families lived at a bare subsistence level, or slightly above, even with both husband and wife employed. The poor, who became destitute in times of crisis, composed as large a part of Philadelphia's population—one-fourth to one-third—as of any comparable European city.[1]

America, and especially the Quaker city led by Benjamin Franklin, has been depicted time and again as the land of opportunity.[2] But laborers and merchant seamen, artisans, shoemakers, and tailors tended to remain propertyless throughout the latter half of the eighteenth century. Their incomes did not increase, nor were they able to move up the occupational ladder. Most poor Philadelphians were either immigrants or native migrants, and one-tenth of them were black; they were an ethnically and racially heterogeneous group from humble backgrounds.

Their migratory patterns meant that laboring families, smaller than the Philadelphia average of 5.2 members, had left their kin behind and therefore could not turn to them for help. That all family members had to work—children gathered firewood, cleaned chimneys, tended cattle—diminished the economic power of men, who in turn empowered their spouses and treated their children equitably in their wills. On the other hand, husbands and fathers perpetrated significant violence in families, perhaps an indication that financial instability affected emotional life.

Between a third and a fifth of lower-class women were pregnant at marriage, a much higher than average figure. They were three times as likely as upper-class women to die in childbirth. Typically in Philadelphia, a woman gave birth every 24 to 36 months for the next 15 or 20 years; a laboring woman, however, delivered only four or five babies during her lifetime, though she did not participate in family planning as some members of the elite did. Half of her children died before reaching adulthood. Her own death, her spouse's, or both might leave children on their own if they were not marked for apprenticeship or the almshouse.

Thus, before industrialization, there existed an urban "lower sort" whose members could be identified not only by their employ but by their lot in life. The toil of children in America was simply taken for granted because they had always worked. But as the circumstances of the urban middle-class young improved, conditions for the progeny of the working class deteriorated, at least relatively if not absolutely. The cause was industrialization.

In the latter half of the eighteenth century, as England's American colonies consciously fostered self-sufficiency, including the home manufacture of clothing, the production of wool and cotton was moved out of the household and taken to a shop for carding and fulling (and sometimes dyeing). The children who had performed these chores at home also entered the shops, which eventually became factories as the entire manufacturing process from raw cotton to yarn was handled by machine. Children seemed designed by nature to tend spindles; their small quick hands easily grasped and knotted the broken threads. The system, which originated in Providence, Rhode Island, in 1791, was reported a quarter-century later to employ 100,000, mostly women and children.

Sometimes entire families were brought into the mill; otherwise, boardinghouses were set up to shelter the young workers, mainly girls. Under the former arrangement, every family member over seven worked from dawn to dusk, six days a week. Wages were determined by age, gender, and task, an arrangement quite unlike that which existed in the household unit of traditional society. The child laborer was not an apprentice or a domestic servant but a wage earner (along with his/her father, mother, and siblings), whose master outside the home was the foreman. The locus of power over the child's life shifted.[3]

It could not have been predicted that this would happen. In England, where the industrial revolution had begun in the mid-eighteenth century, traditional households among cotton spinners were strengthened by climbing incomes and the ability of factory-operative spinners both to hire and oversee the work of their own children and other kin. But by the early nineteenth century, spinning machines had become so complicated that a spinner had to supervise more helpers than could be provided by his family. And since steam engine power now made it possible to locate large factories in cities, rather than country sites using water power, youngsters joined the labor market and could work for spinners other than their fathers. The new situation jeopardized the power of fathers and attracted the attention of school reformers, who

16. Children had always worked, but in a family setting. Now children of the working class became factory hands whose wages were necessary for family support, as this 1900 photograph by Lewis Hine shows. Library of Congress.

were discovering that the young were often not educated or even socialized by their parents.[4]

Conditions for working children in early nineteenth-century America
developed somewhat differently from those in England. Take the Rockdale district, about 15 miles west of Philadelphia, where seven cotton
mills located along a three-mile stretch of Chester Creek sustained about
2,000 inhabitants, more than half of whom were 19 years old or under
and virtually all of whom lived in nuclear families, some as boarders.
Although fathers seldom employed their own children in the mill, the
familiarity of residents in the hamlets meant that adult workers knew the
parents of the children who labored under them and therefore did not
brutalize the young toilers, keeping them in line only through ridicule
and occasional light physical punishment.

But the hours of work were so long that the youngsters, especially
those under 12, were often in pain, fell asleep before having supper, and
sometimes had to be struck to be kept awake at the factory. This was the
doing of the employers, most of whom were evangelical Christians; they
whipped children for tardiness, and although they confessed hours were
excessive and young workers were denied schooling, they nevertheless
justified their practices through reference to marketplace competition
and to the circumstances of parents—as did the local ministers. In the
words of one factory owner, "Education is much neglected about manu-
factories; a large portion of the families employed, are those of indigent
widows, who require the work of their children for support, or of idle,
intemperate fathers ... and these, especially the latter, have but little
inclination to school their children."[5]

However bad the working conditions of children were, their toil was
needed to support their families, since the salary of one worker usually
was insufficient. Boys worked more often than girls, older children more
frequently than younger; boys were paid more than girls, and adults
more than children. Children brought in one-fifth of family income. In
one sense this allowed them to become more independent, since sharing the family burden with parents gave them economic power. But such
independence was circumscribed by the expectation that the young
would subordinate their desires to the family good, an arrangement usually referred to as the family economy.[6]

In the early stage of the industrial revolution it was possible to escape
these working conditions, since factory-employed families could save
money and move west to farm. But such movement was impossible later
on in the nineteenth century, where in a typical mill town working-
class families lived below the poverty line. Although these peoples' lives
were characterized by considerable geographic mobility, such movement occurred because workers lost jobs and needed to look to other

industrial towns and cities, not to rural areas, for employment. The vast majority of Americans still lived on farms, and children did the agricultural work they had always done in traditional societies—but under the direction of their parents, not as pawns in the industrial order. Although in the first stage of the industrial revolution families could sometimes work together in factories, this possibility disappeared with time.[7]

Another profound change in the urban industrial labor force was its increasingly immigrant and ethnic character. The 5,000 newcomers who arrived annually at the beginning of the nineteenth century accumulated to 2.8 million within 50 years. Six million more arrived between 1877 and 1890, and another 18 million before World War I. (Altogether 33 million moved to the United States between 1820 and 1920; about 20 percent returned home.) The earlier immigrants arrived from northern and western Europe; by the close of the century they came largely from the southern and eastern parts of the continent, as well as from Asia (though families were prohibited from accompanying male Chinese arrivals). Working-age males spearheaded the immigrant movement, with men never falling below 57 percent of the incoming tide in any five-year period; their families often arrived later.[8] Immigrants carried cultural baggage—foreign languages and traditional ideas—one of which was that children were subordinate to adults, who were the repositories of wisdom as well as the sources of power.

But in the New World these children learned English and adopted American cultural mores more quickly than their elders, thus challenging the bases for wisdom and power that had existed in the societies of the old country. Adult immigrants, however, attempted to transplant their own cultural heritage to America through the household, churches, schools, newspapers, and social organizations. To the degree that these efforts were successful, children remained the subjects of family authority. Furthermore, ties were strengthened simply by virtue of the fact that it was family members working together that influenced the transition to the new environment.[9] Since different national groups brought to America different cultural traditions, each group needs to be considered on its own terms.

There was a huge German immigration in the half-century before the American Revolution, which then ceased for 50 years, reviving in the early nineteenth century. Until 1900 Germans were never less than one-quarter of the foreign-born population of the United States. But they were not so visible as other ethnic groups, probably because their skills, abetted by such characteristics as diligence and thrift, equipped them well for Americanization. Settling in the middle Atlantic, as well as the north-central states, they worked as farmers and craftsmen, gathering in "little Germanies" in cities such as New York and Milwaukee.

Farming was a family endeavor, and children were the beneficiaries of property accumulated for future generations. But with family continuity also came family control. The father was dominant; his wife and children were subordinate. German women were the least likely of immigrant females to join the industrial workforce and, above the age of twenty, the most likely to be married. German children were held on a tighter leash than other young newcomers, a situation fostered by German rural enclaves that endured into the mid-twentieth century.[10]

The Irish followed the Germans to America, the exodus from the Emerald Isle primarily triggered by the potato famine of the late 1840s, though they had begun leaving earlier and continued later. The famine also altered the Irish family; as the 1851 Census of Ireland observed, "the closest ties of kinship were dissolved." While the famine was cathartic, the demographic trends were of long standing: The population was constantly in decline; marriage was late and infrequent; celibacy rates were high; the genders were not only separated but hostile.[11] Thus, the implications of the famine for America lay not only in the arrival of millions of Irish but also in the composition of the immigrant group. Women, typically young and single, were in the majority (about 53 percent, more than in any other major immigrant group; for example, only 41 percent of German immigrants were women) and children were few (only 5 percent, as compared with 28 percent among Jewish immigrants). The Irish consciously rejected rural life for the city, though this choice did not raise their standard of living. Mortality statistics demonstrate that they held the worst jobs, lived in the most squalid conditions, and were especially susceptible to alcohol.

Marriage, which was almost entirely in-group, dictated that women abandon work and start reproducing; Irish fertility rates were second only to French Canadian at the turn of the century. Hence, economic conditions, already bad (and aggravated by the custom of sending money back to Ireland as a sign of family loyalty), became worse with marriage. Domestic violence was characteristic; the home was no haven. Widowhood was common and, given the hostility between the sexes (responsible for late marriage and nonmarriage) and the fact that divorce was no option among Catholics, male desertion was frequent. The Irish household was typically female-dominated; unsupervised children were early pushed out into the working world; sons were virtually without male guidance.[12]

The situation of the undirected Irish American children was thus quite unlike that of the strongly controlled German *kinder*—and, of course, almost totally different from that of the already-resident middle class. But Irish women got to know middle-class homes through domestic service, an almost universal working experience for the daughters of Erin and one rejected by women of other ethnic groups. Boarding with the bourgeoisie provided healthier living and working conditions than were otherwise available, the money was good, and it allowed these working women to reside away from Irish men. Finally, they could count on learning lessons to be passed on to their own daughters, who might not marry but move into white-collar and semiprofessional jobs such as teaching and nursing.[13]

The Italians were part of a later wave of immigration. Between 1880 and 1920, about 4 million of them arrived, most from southern Italy, and 90 percent settled in cities. In the Old World they had typically been peasant farmers; in the New World they often took up construction work, also seasonal, though women (who, unlike Irish females, seldom became domestics but dominated the garment trades) and children might become migrant workers in the summer. Underemployment was a problem; upward mobility was infrequent; child labor was critical. There was no doubting the operation of the family economy in the Italian American household. And because the work of the young was necessary to the support of the household, Italians opposed compulsory education. Truancy and illiteracy were rife.

These facts did not belie the depth of family affection or the strength of family ties, which were extensive, reaching even to the old country, drawing relatives to America, and aiding old folk returning to Italy. The family of residence, however, was nuclear. It bore the burden of high infant mortality, one child of three, yet produced large numbers of offspring. In Buffalo the average was 11 children per family, as opposed to 7.8 among Poles. Broken homes did not exist. Initially, husbands had journeyed to America alone; by the early twentieth century, families traveled together. The family was father-dominated but mother-centered, with a notably strong mother/son relationship. Girls were expected to live at home until marriage, not date, and tolerate arranged nuptials at young ages. Despite such parental control, some of the newcomers rejected their peasant past and began seeing childhood as a distinct stage of life, thus moving toward the child-centered family of their adopted country.[14]

Poles migrated to the United States at the same time as the Italians; they were part of the "new immigration." Young men emigrated first with the expectation of returning to Poland, which 40–60 percent did before World War I, a statistic best understood in view of the control that family exerted over its members. (The Italian return migration rate, however, was higher.) The Polish family, not nuclear so much as fully extended in the manner of a small clan, existed under the power of strong patriarch. Mothers were weak and, as wives, badly treated. Children were not well cared for, as demonstrated by the high death rate of the young. When children went to work, usually for the purpose of contributing to the accumulation of family property, the jobs they took had to conform to their roles in the family and/or be close to their homes. Poles did not support public education, and girls (who were less encouraged than their brothers) seldom finished elementary school but labored at an early age in sweat shops. Peer groups were feeble.[15]

Jews had arrived before the era of the new immigration and continued to disembark in even larger numbers. Sephardic Jews from the Iberian peninsula and Ashkenazi Jews from central and eastern Europe had met and fused in colonial America. In the early nineteenth century a larger group of Jews, part of the German migration, had settled and integrated well into the capitalist economy of the United States. Immigrants from eastern Europe swelled the ranks of American Jewry in the late nineteenth and early twentieth centuries. Only one-sixth of the 250,000 Jews in the United States in 1880, they composed five-sixths of 4 million Jews in 1920. The newcomers were generally young, skilled (typically in the clothing trades), urban, and part of a family migration that sought a permanent home in America.

From eastern Europe came a tradition of favoring male progeny over female which, given the fact that fathers expected less of their girls, made the father/daughter (and the mother/son) relationship the easier one, although in working-class families older daughters often had to serve as surrogate mothers. But parents, at least mothers, were present, since even working-class women seldom took jobs outside the household, preferring to supplement income by finishing garments at home or taking in boarders. But girls worked, almost never in domestic service but in industrial jobs affording them independence (perhaps to compensate for receiving less encouragement at home than did their brothers).

While not forsaking the religious education characteristic of eastern Europe, Jews in America strongly supported public education and, consequently, assimilation, applauding Americanization in a way uncharacteristic of other immigrant parents. "Education was free," exulted Mary Antin about her arrival in Boston as a child. "That subject my father had written about repeatedly, as comprising his chief hope for us children, the essence of American opportunity."[16]

Despite the diversity of immigrant backgrounds, some generalizations about white working-class parenting are possible. Even if mothers were not working outside the home, they had plenty of domestic duties besides child rearing. Babies were usually breast-fed, but could probably not expect further attention; pacifiers and swaddling clothes served as instruments of control. After infancy it was difficult to inhibit the movement of children; the streets were a place to play, yet there was plenty of work to do as soon as children were able. Wages were so low, however, that children were likely to remain in public school until they reached their teens; boys received higher pay than girls and left school earlier. They also contributed less of their wages to the family economy and were allowed the social freedom to roam the streets in gangs or join neighborhood clubs.[17] As in middle-class families, girls were superintended much more closely and sometimes working-class parents resorted to the law to control rebellious daughters.[18]

In addition to the immigrants coming to the United States, African Americans began moving from the rural Southeast to the cities of the North, a migration referred to at the time as the Great Exodus. Both the rural black family and the family that settled in the cities were lower class, usually with two parents (though one-quarter in northern cities and one-third in southern were headed by women); with the passage of time and persistence of poverty more black families congregated in one household. "Long marriages were common among these rural and urban blacks, and so was the attachment of parent to child," observes

17. Immigrant working-class children did not have nurseries in which to ride hobby horses or play with toys. Library of Congress.

historian Herbert Gutman. As in slavery, the first child was often born before marriage and resided in its mother's household of origin; kin relations continued to be important. Boys and girls were raised similarly, in smaller families than those of the white working class, and they were apt to remain in public school longer.[19]

While the working class, largely immigrant and migrant, sought to survive in the city, the middle class attempted to stabilize a society shaken to its roots by industrialization, urbanization, and immigration. Stabilization was to be achieved, in part, by redeeming the working class, according to middle-class reformers. In the three or four decades preceding the Civil War, there were an unusual number of movements afoot proposing to minister to social problems, some unique to children (such as a dependent's loss of both parents) and others more general (poverty, crime, and insanity). None of these problems was new, but in earlier times such matters had been handled in a family setting (with the exception of crime, which was handled in the community—adults were locked in stocks or hanged). The novel solution of the early nineteenth century was the creation of institutions where the deviant and the dependent would be isolated and rehabilitated. Their reformed behavior would demonstrate to the rest of society how to act.[20] For working-class children this meant going to asylums (for the orphaned, the abandoned, even the poverty-stricken) or houses of refuge (for the convicted offender, the vagrant, the willfully disobedient). Children were also sent to almshouses.[21]

In the seventeenth and eighteenth centuries, when community was small, defined, and familiar, it was the job of the family to prepare its young for life in society outside the household. For those unprepared or unable to sustain themselves, conventionally referred to as "poor" though they could be widowed, orphaned, aged, sick, or insane, the community was willing to take responsibility. They were seldom sheltered in the few existing institutions (such as poorhouses or workhouses) but rather in families where, for example, orphans or socially maladjusted children could be bound out and eventually earn their keep as servants or apprentices (though apprenticeship, already anemic in the late eighteenth century, was gone by the mid-nineteenth).[22]

As this society of small and familiar communities began to be replaced by large and anonymous cities, where mobility rather than stasis was the rule, it was inevitable that social problems would be perceived and faced differently. For the middle class, as noted in Chapter 4, the family became less a place of preparation for society than a haven from it. But working-class families could not supply shelter from the outside world. Indeed, some members of the middle-class viewed the immigrant working-class family as the problem; its corruption and poverty bred dependence and deviancy. Others had less a desire to control others than to define themselves by good works. In either case, bourgeois reformers put forward not only analyses but solutions.

The evangelical answer was the Sunday school. The American Sunday School Union (1824) boasted hundreds of thousands of enrollees, mostly from the working class, while distinct Protestant denominations registered thousands more. Though these reformers talked of a family-centered social order, they often acted on the premise that the Sunday school was superior to the working-class home as a socializing agent. In Sunday school the character of the child would be transformed through exposure to middle-class teachers and, even more emphatically, by experiencing a hierarchy of command, an array of goals (e.g., punctuality), and a regimen of rewards and punishments.[23]

A more radical solution to the perceived degeneration of working-class children was to remove them from the family and place them in an institution. The legal justification for such extreme action—essentially denying that the Bill of Rights protected children—lay in *parens patriae*, a doctrine which in the Middle Ages had given the state the right to intercede in family relations if the welfare of a child was endangered. When in 1838 Mary Ann Crouse was committed to the Philadelphia

18. Some working-class children were institutionalized in authoritarian environments intended to mold their characters in preparation for life outside the asylum. This print features the dining hall of the New York House of Refuge. *Appleton's Journal* (1871).

House of Refuge on her mother's complaint but without her father's knowledge or consent, the judge denied both the father's habeas corpus petition and his constitutional challenge (the sixth amendment promises trial by jury before incarceration), asserting: "May not the natural parents, when unequal to the task of education, or unworthy of it, be superceded by the *parens patriae*." The decision, which gave government the right to assign youths who had committed no crime to a reformatory, was later unsuccessfully challenged.[24]

In the 1820s and 1830s there were established penitentiaries for criminals, insane asylums for the mentally ill, almshouses for the poor, and orphan asylums to accommodate the abandoned, the poverty-stricken, and the victims of intemperate parents, and reformatories or houses of refuge for disobedient and vagrant children.[25] All these institutions shared the beliefs that their young inmates must be trained to deal with a disordered society, else they would succumb to vice and crime, and that human nature was so plastic that children could be reshaped in a specially-created environment. Thus a strict daily discipline, accomplished through absolute respect for authority as evidenced by total obedience, would transform the child's character, preparing him or her for life outside the shelter.[26]

Of course, obedience was the cardinal principle in the middle-class home, but its accomplishment owed something to maternal affection. No one doubted the importance of obedience in the newly constituted common schools, where corporal punishment was receding. The child-saving institutions were more extreme, run in a military manner, a monotonous regime of prayers, meals, lessons, and work, not to mention severe discipline. Children were regularly whipped, handcuffed, ball and chained, and locked away. Incarceration was brief, after which time the children were not likely to be returned to their families of origin, toward whom the authorities were generally hostile, but were apprenticed, sent to sea, or placed on farms, about which places the authorities seemed to know or care little.

New York led the way, setting up a house of refuge in 1825, with Boston and Philadelphia establishing child-saving institutions within a few years. In the 1840s Rochester, Cincinnati, and New Orleans joined in, with Providence, Pittsburgh, Baltimore, Chicago, and St. Louis coming aboard in the next decade. By midcentury, however, the vitality of reform was giving way to the inertia of custody. This was especially evident in the houses of refuge, as overcrowding and harsh punishment raised complaints but did not bring improvement.[27]

Institutions had their critics, none more outspoken than Charles Loring Brace, a young urban missionary who founded the New York Children's Aid Society (1853), an organization devoted to preventative work with the city's poor, vagrant, and crime-prone youngsters. Brace castigated institutions for turning their inmates into robots or hypocrites, ignoring the individual sensibilities of the inmates, and failing to prepare them for real life. (As for urban Sunday schools, he said they served no more purpose than "pouring water through a sieve.") Children's Aid Societies, functioning in major cities, offered industrial schools and night schools—Brace was a committed advocate of hard work—as well as lodging houses. The Societies also sent adolescents to farming families in the West, so-called orphan trains, not because of some romantic or nostalgic longings for rural America but due to Brace's belief that the autonomy he so admired in the city's street urchins would be least fettered there.[28]

Institutions did not go out of business, but they did change their names (training school sounded better than reformatory by the turn of the century), import new living arrangements (cottages replaced cell blocks), and took on the appearance of real life. All three innovations were evident when in 1895 William R. George, long an advocate of the fresh air movement for children, incorporated the George Junior Republic in upstate New York. Both dependents and delinquents (mainly from New York City) were sent to the country, where they created their own government and earned their own money. In the third and forth decades of the twentieth century, the guidance clinic was added, designed to place inmates appropriately and evaluate them constantly during their stay. The institutions remained, but they were not fundamentally reformed: Education did not take place, overcrowded cottages remained prisons, and psychiatric counseling was rarely available.[29]

Meanwhile, middle-class concern for children of the lower class became more evident than ever in the early decades of the twentieth century, the Progressive era, and its most striking expression was in the creation of juvenile courts.[30] Previously, a juvenile coming before a court, if convicted, would be sentenced to an adult institution. (It was conventional knowledge that conviction was often avoided because of the consequences of housing a juvenile offender with adult criminals.) Now juveniles were to be kept out of court if possible, through the intercession of a probation officer who would consider the family situation and the community resources to determine whether a resolution of the complaint against the juvenile was possible. If not, the dependent, neglected, or delinquent child would go to a court inquiry, not a trial, along with family members, perhaps a social worker and certainly the probation officer—an inquiry which had begun while the child was in detention (and separate from adult criminals). Rehabilitation was to take place in the child's home, if the circumstances were appropriate, with the probation officer intimately involved.

Theoretically, the juvenile court was a large step in the direction of empathizing with the child brought before it. A study of its actual operation, however, tells a different story. In Milwaukee the legal and structural framework of the court was well established by 1909. The out-of-court settlements mainly concerned trivial issues. In court, the poor immigrant parents who were hailed to the bench were wary of the probation officers and judges—and with good reason. They and their children were frequently bullied. Empathy was not much in evidence.[31]

Institutionalization was labeled a last resort but, in fact, it was explicitly advocated. A probation officer addressing the National Congress of Mothers, organized in 1897 "to recognize the supreme importance of the child," advised these middle-class matrons that "the [lower-class] women who cannot control their boys of eight or nine years of age should not have the care of them." The juvenile court should have discretionary authority because, he continued, "I want those boys in a reform school; I feel there is no love there in the home, and that his home is no place for that boy."[32]

But such an attitude may have been on the wane. Historian Mary Ann Mason observes that the "new middle-class judiciary, with its idealization of mothers and its tender attitude toward children," extended the concept of the child's best interest (see Chapter 4) to poor children, who "were now more frequently supported in their mothers' home.... If that failed, or if they had no suitable parent, children were increasingly placed in a foster home, which was considered a substitute family ... or put up for adoption by a new family." By the turn of the century, reformers were warning foster parents not to exploit but to nurture children.[33]

The fascination of child-savers with working-class kids, whether orphaned, abandoned, poor, vagrant, or delinquent, did not extend to those children who were physically abused or neglected by their parents, at least not until the founding of the New York Society for the Prevention of Cruelty to Children in 1874. It took the combined forces of humanitarianism, fear of social disorder, and moral revulsion against physical suffering (the SPCA antedated the SPCC in New York by six years) to overcome the naysayers who argued that children must not be taken from their parents. Of course, children had already been removed on other grounds; seldom did the agents of the SPCC go so far as removal—mainly, they were satisfied to merely investigate complaints against drunken and neglectful parents. Indeed, defenders of the SPCC did not oppose corporal punishment, only child cruelty, and it was difficult to draw the line. Nevertheless, as early as the 1880s the Societies were issuing statements that cruelty was on the decline. Virtually all cases handled by the anticruelty societies, which existed in the Northeast and Midwest but not the Northwest, the Rocky Mountain states, or the South, involved working-class or poverty-stricken immigrant children.[34]

A more comprehensive middle-class response to urban problems, one that proved to be ultimately more pervasive in its effect on working-class children than the asylums, reformatories, farms, and private agencies, focused on the public schools. Of course, any modernizing society turns to education to prepare its future citizens in literacy and numeracy, certainly concerns of the middle class for its progeny. But for the working-class young, the objective of the common-school reformers in the early nineteenth century was to promote work discipline and patriotism.[35] Working-class children, however, were usually not pupils but toilers in factories, mines, or homes (their own or those of the middle class), less likely even than African Americans to be in school.

The solution lay in compulsory education. From about 1850 to 1890, as elementary schools drew in more and more children, most states passed compulsory education laws that were ignored. Educators were unenthusiastic about coercing unwilling students into already over-crowded classrooms; school construction could not keep pace with urban growth. Some citizens questioned whether compulsory education was an un-American invasion of parental rights. By the end of the century, the typical child attended school for five years, and the majority of teenagers in school remained in the elementary grades, being forced to repeat. Social promotion was not in practice until the 1920s, which still placed the United States in the vanguard of mass education. At that time, not only was compulsory schooling becoming a more acceptable idea to educators and citizens but laws were providing for more effective enforcement.[36]

Again, as with reformatories, asylums, agencies, and so forth, middle-class reformers supplied the driving force of compulsory education, convinced that immigrant working-class parents were not providing appropriate education for their young. And indeed it was true that middle-class children stayed in school longer than the progeny of the working class, who rarely remained beyond sixth grade. Reformers felt the state should intervene in the heretofore private sphere, providing new adult guidance (e.g., teachers, truant officers), supplementary to if not replacing parents. It is typical of modernizing societies to replace older loyalties (to the family, the ethnic or religious group, to a region) with bonds to the centralized state, and universal education—justified by the concept of an informed citizenry—is a means to this end. Assimilation remained the goal of educationists at least through the 1920s and 1930s.[37]

But there were other reasons as well for the success of compulsory education, whose proponents could boast in 1920 that three-quarters of American children between the ages of 5 and 19 were enrolled. One reason was the growth of an education bureaucracy that, by the early twentieth century, was sophisticated and efficient enough to make coercion work. Another reason was the evident economic benefit of the practice: The investment of money through education for all children, not just the middle-class young, was of long-term advantage to the community—an uneducated mass was a potential burden—even though the enterprise might reinforce society's class structure by offering vocational courses as an alternative to the academic curriculum. A third reason lay in the reformers' ability to show that studying was superior to child labor, although the new urban schools did look like factories.[38]

Fighting against child labor in the mines, factories, and sweat shops, in the streets and on the farms of America, occupied a major part of the middle-class reformers' time. In 1870 one out of every eight children was gainfully employed; in 1900 the figure was one out of six (60 percent were agricultural workers, and over half of the remaining 40 percent were children of immigrants), even though 28 states had passed some child labor legislation. In their crusade against child labor, reformers pointed to the cycle of family poverty, early employment of children, and family poverty in the next generation; they evoked pity for the "slaughter of the innocents"; they cited biological and educational theories supporting a protected childhood; and they argued that a decent childhood was basic to a democratic society. Furthermore, they organized, first on the state but ultimately on the national level, to achieve such legislation as the Keating-Owen Act of 1916, though it was declared unconstitutional two years later. But they were unable to attain a constitutional amendment barring child labor, and children continued to work until the Depression of the 1930s, when adult unemployment effectively ended the practice.[39]

Describing the child world of work is problematical. We have the adult, mainly middle-class, perspective. These folks were scandalized by what they saw or read about, and it is hardly daring to speculate that the more tender-minded reformers felt guilty when they compared their own childhoods and those of their children to the burdensome early lives—or for that matter, the adult lives—of the working class. Jane Addams tells us how guilty she felt when, as a child, she accompanied her father to his mill and recognized how the workers were forced to live. "I had my first sight of the poverty which implies squalor.... I declared with much firmness when I grew up I should, of course, have a large house, but it would not be built among other large houses, but right in the midst of horrid little houses like these."[40]

In an attempt to gain the child's own perspective on working-class existence, historian David Nasaw has studied photos of them ("alive, exuberant—not victims at all"), as well as several oral histories and

19. Middle-class reformers sought to achieve relief for working-class children through legislation and propaganda, as illustrated in this National Child Labor Committee poster by documentary photographer Lewis Hine, c. 1904. Library of Congress.

numerous autobiographies written by kids who went on to success, usually as entertainers, and concluded that these working-class children adapted well to the city and led happy lives.[41]

The record appears to say otherwise. The typical working-class adolescent left the classroom at 12 or 13 because the family needed the supplementary income and the youngster felt guilty if he/she refused. Consider the words of a girl (less likely to leave school than a boy) who recognized her duty to work: "I did have other dreams, it is true. But a child of thirteen has little command over her own existence.... It wasn't so much that I was ambitious as that I had a passionate love for books ... and I begged my mother to permit me to go to high school.... To do mother justice, she understood, a little, my longing to go and would have liked to have me continue, but it seemed neither practical nor sensible to her."[42] It was not only a matter of economic need. Her Italian or Polish or even Jewish parents warned her that too much education would make her unfit for marriage. Furthermore, a girl's school experience was often disagreeable. The culture she had learned at home was not acknowledged, much less respected, in school.

On the positive side, work made it possible to escape the cramped home environment, described by photographer and social critic Jacob Riis in these terms: "The only bed was occupied by the entire family lying lengthwise and crosswise, literally in layers, three children at the feet, all except a boy of ten or twelve, for whom there was no room. He slept with his clothes on to keep warm, in a pile of rags just inside the door."[43] In addition, work was an experience with one's peers that marked ritual passage to adulthood.

Unfortunately, undereducation limited job possibilities, more for girls than boys, and a girl's wages had to be surrendered to parents whereas her brother might pay a token $1 a week for board. Segregated by sex at work, where she learned what was allegedly the American version of female adolescence, a girl was taught again what she had already discovered in her traditional home: She was inferior to her male counterparts. But the adolescent boy's world was hardly better.[44]

In the city the alternative to industrial labor was domestic employment. In the middle of the nineteenth century, most servants were probably teenagers, and some were the recipients of a kind of maternal benevolence which, while it provided warmth and affection, was also likely to be cloying and/or patronizing. One servant described her situation as "the worst kind of loneliness," for she shared in the work of the house but not "in the pleasures and delights of a home." Even though she loved her employer, she opined: "One must remember that there is a difference between a *house*, a place of shelter, and a *home*, a place where all your affections are centered."[45]

In Massachusetts, according to educational historian Marvin Lazerson, "The school dropout problem—limited job opportunities for the uneducated, loss to gross national product, the threat of delinquency among out-of-school, unemployed youth—crystallized the vocational education movement." Sometime around the turn of the century, manual training, which had appeared in the curriculum several decades earlier because it was thought to instill traditional social values through the learning of traditional skills, was replaced by industrial (including clerical) schooling as the preparation for a vocation, for both boys and girls. Soon this movement penetrated the elementary schools, although the class implications were evident. Observed the Boston Superintendent of Schools in 1910: "Because children differ in vocational aim, the schools are now being reorganized for the purpose of providing an education for each child that will best fit him for his future position in life."[46]

Even the kindergarten, which was launched by middle-class reformers who thought immigrant working-class parents could be reached and taught through their children, became in the early years of the century an agency of preparation for elementary school and the workforce.[47]

20. Children of the slums lived in crowded, filthy environments, unbearably hot in the summer, unlivably cold in the winter. This tenement interior in Poverty Gap, New York City, was captured by author and photographer Jacob Riis, c. 1889. Jacob A. Riis, *How the Other Half Lives: Studies Among the Tenements of New York* (New York, 1890).

Whether the preschool years of working-class childhood provided a less dismal experience than the one encountered by older children may be doubted. To be subject to the excesses of temperature in an unheated, unventilated flat and to be undernourished to boot was devastating. Illness—diarrhea and other intestinal disorders, bronchitis, pneumonia—and death were fixtures. About the steel mill town of Homestead, Pennsylvania, social worker Margaret F. Byington wrote: "A comparison of births and deaths of children under two ... shows that among the Slavs one child under two years of age dies to every three children born.... Against many of these deaths was the physician's entry 'malnutrition due to poor food and overcrowding'; that is, the mother was too poor, too busy, and too ignorant to prepare food properly, rooms over-tenanted, and courts too confined to give the fresh air essential for the physical development of the children."[48] There was little in working-class existence to recommend it to children.

Some reformers were convinced that the healthiest possible alternative to the tenement/street/factory existence lay in providing play space for poor and working-class children. What play organizers wanted, however, was not to foster the spontaneous activity that might spring from the imaginations of the young. As historian Dominick Cavallo observes, organizers were convinced that "play was too serious a business to be left to children and parents."[49] Especially not parents, nor even teachers. Committed environmentalists, reformers wanted the opportunity to mold the moral milieu of society by shaping the physical surroundings of the youngest and most malleable citizens.

Unlike their early nineteenth-century predecessors, these reformers did not expect to change human nature but sought to modify behavior. Accepting the idea that human development was a mirror of the evolution of the species, reformers thought it natural that adolescents would be drawn to gangs. These young people were in the "savage" stage of evolution. Rather than discouraging peer association, the male band must be controlled for reform purposes. Indeed, no activity was more appealing than team play (not to be confused with the spectator sports craze so evident in American popular culture by the late nineteenth century, which was escapist rather than reformist). It emphasized community over individualism, thus muting the unrestrained competition characteristic of capitalism with the ideal of cooperation. Hence, team play was nurturant—that is, feminine—and could serve as a counterpart to the immigrant working-class family from which middle-class reformers wished to wean their charges.[50]

Although immigration was a casualty of social reaction in the years following World War I—the National Origins Quota Act of 1924 limited European immigration to 150,000 persons per year, drawn largely from northwestern Europe, and banned Asians—the Progressive reforms for immigrant working-class children continued. Indeed, the most enduring sign of reform at the federal level had been established in 1912: the U.S. Children's Bureau, a division of the Department of Commerce and Labor (in 1913, simply the Department of Labor) and the world's first governmental agency created to deal only with children. Although reference to "the working classes" had been eliminated from the enabling legislation in order to attract rural as well as urban support, the intent of the Bureau's creators to abolish child labor (which surely would not embrace farms), as well as reduce infant and maternal mortality, improve child health, and obtain care for children with special needs demonstrated yet again a middle-class effort to deal with the lower orders. While its initial annual appropriation of $25,640 was ridiculously small, its mandate was so vague as to allow it to move beyond research and dissemination into other areas of child service.[51]

Until this time social welfare issues had been the province of the state and local communities, not the federal government. Julia Clifford Lathrop, appointed chief of the Bureau when women still could not vote, began work on a noncontroversial but deeply important matter. Appalled that of 2.5 million annual births in the United States, an estimated 200,000 babies died, Lathrop directed that the first investigative work should be the study of infant mortality and the advocacy of birth registration (to help understand how and why babies died), meanwhile correlating government data to show the number, location, sex, race, nativity, parentage, and age of America's children. The discrepancies uncovered were striking. Babies born to native mothers survived at significantly higher rates than those delivered to foreign-born women, though infants born to literate rather than illiterate members of the latter group had a markedly superior chance of survival. Age, length of recovery period, outside employment, marital status, and reproductive history were also factors, not to mention the matter that so many of these factors pointed to—the father's income.[52] Poverty, not the inevitable survival of the fittest, explained infant mortality.

Yet what could a working-class mother feel but helpless when she read in a Children's Bureau instructional pamphlet: "Tenements with dark rooms are not fit homes for children. Suburban homes, or those in the outskirts of cities or close to public parks, give to city children the best chance for proper growth and development." When in 1917 the American Association for Labor proposed national health insurance that would include maternity benefits, the Bureau responded with only lukewarm support.[53]

The legislative act which established the Bureau mandated that it investigate and report on child labor, a reform concern that had escalated with the rising number of child wage earners but that remained, none-theless, controversial—and the bailiwick of very uneven state regula-tion, leading reformers to conclude that the solution must lie in the federal realm. It was not clear that child labor could be outlawed, but in the Keating-Owen Act (1916), Congress attempted to discourage the practice through the interstate commerce clause. Two years later, the Supreme Court struck down the Act on the grounds that Congress could not invoke the interstate commerce clause to prevent child labor in the states.[54]

But the Bureau had gained momentum during World War I, attracted attention in the Children's Year (1918), and dramatically increased its funding. Meanwhile, its studies indicated that perhaps 80 percent of American mothers did not receive prenatal or postnatal care and that the problem was most acute in rural America. The Bureau turned its attention to the 1921 Maternity and Infancy—or Sheppard-Towner—Act, which promised $7 million for grants-in-aid to the states "for the promotion of the welfare and hygiene of maternity and infancy." Adopted despite opposition from the American Medical Association (except the dissenting Pediatric Section) as an "imported socialistic scheme," it remained in effect until 1929.[55] During these years, the infant mortality rate declined.

In tandem with the concern for children's physical health emerged a regard for their mental health, embodied in the child guidance move-ment from 1922 to 1945, which initially sought to prevent juvenile delin-quency (now seen to be primarily psychological in origin) but eventually was content to treat mild behavioral and emotional problems in urban clinics funded by a private foundation. Thus, it built on the Progressive legacy of juvenile justice, then moved in the direction of psychiatry, its constituency changing from working-class to middle-class children.[56] During the 1920s, the Children's Bureau also dealt with delinquency as well as dependency and mental and physical handicaps in a series of studies.[57]

Staff members of the Children's Bureau applauded the election of Herbert Hoover in 1928, never anticipating the Depression or his way of handling it through voluntarism. (Indeed, Hoover never embraced the Bureau's "whole child" philosophy and was tied to the American Med-ical Association, an organization always hostile to the Bureau.) While the Bureau lobbied for needy children, the president outright denied its statistics on child malnutrition. Roosevelt was friendlier, although the Child Health and Recovery Program (emergency food and medical care to the neediest), instituted by the Bureau and Federal Emergency Relief Administration, was the early New Deal's only relief effort for young children; it was insufficiently funded for medical and nursing staff.

But under the Social Security Act (1935), children's programs developed that touched more young people than all the investigative and educational efforts of the Children's Bureau during its previous 22 years. Although administrative responsibility for aid to dependent children under Title IV of the Act was not assigned to the Bureau, still its budget was expanded (from $337,371 in 1930 to $8,644,500 in 1938), as was its staff. For the first time a permanent federal agency addressed the needs of poor children, although those with unmarried mothers or even divorced or racially and ethnically disapproved mothers could be excluded. (Furthermore, while old-age pensions were considered insurance, funds to children were stigmatized as welfare.) But child labor went largely unregulated, even though adults often stepped into jobs held by youths, and a constitutional amendment barring child labor ultimately failed.[58]

Most poor children were untouched by the Bureau. Even before the Depression, almost 60 percent of American families lived at or below subsistence. But in the 1930s the traditionally poor, not only the members of single-parent families (10.5 million) but also tenant farmers (8.5 million), the elderly (6.5 million), and the disabled (1.0 million), were joined by the newly impoverished, who were former members of the middle as well as the working class (unemployment moved from 3.0 million in 1929 to 12.5 million in 1932). If family members turned to one another for support, at the same time unemployment undermined the self-esteem of the traditional breadwinner and perhaps the self-respect of the household. Not only wives but also children entered— one might say reentered—the workforce. Divorce declined, but desertion rose spectacularly. The young suffered from malnutrition and the diseases associated with it. During the first two years of the Depression, the number of children placed in custodial institutions rose by half and 200,000 children became vagrants as a consequence of home loss. Couples put off having children, and government policy encouraged family planning. Schools closed. Everyone suffered, but especially the already poor and close-to-poor.[59]

In his work on the Oakland Growth Study, a longitudinal survey whose subjects were middle-class and working-class youths at the time of the Depression, sociologist Glen Elder observed that economic conditions which limited options and resources "are known to foster apathy, restricted needs and goals, and identity foreclosure"—a situation, he judged, more relevant to working-class than to middle-class children from deprived families. Although working-class families had firsthand experience with economic hardship, middle-class parents offered their children "a wider range of problem-solving experience and skills and provide greater emotional support ... [and] tend to know more about the workings of their community ... and are more familiar with available avenues for solving problems." Ultimately, the psychological health of working-class children would be affected more adversely than that of middle-class children by economic deprivation.[60]

But families, and hence children, in both classes were affected. The prestige of fathers declined due to unemployment, especially in the middle class where they had previously been more dominant than in the working class; working-class boys held a significantly more positive attitude toward their fathers through the Depression.[61] Mothers, now often employed, became more dominant—and eventually were resented. Children became more responsible for maintaining the household economy, but boys in both classes resisted parental authority whereas girls accepted parental judgment (girls were sensitive to family relations, whereas boys responded to family status). While boys achieved independence through the autonomy granted by holding jobs, working-class girls had less freedom if the family was economically deprived. (Boys toiled outside the home; working-class girls labored within it; overall, middle-class girls gained liberty during the 1930s, though less than boys.)[62]

The circumstances of the Depression affected family dynamics and, hence, the lives of children in an economically adverse way, more so the young of the working class and the poor. On the other hand, never before the New Deal had the federal government played a major role in guaranteeing family welfare.

The prosperity brought on by World War II—full employment was achieved by mid-1943—also affected all Americans, but now the lowest ranks were the major beneficiaries. Income in the bottom fifth of society rose 68 percent during the war; in the next to bottom, 59 percent. Demographically, the most notable trend was geographical migration. Sixteen million Americans left home for the military service, and almost as many moved in quest of high-paying jobs in the defense industries. Thus, working-class children were better supported financially but not emotionally as the familiarity of community was often lost, not to mention the absence of a father (now in the military—about 183,000 children permanently lost their dads) or a mother (now at work—between 1940 and 1944 the increase of mothers with young children in the workforce was 76 percent).[63]

The Children's Bureau was, of course, in no position to ameliorate the psychological impact of the war on the young. In areas where it could act, its record was mixed. The Bureau held a conventional attitude toward day care—that young mothers ought to remain at home—which did not square with reality but prevented it from generating a program. It was powerless to prevent a return to child labor practices in the face of wartime work needs. It was limited to gathering information on the issue of juvenile delinquency after this behavior escalated during the war. But it did play a role in providing infant and maternal health care for the wives and babies of servicemen (under the Emergency Maternity and Infant Care program), a ministration which the AMA and other critics of the Bureau took as evidence that from its very inception the Children's Bureau had a covert agenda of national health care.[64]

The positive side of the war experience, often forgotten, was the domestic effect of the battle against fascism. One magazine article asked the reader, presumably a mother or father: "Are you a dictator? You are on guard against dictatorship in politics, but what of the management of your own home? Are you training little goose-steppers there?"[65] Already the experience of the Depression was granting more independence to working-class youth, especially boys. World War II, apparently, augmented this trend.

Working-class children were the victims of industrialism, both at home and in society. There is no strong evidence that infants and toddlers lacked mothers and fathers who cared. But parents were preoccupied with work, and living conditions were unsanitary, two reasons for high mortality rates among the young. As children aged, it was expected that they would contribute to the family economy through their labor— doing piece work at home, toiling in mills and factories, even tending to middle-class households. Their existence was otherwise far removed from that of the *bourgeoisie,* as Anzia Yezierska, a Russian immigrant, discovered.

> "Mamma, what's a birthday?" I cried, bursting into the house in a whirl of excitement. "Becky, the pawnbroker's girl on the block, will have birthday to-morrow. And she'll get presents for nothing, a cake with candles on it, and a whole lot of grand things from girls for nothing—and she said I must come. Could I have a birthday, too, like she?"
>
> "Wo is to me!" cried my mother, glaring at me with wet swollen eyes. "A birthday lays in your head?" she continued bitterly. "You want to be glad you were born into the world? A whole lot you got to be glad about. Wouldn't it be better if you was never born already?"[66]

Working-class children did have allies of a sort among middle-class reformers, who established orphan asylums and reformatories, aid societies and juvenile courts, Sunday schools and public schools, all pretty much shaped to adult expectations. Which is to say that the autonomy of the working-class young was not anyone's express goal. That the conditions of the Depression contributed to independence was circumstantial.

Part III
Modern America

Suburban Childhood

I was born in 1934 in Bethlehem, Pennsylvania, and spent my first four years in a city apartment with my stay-at-home mother. My father, an erstwhile college instructor, draftsman/estimator, and employee of the WPA., despite having been a lifelong inhabitant of the steel city, longed to return to his Pennsylvania German rural roots. His dreams were realized when he found a 14-acre farm 10 miles distant. He moved my mother, younger brother, and me (two more boys arrived in 1939 and 1942) into the house, refurbished with a modern kitchen and a two-car garage, then remodeled the barn for my mother's sisters and her parents.

Growing up within the haven of family—a nurturing father, a loving but flustered mother who resorted to spanking, benign grandparents, and intrusive aunts—I spent most of my time playing vigorously outdoors with my brothers and cousins. When a 12-year-old friend died, my mother shielded me from the funeral. I, in turn, protected my parents from any knowledge of my doings away from home. Laissez-faire privacy was the norm, as was church-going, and adolescence brought with it no conflicts.

I attended the local country schools with the children of Pennsylvania Dutch farmers until my parents joined a nearby suburban country club. In this upper middle-class setting I learned to swim and play tennis, activities which served me well at Bethlehem High School and Princeton University, the latter now within financial reach due to Dad's successful career as a builder.

I married my high school sweetheart and began graduate work in Philadelphia, where my son, Joey, was born in 1959, a baby boomer whose rearing would have been approved by Benjamin Spock. We moved to the West Coast, where Joey and his two younger sisters traversed the San Francisco public schools but seldom saw the interior of a church except on television, which was watched without restriction. Parent-child conflict hardly existed, but my wife and I divorced. Joey left home for Europe at 16, studied piano, married a singer, and eventually became an opera conductor. Katie took a nursing course and became a full-time mother. Clara managed a minor adolescent rebellion, majored in art in several colleges, and, still single but (like her siblings before her) living with a "significant other," went into teaching.

In the census of 1920, the United States was declared to be an urban nation. But while more than half of the nation's inhabitants lived in population centers of 2,500 or more, few lived in large cities.[1] By this time suburban development was well under way, a process that was at least partially nurtured by antiurban feelings.[2] The home was a haven for the urban middle class in the nineteenth century, but as the city became increasingly crowded and dirty, and as nature was idealized in a way it had not been in the eighteenth century (when it was still being subdued), the periphery of the city became appealing. "Get your children into the country," advised a real estate ad in 1905. "The cities murder children. The hot pavements, the dust, the noise, are fatal in many cases, and harmful always."

Land developers appealed to the widespread belief that property ownership stood as a mark of prestige, despite the abundance of real estate in America. The unattached house was an added attractive feature of country living, and such a residence was brought within financial reach of the middle class by balloon-frame construction, in contrast to the more expensive European method of building. Furthermore, the emergence of handy modes of transportation, first the streetcar and later the automobile, only made suburbs more accessible and attractive.

Local governments friendly to the suburban middle class funded the track laying and road construction for trolleys and cars. And by the twentieth century, politicians were making it more difficult for cities to annex suburbs. Existing separately, suburbs were free of the racial, ethnic, and class conflicts that characterized the central city. During the Depression, the Home Owners Loan Corporation, in the course of rescuing middle-class citizens from losing their mortgages, developed methods of appraisal (later adopted by the Federal Housing Administration and the Veterans Administration) which were clearly biased against lower-class, often black, neighborhoods. And by revolutionizing the home finance industry, the federal government made it cheaper for members of the white middle class to buy houses in the suburbs than to rent apartments in the city. Finally, the development of a public housing program in the central city had the effect of segregating the races while simultaneously reinforcing the image of the suburbs as a haven from the urban problems of race, crime, and poverty.[3]

The affluent Americans who built suburban homes in the 1920s were encouraged to equip them with electric appliances, telephones, and radios, not to mention garages to shelter their automobiles. The machine had been symbol and reality of the industrial age, so dominant that efficiency experts attempted to transform humans into automatons. But as production was superceded by consumption, a process which affected prosperous Americans by the third decade of the twentieth century, humans began to be characterized as communicators. Sociologist David Riesman argues that the new era of consumption featured a social character that was other-directed, that human "control equipment, instead of being like a gyroscope, is like a radar."[4] In other words, one's behavior toward other people was conditioned by their anticipated responses.

Other-directedness was nourished by the mass media, which coached Americans in what to wear and how to act. The grossly inequitable distribution of income in the 1920s limited the number of people who could afford to follow the fashions of the age, but the economy was clearly headed in a direction that would nurture other-directedness: American workers were shifted out of industrial production into the service sector, that is, into jobs in which responding to others was of critical importance.[5]

But child-rearing advice in the 1920s was not yet calculated to foster other-directedness. Early in the century the best-selling item in the Government Printing Office had been a frequently revised pamphlet entitled *Infant Care*, distributed by the newly established Children's Bureau. This first version of *Infant Care* (1914), true to the nineteenth century, assumed that infant character was malleable; hence, children could and should be trained in the proper habits. Spontaneity was further squelched by the admonition that parents must not play with their babies.[6]

This advice was reinforced in the 1920s by the enormously popular behavioral psychologist, John B. Watson, who ridiculed maternal sentimentality and advocated stern training for the trials of adult life. Reviving from the nineteenth century the idea that the mind of the child was a blank slate, Watson's "habit training" was to be implemented by rewarding good behavior and punishing bad, by rigidly scheduling feeding, play, bowel and bladder elimination, and sleep, by totally controlling the child's relationship to its environment. Thus parents could produce exactly the progeny they wanted.[7]

What was a human but a machine, Watson asked rhetorically, all of whose thoughts and actions could be understood in terms of stimulus and response? His mechanistic turn-of-mind reflected the importance of technology of the 1920s. But Watson was not a scientist. He had never conducted laboratory investigations of children, the certified way to proceed now that systematic experimentation was replacing moral judgment as the basis of child-rearing advice. Observational studies of children had begun in the nineteenth century, prompted by a more benign view of the child, by Darwinian theories that promoted comparisons between animal and human infancy, and by the importance assigned to pediatrics in the 1880s.

Using the most easily measured variable, physical growth, the first investigators had sought to establish its relationship to mental development by looking at groups of schoolchildren. Later researchers had searched for answers to developmental questions in detailed descriptions of individual youngsters, so-called baby biographies. In 1891 G. Stanley Hall, whose work on adolescence emerged a decade later, had initiated the child-study movement (see Chapter 4), sometimes referred to as the first scientific examination of the mental development of the

21. Suburban middle-class Americans turned to professionals for child-rearing advice, increasingly and self-consciously, as the ever-popular artist and illustrator Norman Rockwell demonstrated in this portrait of a mother holding a book titled *Child Psychology*. The portrait served as the cover for the *Saturday Evening Post* on November 25, 1933. Reproduced by permission of the Norman Rockwell Family Trust.

child. By the close of the nineteenth century, there existed an accessible body of knowledge about children.[8]

The Progressive era child-savers of the early twentieth century (Chapter 5) were the beneficiaries of this store of information. They applied the known facts to social problems. (Juvenile courts, for example, were a consequence of this method of reform.) By the 1920s, however, the approach had shifted to one of conducting research on issues as they arose rather than applying already existing knowledge. Furthermore, the attitude of child-savers changed from condescension toward the working-class young, who had been studied as subnormal or deviant, to an assumption that children were generic and, as such, merited analysis without regard to social station. These behavioral scientists reflected the new, increasingly developmental, American-grown approach to psychology. Organized child-saving had become a profession by the early 1930s.[9]

Despite the fact that Watson's *Behaviorism* (1924) was cited by the *New York Times* as having initiated "a new epoch in the intellectual history of man," behavioral scientists soon rejected it.[10] The drift away from Watsonian principles can be seen in the words of psychologist Arnold Gesell at Yale, who observed as early as 1930 in *The Guidance of Mental Growth in Infant and Child* that "the inborn tendency toward optimum development" in the child was "inveterate," surely a rejection of the Watsonian idea that the newborn mind was a blank slate. Rather, the infant was depicted as a being able to choose for itself.[11] But behaviorism, in drawing an analogy between the human and the machine, in stressing the importance of preparing the young for a competitive world, in its environmental approach to the shaping of human personality, remained popular for some time.

For example, the design of toys for early twentieth-century boys idealized technology and the values of competition, traits associated with the industrial age. Girls usually received dolls or other objects designed to train them to become modern housewives and nurturing mothers, to relate to friends and be attractive to adults, age of consumption characteristics. Toys, which were becoming more important to children as the birthrate declined and playthings replaced siblings, also took on a new feature in the early twentieth century: fantasy. Playthings for the first time represented heroes and heroines, drawn from mass culture, which invited the child into the realm of the imagination.[12] This may have connoted parental acceptance of children's self-expression; it also suggests that parents recognized a psychological dimension of play. Fantasy did not figure in Watson's thinking, since he explicitly rejected the idea of an unconscious mind.

Watsonian behaviorism was not explicitly directed to the raising of boys. But its bias was masculine, and as such it pitted itself against changing notions of gender. The middle-class family was in the process of a transition that had begun in the nineteenth century: democratization, with increasing attention focused on child nurture. Fathers in the 1920s were expected to create closer, more personal bonds with their children, to be pals as well as breadwinners. True, mothers remained the real nurturers, as children attested when asked where their allegiance lay. And, in this budding age of consumption, advertisers constantly reminded Dad that his *primary* role was to provide the household finances, not the caregiving.[13]

Unlike the traditional family, however, where the household was the scene of production as well as the classroom, the middle-class family had lost its economic as well as its educational functions, leaving it only the third "e"—its emotional role. This unit, often referred to as the companionate family, featured a less structured, more affectionate relationship between husband and wife as well as parents and children, one in which gender differences were muted.

In this more emotional household, feelings themselves were less gendered than ever before. Men and women were spending more time together, and gender-specific advice declined accordingly. Fear was the first of the emotions to be neutralized. In the nineteenth century, girls were to be shielded from it while boys were to confront it courageously. Now the focus was on early childhood, a time when the vulnerable young of both sexes would need help in overcoming fear. And, indeed, kids may actually have been more fearful, given the decline in the number of siblings (fewer peers to discuss fears with and more time alone to fear the dark), the rarity of death (it became a more fearful matter), and the waning of religion. The prescription given was to deal "not through direct mastery but through benign evasion," and parents were cautioned to master their own fears lest they give disturbing signals to the young.[14] Jealousy, in the nineteenth century a distinctively female trait, now was discovered in young males as well. Anger, which was to be repressed by girls and channeled by boys in the previous century, was last among the emotions to be degendered. Relabeled "aggression," it was targeted as antisocial for all children.[15]

Emotions were not only degendered but, in keeping with the onset of consumerism, they were tied to material objects. A child was to be rewarded for overcoming fear. To cope with sibling rivalry, toys were to be labeled, a youngster was to be compensated with a gift at the arrival of a brother or sister, and hand-me-downs were to be dyed. Dolls were recommended for grief training, even to the point of supplying doll coffins.[16]

As the family became more emotional, it also became more private, posing a problem for the maturing young person: how to make the

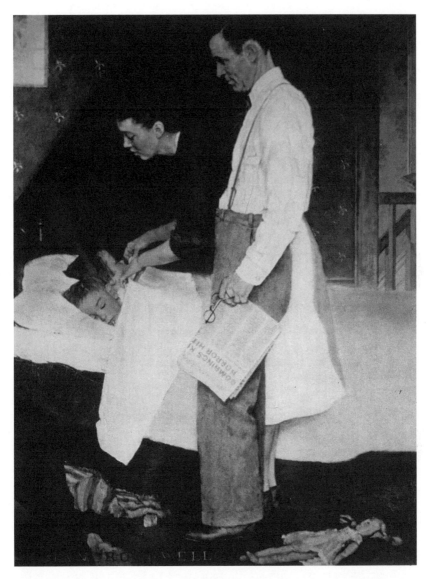

22. As life expectancy rose and the birthrate declined, more parents were available to fewer children. Fathers spent fewer hours on the job and were expected to be more nurturing at home. Norman Rockwell caught the mood of this development in *Freedom from Fear*, illustrating one of four freedoms enunciated by President Franklin Roosevelt as a goal of World War II. Reproduced by permission of the Norman Rockwell Family Trust.

transition from the household, where personal identity was molded, to society, where a social role was assumed. The agents in this transition were the school and the peer group. (The latter, though often denounced for pressuring adolescents to conform, also provided security and thus eased the young person from family affection to the harder social reality of adulthood.)[17] The 1920s, the so-called Jazz Age, is probably best remembered for behavior that characterized only late adolescents from the middle class. Demonstrating a surprising unanimity in their rejection of the social and moral standards of their parents' generation, white, middle-class college students were smoking and drinking and talking coarsely, listening to jazz and wildly dancing, discussing sex and engaging in it as well. The issue is how to interpret this behavior.

In the first place, demographic circumstances directed attention to youth, which was catching up to childhood in numerical importance. As infant mortality and the fertility rate declined and life expectancy rose in the twentieth century, the median age of the population mounted, and the size of the 15–21 age cohort became larger in relation to the under-15 cohort.[18] (The decline in child mortality encouraged Americans to have fewer children, while the ascent in life expectancy contained the promise that more parents would survive to raise their offspring. Thus, more attention could be devoted to each child according to his/her individual needs. This must have contributed to the rise of family affection, already mentioned.)

In addition to the demographic slant, there is a cultural perspective. In the 1920s, American culture was remade. The tension that had long existed between the modern and the traditional was resolved, and youth played a major role, both as the products and the agents of change. And young people were caricatured as a way of understanding and coming to terms with the changes which overwhelmed the old order.[19] Among these changes, of course, were the alteration of the family and the new view of emotions.

In this time of transition, as the family was becoming more affectionate, why would Watson's strictures on child rearing—less sentimentality, more discipline—have found an audience? It seems reasonable to speculate that behaviorism appealed to middle-class parents in the 1920s at least partly because, with youth appearing to be so out of control, a system of habit training held the promise that younger children could be prevented from going the same route.[20] By the 1930s parents gave evidence of becoming more understanding, being drawn to "character education," that is, empathizing with children and teaching them how to forge moral responses to real-life situations. During the Depression, Americans faced the apparent failure of entrepreneurial capitalism, a system that had been linked to behaviorism.[21] While habit training for an entrepreneurial adulthood lost relevance in the 1930s, character education was more appropriate to the reality of the Depression and the struggling household.

The familiar story of the Depression—GNP down 29 percent from 1929 to 1933, unemployment up from 3.2 to 24.9 percent—has not often been examined from the perspective of children. When Social Security became an issue in 1935, Americans were shocked to realize that 40 percent of the people on relief—8 million souls—were children under the age of 16.[22] As noted in Chapter 5, a study of preadolescent and adolescent children in the 1930s concluded that although lower-class children already had experience with economic hardship and its lessons, middle-class youngsters were "better equipped in resources and orientation to work out adaptive responses to the complexities and challenge of change.... Psychological health [was] more adversely affected by economic deprivation in the working class."[23] This observation helps explain the appeal of character education to middle-class parents.

While the Depression was the primary fact of life for Americans in the 1930s, the rise of fascism in Europe could not go unnoticed. In the late 1930s, the democratic nature of the American family was a popular magazine subject; parents were reminded that democracy began at home. During World War II, social scientists studied national character, concluding that obedience and aggression in Germany could be understood in terms of an authoritarian father, a submissive mother, and a child who was subject to a hierarchical system that caused him or her later in life to submit to superiors and dominate inferiors. The American family was (or ought to be) distinctly different. Even an infant was a citizen of this miniature democracy, able to feed on demand. The child was nurtured and thus able to be himself or herself.[24]

At the beginning of the war, only single men were drafted into the armed services. There was a strong resistance to drawing fathers into the conflict, but manpower needs triumphed in late 1943. "Reactions to their absence are as varied and numerous as reactions to their presence," wrote one therapist. Psychologists did agree that the age and gender of the child were critical factors; boys who were fatherless before the age of five showed peer dependency and were less assertive, while little girls appear to have been more aggressive.[25] Plenty of evidence exists that fathers had trouble adjusting to their children when they returned from the war; psychologists concluded that the separation between servicemen and their progeny born during the war had an effect that was both lasting and negative.[26]

But in a benign, democratic, father-present family, life could reflect the war without serious consequences. I was barely seven on Pearl Harbor Day, though I remember it vividly. Soon two older cousins and some family friends were shipped to the South Pacific, but battles in that part of the world seemed curiously one-dimensional. Probably because of my family's German ancestry, the Nazis seemed far more real. My brothers, cousins, and I impersonated Hitler—hair over forehead, comb under nose, right arm outstretched—as we raucously rendered "Right in Der Führer's Face," our jocular cover for more secret fantasies: the life of an undercover agent or member of the Resistance in Paris or Belgrade or, best of all, Berlin, assassinating the leader himself. Not very healthy dreams for preadolescents, but certainly encouraged by both radio and the movies.

My father, a mathematician who had never been in an airplane, taught aerial navigation at a nearby college. We children lay out on the lawn, identifying passing aircraft through long summer days. In the autumn we collected milkweed which, we were assured, would fill life jackets. In winter the girls at school, and even some of the nimble-fingered boys, knitted squares for an afghan, while spring brought drives to collect newspapers, tin cans, and cooking fat. It was a war for all seasons, and we participated fully, at one time staging "This Is the Army" on top of the grand piano in the living room for the gathered relatives. Of course, we all marched proudly in the V-J Day parade, led by the local Chevy dealer astride his dapple-gray, Jim.

We found it hilarious that the emperor Hirohito could not go to work because he had atomic ache. Jokes like this amused rather than frightened us until, years later, the civil defense movement invaded the schools. But surely the implication of the nuclear age, even before the cold war, was that international cooperation was necessary, reinforcing the idea that American family members, by working together, provided a model for the world.[27]

Shortly after the war ended, the most direct assault on Watsonian principles appeared: pediatrician Benjamin Spock's *Baby and Child Care* (1946), which for decades remained second only to the Bible in sales on the American book market. (The Children's Bureau publication, *Infant Care*, which reflected the professional counsel of physicians, psychologists, and social workers, carried a message similar to Spock's and sold almost as well.)[28] Addressing the expectant or new mother in the book's opening paragraphs, Spock reflected on the deluge of advice likely to flow from friends and family and even experts: "Don't be afraid to trust your own common sense. Bringing up your child won't be a complicated job if you take it easy, trust your own instincts, and follow the directions that your doctor gives you. We know for a fact that the natural loving care that kindly parents give their children is a hundred times more valuable than their knowing how to make a formula expertly."[29]

He echoed the thinking of behavioral scientists such as Arnold Gesell when he assured parents, "Your baby is born to be a reasonable, friendly human being." And he promised that if the child was loved, enjoyed, and appreciated "for what he is," the youngster would grow up happy and confident. Strictness or permissiveness was not the basic concern. "The real issue is what spirit the parent puts into managing the child and what attitude is engendered in the child as a result."[30] Spock's genius was to inspire confidence by making it clear that the parent need not be a laboratory scientist to succeed; the democratic family could be run by its own citizens in the spirit of love and trust. And when in doubt, call the family physician. Pediatricians were hardly available in the early years of the century, but when World War II began there were 2,400 of them, a figure which doubled during the 1940s.[31]

Although physicians concerned themselves with preadult diseases at least as early as the eighteenth century—Benjamin Rush, for example, wrote about infant cholera in 1789—the practice of pediatrics is usually dated from the work of Abraham Jacobi, a German who reached New York in 1853 with a fresh medical degree from the University of Bonn. He gradually concentrated his practice on the young and became the first professor of children's diseases at Columbia, a founder of the American Pediatric Society (1888), and its first president. By the early twentieth century, medical schools were offering pediatric specialties and allying themselves with children's hospitals. Meanwhile, better sanitation, coupled with immunization (first against diphtheria, then tetanus and pertussis) and the use of chemical agents to control bacterial infections, significantly reduced infant mortality. It was an appropriate moment for pediatricians, organized in 1930 as the American Academy of Pediatrics, to turn their focus from childhood illness to preventative medicine (through well-baby clinics and immunization programs), diagnosis and counseling regarding normal growth and development (by this time Arnold Gesell had initiated his longitudinal studies of children at Yale), and the problems of prematurity, genetic transmission, and mental and behavioral matters.[32]

But illness remained a real problem. Immediately after World War II, the AAP officially observed that three babies under the age of one had died for every two soldiers killed in the war, a situation accentuated among minority groups. The fault, it was concluded, lay primarily in the facts that general practitioners, who handled three-quarters of the private medical care of children, were terribly underprepared in pediatrics, and that medical care in remote areas did not match modern standards. (President Harry Truman, on the other hand, asserted that the major reason Americans failed to receive needed medical care was its cost.)[33]

Within two decades, the development of antibiotics, the prevention of childhood diseases (especially polio) through immunization, the diagnosis and surgical correction of congenital heart disease, the discovery and treatment of new diseases, the emergence of neonatology (and all it implied), not to mention the positive attitude of the federal government expressed through the National Institutes of Health, gave the AAP cause for a qualified optimism. It observed that "more American children receive optimal health care than the children in any other country. But in fact a tragic paradox exists.... many American children do not have *access* to high quality medical care and many do not have *access* to child health supervision." Again, the major problem appeared to be one of health care delivery. The number of physicians had increased 157 percent over the past two decades, but the general practitioners (who in 1949 had handled most children's cases) had dropped from 80 percent to 20 percent of the medical profession while pediatricians had risen from 3 percent to only 5 percent—and almost a fifth were not delivering primary care.

Furthermore, physicians had been migrating from rural areas and city centers to suburbs and middle-sized cities. The AAP concluded its report with the observation that if the infant mortality rate—higher in the United States than in any other developed country and much higher in the nonwhite U.S. population—was to be reduced, there would have to be "broad changes in the economy of the society as well as in the health care delivery system."[34] The American Medical Association, which in 1939 had adamantly opposed a National Health Bill that threatened to provide federal grants to assist state programs in child health care, would never have endorsed such a statement. Nor, of course, could the AAP implement it.

Benjamin Spock's endorsement could hardly have helped. By this time he was well known as a radical and about to be the presidential candidate of the People's Party, a coalition of left-wing groups. In the 1960s Norman Vincent Peale, a nationally known dispenser of spiritual advice, had applied the label "permissive" to Spock, asserting that the most popular of pediatricians was responsible for the current youth rebellion.[35] In fact, his child-centered first edition had moved to a parent-centered second edition in 1957; Spock sensed that mom and dad needed reassurance.[36] But the "permissive" appellation stuck not only because it provided such a simple explanation for a confounding phenomenon but also due to the doctor's antiwar activities, precipitated by his search for a nuclear test ban. Yet discerning readers of *Baby and Child Care* recognized Peale's misperception.

It was evident in Spock's observation that books about child care focused on the requirements of children to the exclusion of "the genuine needs of parents, the frustrations they constantly meet."[37] Pointing out that rearing offspring was not only hard work but expensive and demanding of sacrifice, Spock argued that mothers and fathers should expect in return from their young "considerateness, affectionateness, and willingness to accept the parents' standards and ideals." Because elders were apt to become cross with bad behavior while their progeny preferred to be good, parents were advised to keep their young ones under "reasonable control" through firmness—"Firmness, by keeping children on the right track, keeps them lovable," Spock observed. "And they love us for keeping them out of trouble." When trouble threatened, disapproval was a reasonable deterrent.[38]

An unrelenting advocate of affection toward children, Spock emphatically denied that all kids needed was love, an erroneous assumption parents could harbor through feelings of guilt, causing them to expect too little of their children and too much of themselves. They should not, for example, rein in their feelings of anger (nor should the kids) but, rather, be capable of controlling their aggressive feelings. They should be friendly in their firmness, but not be called upon to explain prohibitions to their offspring. And they should permit themselves to punish. Punishment, while never the main aspect of discipline, could be gauged by the test of "whether it accomplishes what you are after, without having serious effects." By which he meant negative effects, since his tolerance of corporal punishment was predicated on a positive outcome. "I'm not particularly advocating spanking, but I think it is less poisonous than lengthy disapproval, because it clears the air, for parent and child."[39]

Spock spoke to an era filled with parents and children. The postwar baby boom temporarily reversed a centuries-long decline in the birthrate. The grim conditions of the Depression during the 1930s pushed the fertility rate in the United States to an all-time low, and the absence of men during World War II also served to limit reproduction. Hence, in 1945 there was a large cohort of women waiting to have children. In addition, during the 1940s and 1950s more Americans were marrying than previously (in 1940, 15 percent of women reaching 30 had not wed; by 1960 the figure had dropped to 7 percent), and they were marrying younger (the median nuptial age for women dropped from 21.5 in 1940 to 20.6 in 1956). Thus, in the postwar years, two different age groups were producing babies at the same time.[40]

The prosperity of the postwar period supported the urge to reproduce, as did the hope fostered by consigning the Depression to the past, feeling reassured by the war victories, and marveling at the technological prospects of modern times. The consequent torrent of tots burst forth in 1946, responding to the return of the GIs from World War II, and produced over 4 million infants per year from 1946 to 1964, or over 76 million babies in its nineteen-year duration.[41] Postwar parents believed that prosperity was permanent, guaranteeing the brightest future for their offspring. The new arrivals were thus inspired to believe they were special. And *they were*, especially in the initial years of the boom, since so many of them came into the world as eldest children, with all the self-esteem that a number-one birth position confers. For the baby-boom generation was not the product of many larger families but, rather, of more small families—and, hence, more eldest children—as fewer people remained single, and those who married were not content to remain childless.[42]

Hand-in-hand with this behavior was the popularization of the idea that women were meant to be mothers, despite the fact that during World War II they had assumed significant work roles. Books, popular magazines, films (though they began to turn away from family themes in the mid-1950s), and especially television shows—TV having initially been touted as family entertainment—popularized the concept of mothers as natural nourishers—and often included fathers as nurturers as well. Not only was the birthrate high, but so was the marriage rate, while the divorce rate was stable, and the age of marriage fell well below the previous average.[43]

Spock recognized that most mothers, especially those raising a first child, were primarily concerned with well-baby matters, the day-to-day tasks of feeding, bathing, diapering, clothing, entertaining and playing with, training, and bedding their children. At the time *Baby and Child Care* was published, providing nourishment was a major issue and rigid scheduling (as well as bottle feeding) was typically advised, as prescribed by Watson. Spock pointed to recent research which showed that most babies could choose their own feeding times and remain healthy. Nevertheless, he continued, parents brought up in a stringent regime who felt most comfortable maintaining a familiar level of strictness could do so as long as they remained "basically kind" and their children were happy. He was less flexible on the issue of bottle versus breast, believing the latter to be a more natural and therefore superior method "unless you are absolutely sure you have a better way."[44]

Behind Spock's plain talk about day-to-day matters were sophisticated psychoanalytic ideas known to an American elite but not popularized in terms of child rearing in the United States until he broadcast them in 1946.[45] Infrequently Spock explicitly related his advice to Freud's tenets (as in his cautions against "frightening a child about sex"). Far more often he simply incorporated these ideas into his homespun prose. Few readers were apt to connect Spock's treatment of thumb-sucking to Freud's concept of oral sexuality. Similarly disguised are sibling rivalry and Oedipal conflict, the castration complex and penis envy. In dealing with bed-wetting, nightmares, masturbation, and nudity, Spock relied on Freudian formulations of the unconscious, regression, and child-hood sexuality, which had not appeared in earlier child-rearing litera-ture. He later recalled, "In pediatric practice I was trying, with difficulty, to reconcile concepts gained in psychoanalytic training with what moth-ers told me about their children.... After ten years of that, I was able to write *Baby and Child Care*."[46]

The baby boom guaranteed Spock a huge audience, though it was concentrated in the middle class in the suburbs where, in 1960 for the first time, as many Americans lived as in the city. And the audience was affluent: by 1960, 60 percent of Americans owned homes, 75 percent possessed cars, and nearly 90 percent had television. The 6 percent of the world's people who lived in the United States consumed almost half the world's manufactured goods.[47] The new affluence and the conve-niences it bought provided the conditions for more relaxed child rear-ing, just what Spock was advocating. Dependable bottled milk allayed anxieties about breast-feeding (Spock's counsel about breast-feeding notwithstanding), washing machines and (later) disposable diapers diminished the urgency of toilet training, central heating made dressing the kids in heavy and restrictive clothes unnecessary, larger houses provided greater privacy, younger parents (for wealth made earlier marriage feasible) facilitated intergenerational understanding, not to mention allowing for the leisure time necessary to respond to the child. Needless to say, as this child matured, he or she would not carry the burden of economic responsibility typical of earlier generations, while better health and nutrition, as well as sensitivity to the mass media and a pattern of early dating, brought him or her to physical and social maturity sooner.[48]

A prosperous economy might tip the scale toward autonomy. As his-torian David Potter wrote in his provocative book, *People of Plenty* (1954), "No longer a suppliant, the workman found submissiveness no longer a necessity and therefore no longer a virtue.... Finding that the most valuable trait in himself was a capacity for independent decision and self-reliant conduct in dealing with the diverse opportunities which abundance offered him, he tended to encourage this quality in his children."[49]

Yet abundance had other consequences, not consonant with the results Potter described. An economy whose watchword was "produce" had created an industrial plant and generated personal wealth that called for consumption. Since the major economic activity of Americans had shifted from the manufacturing to the service sector, children as future consumers needed to be taught an awareness of fad and fashion, a sensitivity to the opinions of others, and an ability to alter themselves accordingly. Youngsters headed for the service sector, where handling people was more important than producing goods, also needed coaching in other-directedness. These would *not* be lessons in self-reliance; autonomy is another question.[50]

The mass media that broadcast the advertisers' message was critical to the success of the consumption ethic, which waxed in the upper middle class during the 1920s and waned during the economic hard times and rationing of the 1930s and early 1940s, before it blossomed in postwar prosperity. (Both the telephone and the automobile, though not classified as media, obviously facilitated the interpersonal communication so fundamental to other-directedness.) Movies, which had been a working-class phenomenon in the earliest decades of the century, were by the 1920s self-consciously attempting to replicate middle-class values. The radio was making its way into the home, replete with commercial messages, as magazines and newspapers had been for decades.[51]

But the real household intruder was television. Combining the incessant audio power of radio with the fascinating visual power of the film, and fueled by commerce, it was a never-ending advertisement, mesmerizing while merchandising. Reaching only a faint 3 percent of American households in 1950 but promising wholesome family entertainment, it was able to clutch 86 percent of the nation's homes in its electronic embrace by the end of the decade.[52]

At the outset the networks presented almost 30 hours a week of children's programs. In the first major survey of TV's effect on American kids, Stanford researchers wrote in 1960 that "along with the home and the school, it has come to play a major part in socializing the child"; problems were recognized in the violence evident and the distortion of reality.[53] As shows such as *Howdy Doody* and *Captain Kangaroo* began to be supplemented and even replaced by cartoons (sometimes very old cartoons) that offered merchandise for children, it became apparent that kids' TV was no exception to the market-driven energy behind the medium. Despite massive academic research detailing TV's shortcomings, especially regarding the young, not to mention books and lobbying organizations calling for regulation of television, it became clear that the networks had almost carte blanche on programming.[54]

In 1952 the Federal Communications Commission reserved 242 channels for education, largely UHF and thus beyond the reception of most viewers. Initially, educational TV for kids was closed-circuit, but the Educational Facilities Act (1962) and the Ford Foundation provided funding for higher quality presentation. The formation of the Corporation for Public Broadcasting in 1967 brought about the Children's Television Workshop a year later, which showed the way to imaginative instruction through *Sesame Street.* Targeting preschool kids from inner-city, low-income families, *Sesame Street* not only provided the culturally rich fare

23. Television, a technological innovation billed as family entertainment, quickly found its way into the American home. Its interest in children as consumers far exceeded other concerns for the young. National Archives.

that middle-class children were apt to receive at home but also reached into those very middle-class households.[55] Kids did not desert commercial TV, of course, and stinging critiques continued to emerge from reputable places.[56] In 1980 the FCC deregulated cable TV, which increased both the problems of and opportunities for child advocates; it also wed the worried networks to formulas that had worked. The Children's Television Act of 1990 summoned broadcasters to serve the "educational and informational needs of the children through programing," to which the networks responded by asserting that programs such as *The Flintstones* were educational. The FCC agreed, only to reverse itself in 1993.[57] Still, it would be an exaggeration to say that TV was child-friendly.

Television, in turn, affected the toy industry. (Whether children's play has survived television and whether the folklore of earlier societies continues to have a significant effect on children's rhymes, songs, and games are separate questions.)[58] Essentially, two types of toy were available: One planned the future of boys (machines) and of girls (dolls), while the other appealed to dreams generated by radio and films. There were also educational toys, which were intended to reinforce both parental authority and a child-centered culture. Pressure from parents pushed these toys into the category of planning-for-the-adult-future, turning child's play into work. But children got their revenge when TV advertising undermined parental control by bringing toys into the living room and appealing directly to the child's imagination (and the emerging consumption ethic) with Barbie (carefree buying) and GI Joe (heroic action), to mention only the most popular playthings.[59]

Music was a critical ingredient of the movies, radio, and TV. The changes in its content and audience are instructive concerning the rising power of the young. Before World War II, the sentimental syrup labeled popular music, for example, Bing Crosby singing "Ida, Sweet as Apple Cider," was intended for whole-family consumption. Other musical genres—folk, spirituals and blues (or "race music"), country and western—were consigned to regional and ethnic ghettoes. The migration of white "hillbillies" and black sharecroppers to cities during the war, as well as their congregation in the armed services, made it possible for the first time to hear all sorts of music across the radio band. Inevitably there was fusion. At the top of the charts in 1951 was "Goodnight, Irene," written by a black bluesman, sung by a folk group, and prettified for popular consumption. The whole family was still listening to, and soon watching, *Your Hit Parade*. But the music was changing.[60]

The most dramatic transformation came with rock 'n' roll, formerly "race music" and explicitly sexual. Now teenage girls in mixed-race audiences screamed and swooned at the appearance of Elvis Presley, a white crooner who sounded black. Middle-class parents were appalled while adolescents were enthralled, reinforced in their rapture by the new power of peer pressure. Abundance meant the young formed a huge market for concerts and recorded hits. By the late 1950s the term "popular music" often referred to youth music.

Adults had been both fascinated and appalled by teenage behavior in the years immediately following World War II—the way they dressed, talked, and associated with one another seemed bizarre and ever-changing. But by the mid-1950s there was real consternation, allied with the belief that the mass media, the vehicle of a new peer culture, had erected a barrier between parent and child. (An examination of the magazine Mad, created in 1952 and ever popular for its derision of adult society, would certainly support this argument.) If the older generation could not impress its values on the younger, that explained widespread misbehavior and delinquency. By the late 1950s, social commentators were arguing that teens had taken over popular culture and were dictating their vision to elders.[61]

The divide between generations in the 1920s differed from that in the 1950s because earlier "youth" had signified white, upper-middle-class college students. Now the prosperity of post–World War II America had raised many working-class families into the ranks of the bourgeoisie, unleashed a veritable army of youngsters from after-school jobs, congregated them in suburbs, assembled them before the media, predisposed them to seek one another's opinions—in other words, created the conditions for the flourishing of a peer group, much larger than in the 1920s, that challenged the influence of the family.

The young were still economically dependent on their parents. The increasingly sophisticated world of work demanded a longer schooling than ever before; students stayed, parents paid. Yet these mature students were prepared for adult sexual roles. They had experienced an earlier puberty than their elders due to improved nutrition and health, affluence had fostered early dating, and the mass media advertised sex. Such conditions created an audience ready for rock 'n' roll, as well as eager participants in the sexual activity it celebrated. In the 1950s, sexual intimacy was restricted to marriage; heavy petting was approved, but virginity was expected to be carried to the altar. By the late 1950s, or at least by the early 1960s, sexual intercourse was permissible if the participants were in love (and for the first time oral contraceptives were available). By the late 1960s, love and the prospect of marriage were not a necessary prelude to sex, and the female rate of intercourse caught up to the male.[62]

Needless to say, most middle-class parents were unlikely to view their children's behavior in terms of abstractions such as affluence, demographic change, or an emergent new popular culture, though they were sensitive to class differences and antagonistic to what they perceived as the spread of lower-class culture. A report from the White House Conference on Children in 1950 observed, "There arises the possibility that the standards of the lowest class can through the children reach some of the boys and girls of other social groups." Race as well as class was probably involved. The percentage of blacks finishing high school doubled between the early 1940s and the late 1950s, so that by the early 1960s the percentage rates of whites and blacks finishing high school were almost equal. And parents could not help but notice that it was at the high school, more than any other place, where youngsters met and mixed.[63] (As a result of the GI Bill, the colleges were also diversified, though much less than the high schools.)

But while the middle-class American family was becoming more benign, more mutually sensitive, more democratic, the internal structure of the American school remained largely unaltered. There was a dramatic ascent in the number as well as in the variety of children attending. (High school enrollments were more than 10 times what they had been in 1900, partly stimulated by the Depression. Similar growth was also experienced at lower levels of education.)[64] And there were changes in instructional materials, architecture, curricular offerings, and even in discipline. But these changes had not liberated the classroom. Earlier in the century John Dewey, the progenitor of the Progressive thinking which had allegedly taken over the schools, had been as child-oriented as Benjamin Spock. Believing that the young must be nurtured in an atmosphere commensurate to their social responsibilities, Dewey had stated that they must not be trained to take orders. "Children in school must be allowed freedom so that they will know what its use means when they become the controlling body, and they must be allowed to develop active qualities of initiative, independence, and resourcefulness, before the abuses and failures of democracy will disappear."[65]

Despite Dewey's eloquence and his appeal to professors of education, regimentation was the norm in schools in the mid-twentieth century. In the 1950s, the teacher was firmly in command, more often than not passing out moralistic advice along with uninspired lessons. (The profession was partly redeemed by talented women who had almost no other career open to them.) Extracurricular clubs and sports did lighten the atmosphere for students and for the community, which was more interested in the strength of the football team than the quality of the English department.[66]

Americans turned to these rigid institutions with a multitude of issues in the postwar period. The baby boom raised the problem of rapidly expanding enrollments; schools became larger, more bureaucratic. Meanwhile, parents in the child-centered family expected special attention for their children, which could not be delivered as classroom size grew. McCarthyism subjected teachers to accusations of subversion. The technological demands of the cold war prompted Americans to demand scientific preparation of students beyond the capacities of most schools; critics accused schools of wasting time with "life adjustment" courses. And schools were expected to resolve the nation's shameful racial situation through integrated classrooms. Historian James Gilbert has referred to the American high school in the 1950s as "the symbol of hope and trouble in socializing American youth."[67] It turned out to be more trouble than hope.

First of all, school administrators and teachers were largely insensitive to the changing demeanor of the young. Cold war pressures, most notably the launching of Sputnik, led to tougher courses and a stronger emphasis on math, science, and foreign language in the late 1950s and early 1960s. But such courses as basic U.S. history remained unaltered, as did the school culture of compulsory attendance, isolation of departments within the curriculum, and graduation based on number of course credits. School discipline was affected, however, by the migration of African Americans from the rural South to the urban North and West during World War II; administrators had to grapple with the problem of rowdiness, and to their credit they paid attention to sociological and psychological explanations, labeling what had once been called mischief and belligerence as deprivation and disadvantage.[68] But tolerance of youth in the schools came only slowly.

Also, changes taking place outside the classroom were close to overwhelming.[69] To the lure of alcohol had been added drugs; by the late 1960s, 10 percent of high school students were attending classes high on marijuana. Sixteen- and seventeen-year-olds (re)joined the labor force (a move recommended by prestigious commissions who thought youth would thus develop an attitude of social responsibility), usually in boring, dead-end service sector jobs, thereby diverting them from homework, affording them automobiles, and stigmatizing work.[70] Television and music were time-consuming pastimes, and by the 1970s sexual intercourse was an acceptable but diversionary activity for middle-class youth.

A youth revolution was under way. It had many explanations, not least of which was demographic: The baby boom of the late 1940s was inevitably followed by an adolescent boom beginning in the 1960s. Between 1960 and 1970 the 18–24 age group expanded 53 percent. Adolescence in modern America has been the transitional period between childhood and adulthood, during which time youths have been badgered by adults to adopt mature (that is, the adults') thought and behavior. In the 1960s the adult task was more arduous than usual because the ratio of young to old had risen—and more difficult still because many middle-class adults were themselves in transition from one set of values to another.[71] Adults in turmoil were less able to sustain a united front based on traditional values that many of them no longer honored.

Finally, and fortuitously, issues arose concerning race and war to which adults were especially vulnerable. At least some young activists developed a political agenda embodying ideas they had first heard at home, challenging liberal middle-class parents. Mom and Dad believed that every American, regardless of color, deserved first-class citizenship; they revered Martin Luther King, Jr. Why then didn't they support the destruction of every vestige of segregation, not only in Mississippi (where their carpetbagger children's lives were in danger) but also in Columbus (where Dad's golfing buddy was part owner of a hotel in which Negroes held only menial positions)? Dad fought in World War II and agreed with the Roosevelt administration that self-determination must replace colonialism, and both he and Mom deplored McCarthyism as an excess of the cold war. Why then couldn't they see that the so-called containment of communism in Southeast Asia ran contrary to their principles, that the Vietnam conflict was truly a war of national liberation?

Of course, the stance of many of the young showed little of the restraint characteristic of their elders; it seemed a sign of weakness for parents to opt out of the antiracism and antiwar movements. Having been coached in autonomy in the family environment, youth simply took the initiative, staging sit-ins for racial integration and attempting to block troop trains and induction centers (where protesters encountered more conventional members of their generation). Indeed, it came as a relief to leave behind the stodgy suburbs, where there was not even a place for them to congregate unobserved.[72]

A founder of the Students for a Democratic Society later recalled that members of the New Left shared values with their parents, but only to a point (hence *New* Left, to distinguish the current political movement from the older Left of the 1930s), and that the SDS itself became a surrogate family, not surprising considering that as many as half the organization's leaders came from broken or unstable families.[73] The apolitical youth rebels of the 1960s, the "tune in, turn on, drop out" hippies, were even more drawn to so-called family life—and were christened "flower children" by the media.[74] Although critics of the young seldom made a distinction between explicitly political and implicitly apolitical rebellion, it was the hippies whose influence on youth culture was probably longer lasting. But both groups, by 1970, were having an impact on school life, as dress codes were loosened, social issues were subjects for deliberation rather than punishment (for example, alcohol and pregnancy counseling), student rights were supported (especially after the *Tinker v. Des Moines* decision, in which the Supreme Court ruled that students had freedom of speech), and integration was enforced (largely because of the 1964 Civil Rights Act).[75]

If schools seemed suddenly (but briefly) flexible on the youth issue, social commentators—or at least some of them—were not. The 1970s abounded with predictions of the death of the family, killed not only by the rebellious young but also by bad-behaving elders.[76] The proximate villain in the middle class was divorce. Women's entrance into the labor force had a profound impact on that institution so often paired with post–World War II plenty: the happy two-parent family. Although the divorce rate had risen steadily through the twentieth century, the trend did not become obvious until the dramatic ascent which began in the 1960s, causing the divorce rate to double by the mid-1970s. Sociologists Frank F. Furstenberg, Jr., and Andrew J. Cherlin see the reason for this gigantic change in gender relations created by the growing number of married working women, which broke down the domestic division of labor. As men lost the traditional privilege of being taken care of in the home, and as women who could support themselves became less tolerant of an unhappy relationship, family breakup was the result.[77]

If the economic independence of women made divorce more possible, this is not to say that finances were the sole cause of breakup. Furstenberg and Cherlin conclude that "emotional gratification has become the sine qua none of married life. It is the main glue that holds couples together."[78] Hardly any scholar would dissent from that judgment, and of course those same feelings of affection embrace the children. "Both fathers and mothers have come to want and need warm relationships with their children and to feel inadequate without them. Love and warmth form the new basis for socializing children," according to the authors of *The Inner American*, who place this emotionalism in a broader context. "Between 1957 and 1976 our culture underwent what can reasonably be described as a psychological revolution," a judgment based on extensive national polls carried out in both of those years.[79]

This emotional climate, combined with the rising divorce rate, was a challenge to the mental health of the young. In the face of parental conflict and household breakup, boys were inclined to become aggressive and act out, while girls were more likely to become internally distressed. Both sexes tried to intervene and mediate. Children reacted, yet the long-range effect of divorce was not clear and certain. Psychologist Judith Wallerstein's pioneering study, focusing on sixty families through the course of twenty-five years, supported the conventional wisdom that family breakup was fundamentally harmful. Dissenters quarreled with the evidence gathered to make this judgment.[80]

But unanimity existed that the disposition of the children of divorce was badly managed. Since the nineteenth century, custody had been decided on the "tender years" doctrine, which assumed that children needed the nurture and stability of a primary parent, almost certainly the mother. This child-centered policy gave way in the 1970s to joint custody, largely a response to feminists. In 1967, for example, the National Organization for Women rejected the idea "that home and family are primarily a woman's world and responsibility.... We believe that a true partnership between the sexes demands ... an equitable sharing of the responsibilities of home and children." Judges and state legislators took this message seriously. Though the term "best interests of the child" was bandied about, neither the developmental needs of the child were heeded nor even the voice of the child heard in lawmaking and judicial decisions which now favor fathers (even unmarried ones) who, evidence suggested, were often less interested in sharing custody than using the threat of sharing to reduce child payments.[81]

This sort of behavior did not contradict the new meaning of family. Americans moved from the traditional household where values were shared to an emotional dwelling whose members wanted warm relationships, parents with children, husbands with wives. And this transformation made the family a more volatile unit, vulnerable to separation if feelings were unfulfilled, open to resentment. Ironically, as the family became more loving, it became more fragile; as parents cared more for their children, they were more apt to lose them—if not by divorce, then through time spent away from home earning the income that would give their kids the very best.

And time away from home became increasingly necessary; possibly more damage came to children from the economy than from divorce. In the face of a weakening financial situation beginning in the early 1970s, even families that remained intact frequently required two wage earners to maintain the standard of living Americans had grown used to during the postwar era of prosperity. While less than 20 percent of mothers were employed outside the home in 1960, the numbers rose as the economy declined: 30 percent (1970), 45 percent (1980), 57 percent (1990). Without women's contribution to household finances, the gains of the 1960s would have been completely offset by losses between 1970 and 1990.[82]

The economic problems of the middle class, arising in the 1970s, were accentuated during the following decade when the rich got richer and everyone else suffered. Kevin Phillips, once a political analyst for the Republican Party, minced no words about what happened. "America's heyday practices of the 1980s were, for the first time, those of a weakening great economic power, risking its credit and its future and abusing its middle-class citizenry for the benefits of elites and special interests."[83] This was the program of the Reagan Republicans who publicly shed tears for the decline of the family.

It was only the presence of women in the workforce that allowed the median income per child to increase from $4,123 in 1960 to $6,917 in 1988. The rate of increase was much larger from 1960 to 1970 (2.8 percent/year) than from 1970 to 1988 (1.3 percent/year). Also unsurprisingly, the inequality of income for children grew rapidly from 1970 to 1988.[84] The reason for this inequality is partly economic, as already observed, and partly demographic.

As the economy slumped, the American population aged. Only 4 percent of the population was over 65 in 1890, but almost 11 percent was in 1980. Seniors, like youths, are not part of the workforce in modern society (and the places of retirees were largely filled by women in the late twentieth century). Hence, the old and the young have become competitors for the largesse of society, creating a barrier in the path of adolescents who must move from childhood dependence to adult independence, the latter sustained by self-supporting work.[85] The alternative development, that the increasing number of adults would take care of children, whose numbers have remained steady since 1960, has not happened.

Rather, in the privatized home, children are apt to be without parental guidance much of the time, a situation due to nonmarriage, divorce, and the economy. Of course, the government, federal, state, and local, allots goods and services to children (such as schools) as well as to adults (such as Medicare), both of which increased in the late twentieth century but faster for adults (who could vote) than for children. Household income devoted to children also rose, but more before 1973 than after, a situation worse for families on the bottom as the inequality in income distribution widened. When women stepped in to supplement household revenue, parental goods and services for children inevitably declined. Who, for example, would help kids with homework?[86]

Even though parent-child interaction occupies less than 1.5 hours of a youngster's waking day, there are activities such as television watching (3–4 hours a day) or chores (less than an hour a day) that are sometimes carried out together. Only 2–3 hours a day in the interval between school's end and bedtime is a child on his/her own.[87] As the number of single-parent families increases, should the community provide more organized activities to keep the young out of trouble?[88]

Americans are divided on the issue of what to do about the changing family. Conservatives, notably those affiliated with religious groups, call for a return to the traditional family: Mothers should be home, regardless of whether the household needs the income or women deserve choices as to how they use their time. Liberals favor government programs directed to children, which would mean a reallocation of resources from old to young, a change which does not appear politically feasible.

Meanwhile, the children are spending yet more time at school. By 1980 some 98–99 percent of youngsters between the ages of 7 and 13 were in school, and a high number were staying there: for every 100 pupils in the fifth grade in 1972, 89 entered the eleventh grade in 1978 and 75 graduated from high school. (Most elementary schools served their neighborhoods, while most secondary schools were comprehensive, which is to say that in cities the former were more segregated by class, race, and ethnicity than the latter. In either case, the most shared experience of the students and their teachers was television.)[89] Americans, publicly more worried about schools than about families, probably held unrealistically high expectations regarding education's accomplishments. Yet it was difficult for critics to diagnose the reasons for their discontent (not that they were ever without opinions), since the schools had so many components: students; teachers; principals; district, state, and federal officials; parents; and, of course, the purveyors of mass culture.

School achievement was not easily measured. National test results were quoted facilely, but their interpretation demanded in-depth understanding. Scholastic Aptitude Test scores dipped in the early 1970s, leading to public demand for better instruction in science and math when, in fact, the largest decline was in civics. Among the get-tough responses were longer school days and longer school years, not to mention invidious comparisons between lazy American teens and industrious Japanese students. In other words, not only were the scores misread but the students were blamed. Such an eminent commentator as Robert Bly, who provocatively argued that contemporary parents are failures at raising children because of the leveling that has taken place in the family (and, hence, society), also observed: "By 1980 most high schools were being run by their own students."[90]

Studies showed, however, that while elementary schools had become more and more student-centered, the high schools remained teacher-centered.[91] The change was not in the locus of authority but in the structure; the comprehensive high schools recommended in the late 1950s on the principle that bigger was better were transformed, in a concession to the consumption ethic, into shopping mall high schools, which featured "an amalgam of elementary education, university instruction, technical education, and adult education, plus the offerings of mental health and social service agencies."[92]

Even the most sympathetic observers of the schools found obvious fault with them. Some noted flaws in daily practice: "the rushed procession of fifty-two-minute classes; the jumble of 'subjects'...; the predominance of teacher-talk and student-listen...; the reduction of the goals for a school to the collection of credits...; and the procession of mindless, brief tests." Others were critical of the deep-seated structure: "As long as the public schools' dominant social role in the culture (i.e., to bolster the economy and national defense, to solve major social ills, and to select those students who can succeed academically) remains unchanged, and as long as schools remain organized as they currently are (age-graded, with hierarchical authority flowing down from the top, etc.), teacher-centered instruction will remain." In either case, little hope of reform was tendered, not because the problems were hidden but because of built-in conservatism and, disturbing but somehow unsurprising, the complacence of the parties involved.[93]

But complacence may have been but a cover for the ambiguous feelings adults developed toward adolescents over the course of the twentieth century. It was evident from the beginning discussion, G. Stanley Hall's trail-blazing two-volume *Adolescence: Its Psychology and Its Relations to Physiology, Anthropology, Sociology, Sex, Crime, Religion, and Education* (1904). This stage of life was a "new birth," Hall wrote, initiating a period of "storm and stress" during which the young person alternated between overactivity and inertness, between sensitivity and hard-heartedness, between a desire for freedom of expression and development of potential coupled and a need for control and direction, especially in the realm of sexuality.[94] At that time only one-tenth of high-school-age youth actually attended high school, which offered skills training that obsolescent parents could not teach in a modernizing society, and just half of these adolescents were being educated 30 years later.[95] But the trend was unmistakable, and so, too, were the consequences of peer isolation, with virtually all teenagers in school: Control and direction could slip from the hands of adults.

The response of oldsters has been ambivalent. On the one hand, adults have been willing to grant adolescents freedom. For example, young people can drive at 16 and vote at 18. On the other hand, the older generation has curtailed the rights of the young. The drinking age has been raised to 21, pregnant teens must gain parental consent or a court order to obtain an abortion, and mothers under 18 are no longer eligible for welfare without a parent or foster home sponsor. And the student right to free speech, seemingly settled by the *Tinker v. Des Moines* decision, was curtailed in later decisions such as *Hazelwood School District v. Kuhlmeir* (1988). All in all, the ambivalence regarding adolescents has led to more restriction than expansion of rights.

From its beginnings, suburban America was a place of privilege. The middle-class family nestled into it became wealthier, smaller, more private and emotional, thus allowing for a longer childhood, more parental love and attention, and a greater space to grow. Under these benign conditions, children could be expected to prosper as independent beings, especially under the kind regime of Benjamin Spock and his followers. There were, however, inhibiting factors. The adult workplace continually demanded more school, where adolescents encountered peer pressure to conform, institutional restraints against intellectual and social growth, and, as they pushed on to college, the frustrations of remaining financially dependent while becoming physiologically mature.

Inner-City and Rural Childhoods

Brent Staples grew up, the seventh of nine children, during the 1950s in the industrial town of Chester, Pennsylvania, poor but not on welfare—just as urban African Americans began to be identified with both poverty and handouts, not to mention violence. His parents had migrated to Chester from rural Virginia during World War II, lured by the economy.

Sometimes Brent's alcoholic father was in the home; often he was not. The family moved from one run-down residence to another, unable to pay rent for any length of time. "We went on and on like bedouins with couches, tables, and mattresses jumbled in the backs of pickup trucks." Brent had a street life, but he never missed school, just as he filled a responsible place in his family. In the classroom, his mind was often elsewhere, but a few teachers influenced him.

Several Quakers had established a community house in Chester, where Brent began hanging out. There he met black students from nearby Swarthmore College and soon visited the campus; it was safe when social events in Chester were dangerous. Thoughts of continuing in school and advice from a friend led him to apply to Pennsylvania Military College, a local institution with an outreach program for blacks. Although he could not afford tuition, he was nevertheless admitted, and he went on to earn a Ph.D. at the University of Chicago. He was a lot more fortunate than his younger brother, a drug dealer murdered at the age of 22.[1]

There is a persistent myth in America that its citizens inhabit a classless society. Secondary school history books are mute on the subject of socioeconomic division; the word "class" goes unmentioned. It is almost never uttered by politicians, who sometimes take offense at the very use of the term, unless reference is being made to the middle class, which is assumed to include everyone. Class is defined by personal income; the assumption is that anyone in our open society has access to a fluid economy and, with a little effort, may join or remain a member of the middle class. This mythology could not be maintained during the Depression of the 1930s, but it was reasserted in the cause of unity during World War II and the cold war.

Prosperity is applauded because it is expected to affect all of us ("a rising tide lifts all boats"); its limits are frequently unnoticed. We proudly claim that after World War II the nation was rich. The gross national product, $212 billion in 1945, rose spectacularly to $503 billion in 1960 and kept moving up. A majority of Americans did, in fact, belong to the middle class: Their jobs were secure, they owned cars and homes and TVs, and they could send their children to college.[2]

And yet after World War II almost a quarter of the nation's families lived below the poverty line officially set by the federal government. A third of them were rural people—tenant farmers, sharecroppers, migrant farm workers. The remainder resided in the inner city, migrants from rural America, as well as from Puerto Rico and Mexico, who took the places left by those exiting to the suburbs. African American and female-headed households were conspicuously poor.[3]

Middle-class America was taken aback by the portrait of the poverty-stricken vividly drawn in 1962 by Michael Harrington in *The Other America*. Pointing to the invisibility of the poor, Harrington argued that they "are increasingly slipping out of the very experience and consciousness of the nation." (In truth, there were in 1962 a lot fewer poor people in the United States than there had been before World War II.)[4] The most impoverished age group was the almost 10 percent of the population over 65, some 8 million (or roughly half) of whom lived on less than $1,000 a year (when the poverty line was $3,000 for a family of four), frequently without adequate food, housing, or medical care. But minorities had not participated in the prosperity of the postwar years, either. Millions of children, white as well as black, brown, and yellow, lived in poverty. In addition to the 24 percent of the child population living in "relative poverty" (less than 50 percent of median family income), 18 percent existed in "near-poor frugality" (between 50 and 75 percent of the median). They were more likely than adults to live in deprived economic circumstances.[5] Dr. Benjamin Spock's *Baby and Child Care*, in its third edition by 1960, did not mention the words "class" or "poverty."

The infant mortality rate for poor children was roughly twice the national average. The survivors lagged considerably behind others in basic measures of physical development, such as height and weight, and were more susceptible to disease. And, of course, medical care was limited in both availability and quality. Malnutrition was common, leading even to brain damage or death. Later in their young lives, they were more prone to accidents, homicide, and suicide.[6]

Child poverty had been confronted earlier in the century. At the 1909 White House Conference on Dependent Children, delegates argued that needy youngsters should be taken care of at home rather than in institutions. Their campaign, the widows' aid or mothers' rights movement, was first successful on the state level, when Missouri in 1911 passed a statute enabling counties to provide cash to mothers with dependent children. In 1935, by which time all states but South Carolina and Georgia had laws similar to Missouri's, Title IV of the Social Security Act established a program of Aid to Dependent Children. (One dollar of federal money was contributed for every two dollars spent by the state on children—and children only, since mothers were not included until 1950; until 1967 any maternal earnings were subtracted from the relief check.) In 1961, ADC was amended so that families with unemployed fathers could receive aid, though half of the states did not take advantage of this option. At this time the average ADC payment was $124 monthly or $1,488 annually, an income less than half the poverty level and way below the $5,464 "minimum comfort" standard established by the Bureau of Labor Statistics.[7]

Middle-class Americans, if not oblivious to poverty and the circumstances frequently surrounding it in the postwar period, optimistically believed that economic progress would wipe it out. It was not their problem. (Nor was it unique to the postwar period.)[8] For example, many social workers, members of the bourgeoisie who might have been the natural allies of destitute kids, were drawn into private practice in the postwar years, where they worked with well-heeled individuals and families rather than wrestling with public policy. And public policy reflected the moralism of the comfortable. The states, where welfare was administered without regard for national uniformity, were at one when it came to denying funds to families if it was suspected that absent fathers lived nearby and could, in fact, provide; meanwhile mothers were surveilled to ensure that they kept suitable homes. This attitude also appeared in the media, where welfare chiselers and immoral moms came under frequent attack. Polls revealed that middle-class Americans ambivalently felt that welfare was wasteful and demoralizing, yet people in need should be given public assistance.[9]

If class was a foreign term and poverty went too often unaddressed, the relationship between income level and child-rearing practices was similarly obscure. Robert S. and Helen Merrell Lynd, authors of the classic sociological study *Middletown* (1929), had pointed to division between the business and the working classes on many issues in the community (Muncie, Indiana) but had seen little conflict in the arena of child rearing.[10] However, a report from the White House Conference on Child Health and Protection summoned by President Hoover in 1930 had observed:

> The evidence for the existence of differential environments so far as the child is concerned is overwhelming. When the population is divided on the basis of

socioeconomic status and the practices of the resulting groups are studied in detail, a picture is obtained of a society composed of a series of cultures. . . .

Moreover the differences in these practices begin at birth. They affect the medical care the mother receives, and the diet and sleep of the infant. As the child develops, they affect every aspect of his life. Only a few phenomena seem to be independent of the socio-economic factor.[11]

Yet a separate committee report from the same conference muted the effect of this stark statement, observing that socioeconomic status was unrelated to personality or conduct.[12]

Sociologists who did recognize socioeconomic diversity after World War II battled over the question of whether working or middle-class households were more permissive in their child-rearing practices.[13] It now appears that during the 1930s and early 1940s working-class mothers were more permissive: they breast-fed on demand, weaned late, and were lax about bowel and bladder training. But by the late 1940s these practices were labeled middle-class, partly because so many working-class Americans, the beneficiaries of postwar prosperity, had risen to the middle, and partly because of the influence of the new child-rearing literature, especially Benjamin Spock's *Baby and Child Care* and the Children's Bureau publication, *Infant Care*.[14]

The cultural gap between middle and working classes was blurred, although the latter more often resorted to physical punishment, while the former disciplined by such effective methods as withdrawing love. Middle-class fathering was less authoritarian and more nurturing, though these dads were seldom engaged in the daily care of their young—not to mention housework. But working-class fathers were less affectionate, encouraging, and engaged with their children. (Fatherhood continued to be a point of class distinction through the 1970s and 1980s.)[15] Black families, few of whom had yet attained middle-class status, more often resorted to physical punishment than white families, were more rigorous on toilet training, more prudish regarding nudity and masturbation, but more permissive on feeding and weaning.[16]

Surely the American public was even less aware of the academic literature on comparative child rearing than it was of the matters of class and poverty. But it was being educated on a third issue, civil rights, which led indirectly to a broader knowledge of race and class, wealth and poverty, family and childhood (as noted in Chapter 3). In fact, the most famous event of the early civil rights movement concerned children: the 1954 Supreme Court case of *Brown v. Board of Education of Topeka*, the legal anchor of school desegregation.

Oliver Brown's eldest daughter, Linda, attended the Monroe School, a public elementary school in Topeka for black children, a mile from her house, which involved her leaving home at 7:40 A.M, walking through the Rock Island Railroad switching yards to catch a bus at 8 A.M. and riding 30 minutes to school, which opened at 9 A.M. Waiting for the often tardy bus and waiting to enter Monroe meant standing in any sort of weather. The Summer School for white children was a pleasant seven-block walk from her house, and her father thought she should be allowed to attend there. The NAACP agreed when it included Oliver as one of several dozen parties to the lawsuit against the Topeka Board of Education.[17]

The argument advanced in 1954 against the reigning separate but equal doctrine, declared by the Court in the 1898 *Plessy v. Ferguson* decision, was that separate schools, even if equal, violated the Fourteenth Amendment by inflicting psychological damage on African American children. The Court's unanimous finding was that separate facilities were "inherently unequal" and, further, that dividing children solely on the basis of race "generates a feeling of inferiority as to their status in the community" that may become permanent.[18] Legal scholar Robert Mnookin has observed that black children's feelings of inferiority were a response not to school desegregation but "instead to the totality of their experience in a society plagued by racial prejudice." Nevertheless, the *Brown v. Board of Education* decision not only got the lower federal courts involved in dismantling dual systems of education but marked a turning point in the expansion of judicial power.[19]

Although desegregation was to proceed "with all deliberate speed," inertia in the White House and resistance in the Deep South dictated otherwise. But when nine black youngsters attempted to integrate Little Rock High School in 1957, the federal government finally stepped in to restrain the segregationist mob. In 1960 it was again African American students, this time in Greensboro, North Carolina, who initiated a sit-in movement. The 1964 Civil Rights Act, though it pertained mostly to adults (no segregation in public facilities, an Equal Employment Opportunity Commission, protection of African American voting rights), was very much the product of young people's activities and owed its implementation at least partly to the work of youth in the South (see Chapter 3), especially in Mississippi.[20]

With so much attention focused on the overt segregationist policies in the South, most white Americans were surprised to confront a racial crisis in the cities of the North and West, where segregation existed de facto, but school officials claimed to be color-blind. When civil rights groups pointed to conditions that belied that claim, the officials responded by defending the sanctity of neighborhood schools. Black protest continued. Studies were undertaken, and often agreements were reached whose terms were later unmet or only minimally fulfilled. Finally, busing was introduced—and hotly contested. In some cities, such as San Francisco, major opposition came from other than black minority groups. These conflicts stretched into the 1970s.[21]

As white America's consciousness was being raised about race, John F. Kennedy was elected, bringing to his short-lived presidency an interest in poverty, for which there were no studies or programs nor any official estimates of its nature and extent. But it was his successor, Lyndon B. Johnson, who declared a War on Poverty, with an agenda weighted in favor of helping children: education programs (Head Start, Follow Through, Upward Bound, Teacher Corps, Title I of the Elementary and Secondary School Act), skills training (Job Corps, Neighborhood Youth Corps), food and health assistance (a school lunch service, Medicaid), and Community Action and Legal Services programs.[22] The Economic Opportunity Act of 1964, the first shot in the battle, featured VISTA, a domestic Peace Corps; the Job Corps, where high school dropouts could obtain vocational training; and Community Action Programs, out of which Head Start was born as an early intervention program meant to "overcome a lot of hostility in our society against the poor in general and against black people who are poor in particular, by going at the children."[23] The mayors of San Francisco and Los Angeles accused the Office of Economic Opportunity of "fostering class struggle."[24] But for the next decade poverty declined, social spending rose, and the welfare rolls ballooned.

24. Black children may have played with white youngsters during slavery, but their entrance into southern white schools in the 1950s traumatized American society. Illustration by Norman Rockwell. Reproduced by permission of the Norman Rockwell Family Trust.

Head Start was based on the idea that education provided an antidote to poverty. Although there was no precedent for meeting the needs of poor preschoolers and little data concerning those needs, it was thought that a program must affect not only the youngsters (by aiming for sound physical and psychological health as well as academic achievement) but also their families (through parental participation). Head Start graduates in kindergarten through third grade could enter Project Follow Through, a less known and less successful endeavor. The Elementary and Secondary Education Act of 1965 contained a Title I, through which "educationally deprived," low-income children could get help, a piece of legislation so influential that President Johnson's observation— "I believe no law I have signed, or ever will sign, means more to the future of America"—seems hardly hyperbolic.[25]

And the legislation's sponsors, convinced that childhood experience mightily influenced adult thought and action, could find vindication among behavioral scientists. Almost a century previous, Sigmund Freud had located the origins of middle-aged hysteria in childhood events. Indeed, he portrayed the first five years of a person's life as critical to the remainder, virtually claiming that the unconscious mind was the child manifest in the adult. Even John Watson, the behaviorist who denied the existence of an unconscious, argued that he could mold the formless infant into any character he wished, thus sharing with Freud a belief in the determinative nature of early childhood.

The idea that a child's experience shapes his or her adult thought and behavior did not originate with Freud. Seventeenth-century Puritans, imbued with and acting on the belief that a person was nothing in the sight of God, sought to instill in their children the same credo through harsh discipline (Chapter 2). They saw an analogy in the parent-child relationship to the God-person relationship. The Reverend Francis Wayland, for example, observed, "In infancy the control of the parent over the child is absolute; that is, it is exercised without any due respect to the wishes of the child." Whatever his reasoning, he felt justified, as did many before and after him, in breaking the will of his 15-month-old son as a means of preparing him for a life of religious humility.[26] (However, as noted in Chapter 4, many American parents were beginning to abandon the battle-of-the-wills stance toward their children even as Wayland was disciplining his son, not because they ceased to value the shaping force of early experience but because circumstances changed: The home became a haven from the dangers of the city, and young children were perceived as the home's innocent and vulnerable inhabitants, hardly the targets for intergenerational combat.)

The persistence of Wayland's point of view was evident in the child-care advice of radio personality James Dobson, founder of the Christian

Right's Focus on the Family nonprofit (but politically potent) organization, who wrote in 1970 that "developing respect for the parents is the critical factor in child management" because it will shape his/her attitude toward authority for the rest of life and also because "Christian parents who wish to sell their concept of God to their children ... must first sell themselves." Dobson, like Wayland, depicted relations between parents and children as an ongoing battle of the wills.[27]

Long before Dobson, who held a Ph.D. in psychology, the orthodoxy about early childhood experience had been put to the empirical test when research centers established by child-savers in the 1920s conducted longitudinal studies of children, typically from birth into adulthood. Although the purpose was to study growth rather than the effect of early experience, inevitably conclusions about the latter were drawn. A member of the Berkeley project since the late 1920s, Jean Macfarlane, admitted in the early 1970s that she and her colleagues had "unquestionably overestimated the durability of those well learned behaviors and attitudes" from the past; what they witnessed were adaptations "along the whole lifespan."[28] Jerome Kagan, who helped direct another of the longitudinal studies, saw only the faintest continuities in behavioral patterns over time.[29]

By the time these disparaging results were under consideration, the importance of early experience was being invoked by psychologists more empirically oriented than the child-savers. William Goldfarb and Rene Spitz studied the institutionalization of infants and pointed to its deleterious effects on mental (and physical) development. Considering these studies and others, psychiatrist John Bowlby reported to the World Health Organization in 1951 that maternal deprivation critically retarded the growth of children under 30 months of age who were institutionalized. "Mother-love in infancy and childhood is as important for mental health as are vitamins and proteins for physical health," Bowlby warned.[30]

Of course, it was unconscionable to deprive human infants of care for purposes of research on this issue. Such moral strictures did not apply to animal laboratories. At the University of Wisconsin beginning in the late 1950s, Harry Harlow raised rhesus monkeys in isolation, fed by surrogate mothers. Introduced to monkey society, these pitiful primates were incapable of relating to or mating with their peers; when some of the females finally reproduced, they could not mother. But when Harlow later conducted similar experiments, he was unable to validate the determinative effect of early experience; the longer the monkeys were in isolation, the longer it took for their rehabilitation, but they did recover.[31]

However, Konrad Lorenz's work in the 1950s with imprinting in goslings—based on the discovery that a newly hatched gosling, if its initial contact was with a human, would permanently retain that attachment in preference to association with other geese—led him to write about a "critical" period in development (not a learning period but one in which an instinct was acted upon; usually, of course, the attachment would be to the nearby parent). Imprinting obviously gave credence to the determinative effect of early experience, and it appeared consistent with the concept of stage development. It was seized upon by some psychologists as evidential for humans as well as animals, though with the passage of time and conduct of more experiments, the word "sensitive" seemed more accurate than "critical."[32]

The effect of early experience was also tested by looking at the alteration of brain biochemistry through the introduction of an enriched environment and by measuring the long-term consequences of sensory deprivation. In neither type of empirical analysis did the impact of initial stimulation or lack of same have a determinative effect on the future.[33] Such experiments had to be conducted with animals, but it was possible to find children in situations—in orphanages, for example, or the victims of deranged parents—where scientific investigation could yield respectable answers. Again, the consequences of early experience were not found to be permanent, though it could be said that a person becomes less malleable with age. Behavior seemed to be less the product of first encounters than the result of environmental continuity, whether good or bad.[34]

Considering this body of investigation, not to mention a popular belief in the beneficial effects of a changed environment, it was hardly surprising that the long-term effects of Head Start should be examined. In fact, the cognitive advances fostered by Head Start seemed to fade out in elementary school (the more reason for Project Follow Through), a finding which brought the program into jeopardy even though raising IQ was only one of its aims. However, another goal of the program, social competency (high school completion, employment, avoidance of juvenile delinquency and teen pregnancy), was accomplished by program participants.[35]

The record of the Job Corps, on the other hand, was undistinguished. One-quarter of the nonwhite teenagers in the inner cities of the twenty largest metropolitan areas were unemployed at the zenith of the economic boom in 1969. Two years later, with the adult white unemployment rate at 4.6 percent, the black teenage jobless rate in poverty areas was 39.1 percent. An estimated 100,000 or more young ghetto jobless residents were excluded from the totals, not to mention that "employed" embraced the under-employed, usually in dead-end jobs, and rates were higher in rural areas![36] A dozen years later the situation was worse, with 55 percent of black males aged 16 to 21 not working, as compared with 27 percent of white males the same age.[37]

The discovery of poverty in the early 1960s also affected Aid for Dependent Children. In 1961 ADC funds became available for foster care when children were removed from "unsuitable homes," as well as for children whose able-bodied but unemployed parents were no longer eligible for unemployment benefits and earning less than an essential income. A year later ADC was changed to Aid to Families with Dependent Children, which aimed at getting families off welfare. The War on Poverty expanded the AFDC rolls greatly (this was partly a reflection of the baby boom, but also due to a real effort to eliminate destitution), provided food stamps and new medical aid, and sponsored local action (including neighborhood legal services) as a way to involve the poor in their own fate. Testimony to the success of involving the local people was the formation of the National Welfare Rights Organization, the core of which was poor black women. The Supreme Court aided the NWRO by declaring in 1968 that federal assistance could not be denied to destitute children simply because there was a man in the house. And in 1968 the Court struck down state residency requirements. The number of eligible families who applied for aid and were, in fact, assisted rose from 33 percent in the early 1960s to over 90 percent a decade later.[38]

By the mid-1970s, AFDC embraced almost 11 percent of American families (5 percent more than the late 1960s), raising them above the

25. Although Aid to Families with Dependent Children substantially reduced the poverty level, it was unpopular with many middle-class Americans who lived oblivious to the plight of poor children. Photograph by Shelly Rusten.

poverty level through cash payments and in-kind services such as food stamps and Medicaid. The number of poor Americans had dropped from 22 percent of the population in 1959 to 11 percent in 1973. Instead of being proud of this revolution regarding poverty, many Americans—most if not all of whom received tax relief—regarded welfare as close to criminal.[39] In fact, means-tested programs targeted at the poor (AFDC, food stamps, public housing, and the like) never totaled even 20 percent of welfare spending between 1965 and 1975. The really costly programs were unemployment compensation, Social Security, and Medicare, which affected four times as many nonpoor as poor but helped the latter enormously.[40]

Yet the very fact that the welfare rolls included so many African Americans (close to 50 percent of the rolls by the late 1960s), and that so many were unwed (over 25 percent), provoked a backlash.[41] In 1967 AFDC was amended to require recipients with children over six to register for work and training. The Work Incentive Program was based on the theory that the poor could work their way out of poverty, an idea that has always been popular, although its implementation failed to reduce the welfare rolls. But the amendment changed the meaning of the program: When ADC was created in 1935, it was aimed at keeping mothers *at home* to care for children.

Conservatives who publicly hated welfare continued to agitate for change. During President Reagan's first term, households earning less than $10,000 annually suffered a major cut (about 8 percent) in AFDC and related federal benefits (e.g., school lunches); households receiving over $40,000 saw no reduction in federal aid. Payments continued to decline into the 1990s. On July 1, 1997, AFDC became Temporary Assistance for Needy Families, the emphasis shifting from welfare to work, with the states taking on the role of administering it.[42]

The civil rights movement played a major role in bringing employment and living conditions to national attention and in prodding politicians to respond.[43] As scholars probed the reasons for joblessness and poverty, they looked beyond economic to cultural factors, and in doing so one member of the Johnson Administration struck a raw nerve. When Daniel Patrick Moynihan, assistant secretary of labor, published *The Negro Family: The Case for National Action* (1965), the confluence of national prosperity and the civil rights movement prompted him to observe that "the Negro family is dividing between a stable middle-class group that is steadily growing stronger and more successful and an increasingly disorganized and disadvantaged lower-class group." The latter was characterized by divorce, single-parent (usually female-headed) households, illegitimacy, and welfare dependency. In other words, family disintegration.[44]

It was nearly unanimous opinion at the time Moynihan wrote that the black family was weak due to the continuing effect of slavery, a condition that followed the family out of the South. Six and a half million African Americans moved to the North between 1910 and 1970, 5 million after 1940. Not until 1976, when historian Herbert Gutman established that African-Americans began their great migration to the North in the early twentieth century as two-parent families—families which lasted until urban unemployment destroyed them—did this point of view on the historic weakness of the black family start to wane.[45]

But what made the Moynihan Report controversial was not its history but its reference to the black family as "a tangle of pathology" (though the African American psychologist Kenneth Clark had already applied the same words to the black family) at a time when most African-Americans and their sympathizers were bound to take umbrage. Had Moynihan chosen his title more sensitively—say, *The Impoverished Negro Family*—he might have made his point about class as much as race, about poverty as well as ethnicity.[46]

For there was now a black middle class to be reckoned with. Ironically, the upward mobility of some African Americans, acknowledged by Moynihan, played a part in the failure of others. In the pre–civil rights period, residential segregation had meant that black professionals, as well as middle- and working-class blacks, lived in the same area as the lower class, maintaining institutions (churches, schools, stores), providing role models (for family life, educational achievement, careers), and even furnishing marriage partners for less fortunate members of the community. As the civil rights movement broke down racial barriers, the more successful African Americans moved to better neighborhoods, leaving the ghetto to decay in the hands of the unsuccessful.[47]

Moynihan expressed concern that a quarter of black families were headed by women and that a quarter of black children were born out of wedlock. (He might have added that family formation patterns *throughout* the United States showed more divorce, more births out of wedlock, more nonfamily living arrangements.) In addition to family dissolution and welfare dependency, there was crime, with a disproportionate number of black perpetrators and victims. The context for these developments was the ghetto, and the most salient feature of the ghetto—Hispanic as well as black—was poverty. The cause of poverty was unemployment. Sociologist William Julius Wilson has pointed out about these "truly disadvantaged" people: "The problems of male joblessness could be the single most important factor underlying the rise in unwed mothers among poor black women." But the federal government proved far more successful at distributing welfare than creating permanent jobs.[48]

The dismal economic situation appeared to be compounded by the demographics of black inner-city life. Most observers agreed with Moynihan's depiction of family disintegration caused by high rates of divorce, illegitimacy, and single-parent households.[49] The minority view held that most observers, wed to census data and a conventional view of what the family ought to be, based on the nuclear family model of the white suburbs, simply missed the point. The welfare poor in urban ghettos were constantly helpful to one another, pooling personnel and resources to create a sort of community family.[50] It was certainly true that grandparents played a larger role in child rearing among African Americans than among whites. Furthermore, studies of urban poor youth found no association between fatherlessness and psychopathology, personality, self-concept, achievement, or IQ.[51]

Still, something seemed to have gone wrong. Historian Carl Nightingale noticed two changes that occurred in lower-class black life in Philadelphia about 1960. Two-parent households had predominated for a century (if there was only one parent, it was usually a widow) when, quickly over the next 25 years, single parenthood became characteristic of a quarter of the families. And 1960 was the first year when homicide was the leading cause of death among young African American males: from 1960 to 1970 the murder rate in black Philadelphia more than doubled. Moving into one of Philadelphia's ghettos and making friends with the local boys, Nightingale witnessed "two deeply confusing and painful personal struggles whose outcomes greatly determine the extent to which they make aggressive behavior part of their own daily habits and social styles." On the conscious level existed a conflict between street smart values, cynical and manipulative, and ethical traditions, cooperative and responsible. On an unconscious level were painful emotions, feelings of "sheer humiliation and embarrassment, disappointment and frustration, grief and loneliness, and fear and anxiety (especially concerning suspicion, rejection, and abandonment)," some of which could be attributed to frequent corporal punishment and a corresponding lack of parental empathy.[52]

Even where empathy existed, the situation was grim. In 1987 Lafeyette (11) and Pharoah (9) Rivers lived with their warm and generous mother, LaJoe (35), and their four-year-old triplet brother and sisters in a rundown, unpainted, toilet-clogged flat in the Governor Henry Horner Homes, a housing project close to downtown Chicago. (Three older children, all with drug and jail records, did not live at home, nor did Lajoe's husband, father of all the children). The high-rise had no lobby, simply a tunnel through the middle of the building, dark but no darker than the corridors (residents carried flashlights). The neighborhood housed no library, cinema, or similar facility, and it offered almost no jobs. Playing outside was dangerous; children were frequently the victims of gang warfare, with male adolescents most in danger. When LaJoe temporarily lost her meager welfare benefits because social services learned her husband occasionally visited her home, she shared her upset with Lafeyette, who was no child in the middle-class sense of the word. Both he and Pharoah had seen at least one murder.[53]

Next to his close family associations, school was the brightest aspect of Pharoah's life. Of course, he knew only what it was, not what it might have been. The several late twentieth-century mayors of Chicago who sent their children to private schools had a larger perspective, as did a city alderman who stated, "Nobody in his right mind would send [his] kids to public school." These places of education could be judged on the basis of plant maintenance, student discipline, or teacher-student ratios. No vantage point, however, was more basic than funding, that is, the local property taxes which were the mainstay of the schools. Comparing the tax base in Chicago with that of one of its wealthy northern suburbs (not to mention comparative property-tax and mortgage-interest deductions for parents), it was easy to see why per pupil spending was 50 or 60 percent higher outside the city, why suburban school kids had up-to-date books and other supplies, higher paid teachers, libraries, guidance counselors, science labs, and so forth. Unsurprisingly, in Chicago the dropout rate was much higher, the reading level much lower. Compensation for middle-class Chicagoans came by way of magnet or selective schools, a sort of private school system within the public realm which most poor and minority children never experienced and maybe did not even know about. Nowhere did the class system operate more effectively than in the public schools.[54]

For the African American children submerged in the ghetto, it was unnecessary to separate class from race; the combination was overwhelmingly oppressive. Blacks who surfaced in the middle class had overcome one of these obstacles only to find themselves still faced with the other. African American psychiatrists James P. Comer and Alvin F. Poussaint confronted this issue in *Black Child Care* (1975), written in response to white attitudes and policies "often antagonistic or indifferent to the needs of blacks." But rather than proposing a class solution, they argued that African American children needed the security of belonging that could be found only in blackness, a "psychological place ... where we are accepted, respected, and protected."[55]

Comer and Poussaint did not reject conventional, that is, white developmental psychology but placed it within an African American context. It was well known, for example, that blacks frequently resorted to corporal punishment. Thus, in Comer and Poussaint's rendering: "Children who were spanked by thoughtful, loving parents rarely have problems as a result of spanking. But if your child can achieve good control and behave well without spanking, why do it?"[56] On the issue of aggression—or "raw physical energy" (Freud called it instinct) which should be turned into "the fuel for curiosity, determination, learning, work, and play" (sublimation, according to Freud)—Comer and Poussaint observed that black parents in the past, facing a hostile white world, were apt to repress any aggressive tendencies in their children while today's parents might mistakenly overcompensate by allowing negative behavior and anger to go unchecked. Children benefited most, they thought, from the development of inner controls that would foster autonomy.[57]

Comer made clear his belief that not only black children of the middle class but also those from low-income families could succeed in America *if* their parents became involved in their school lives and *if* the schools responded appropriately—his own experience as a poor African American child.[58] But a school principal in the Bronx commented: "Will these children ever get what white kids in the suburbs take for granted? I don't think so. If you ask me why, I'd have to speak of race and social class." Thirty-five years after the *Brown* decision mandating desegregation, social observer Jonathan Kozol traveled through the nation for two years visiting schools; he failed to find nonwhite children in large numbers integrated with white children anywhere or any influential people concerned. And the nonwhite schools he reported on often had not the resources to respond appropriately to their students.[59]

Like African Americans who moved to the North and West (and many who remained in the South), Hispanics were also being urbanized. *El barrio* was as poor as the black ghetto; a Hispanic middle class had yet to emerge. The victims of poverty but never of slavery, preassimilation Hispanic families were classically traditional. The father was dominant, earning the living and issuing orders, while his wife was submissive, though she carried the full burden of child rearing. Children were a sign of his machismo. Hardly expecting fidelity or even company from her husband, the mother regarded her children as her world, and she bound them to her through love and feelings of guilt. The nuclear household, though not without community ties, was relatively isolated. *El barrio* was a closed community, though the public school might lie outside it (and, of course, television intruded into the home itself). To encourage success at school was to risk losing a child to Anglo culture. Less than a quarter of children aged three and four were in preschool programs, while only 43 percent of Latino youths graduated from high school, compared with 51 percent of African Americans and 75 percent of Asian Americans.[60]

Because Asian Americans have gotten more education and become upwardly mobile, their inner-city origins are sometimes forgotten.

Largely immigrant, the family structure was traditional (extended, patri-archal) and child care involved close contact (including breast-feeding) with and permissiveness toward infants and toddlers; corporal punish-ment and repression of aggressive behavior came later on.[61] The father's assumption of the role of disciplinarian when his children reached the age of five or six, as well as the importance of family and the shame of disgracing it through inappropriate action in the social world, condi-tioned school behavior in a manner helpful to the success of the Asian American pupil, as reflected in the label often applied, "the model minority." Maxine Hong remembered her mother's explanation for cut-ting the frenum of her daughter's tongue. "I cut it so you would not be tongue-tied. Your tongue would be able to move in any language." But when Maxine entered kindergarten and was faced with speaking English for the initial time, she said nothing. "During the first silent year I spoke to no one at school, did not even ask before going to the lavatory, and flunked kindergarten. My sister also said nothing for three years.... I did not speak and felt bad each time that I did not speak.... When my second grade class did a play, the whole class went to the auditorium except the Chinese girls.... Our voices were too soft or nonexistent.... One of us (not me) won every spelling bee, though." After American school she attended Chinese school for two and a half hours. "There we chanted together, voices rising and falling, loud and soft, some boys shouting, everybody reading together and not alone with one voice."[62]

In the early years of the twentieth century, the city had been the habi-tat of those who had recently immigrated from Europe and Asia, who became the concern of middle-class social workers. The composition of the inner city changed with the movement of African Americans and Hispanics from the rural South and Southwest to the urban North and West, not to mention the post–World War II suburbanization of second- and third-generation Europeans. While internal migration accelerated, immigration remained tightly controlled from the early 1920s until 1965. In that year, the Immigration Reform Act permitted 120,000 immi-grants per year from the Western Hemisphere (Hispanics) and 170,000 from outside it (largely Asians) without reference to nationality.[63] (The U.S. population rose from 227 to 248 million between 1980 and 1990; almost 40 percent of the growth resulted from immigration.)

Special encouragement was given to the well educated, and the gates were opened to refugees from Southeast Asia and Central America.[64] The children of these immigrants, maturing in the final decades of the twentieth century, were of uniquely diverse social and economic back-grounds ranging from professional (about one-third) to poor and illit-erate. Two-thirds lived in two-parent, intact households; persistence of parental authority was related to acculturation. (Mothers and fathers remained strong if there was little acculturation or the same rate of acculturation in both generations or the immigrant community encouraged selective acculturation, while dissonance occurred if the second generation was neither guided nor accompanied in change.) They were likely to be children of color, fluent in English. Hispanics, primarily from Mexico, composed the largest group among the newly arrived, with Asians—Vietnamese, Koreans, Filipinos—next. Immigrants had accounted for 14.9 percent of the American population in 1910; in 1990 they added up to 7.9 percent.[65]

Because of their initial poverty, the new immigrant households were concentrated in metropolitan areas where they came into contact with the urban underclass. For example, in Los Angeles students of Mexican background were divided between the recent newcomers, influenced by their experience in the native country, and the second- and third-generation Mexicans (Chicanos), whose loyalty was primarily to an in-group at war with Anglo culture. The former were strongly guided by parents and extended family, were looked on favorably by teachers, and tended to do well in school. The latter, especially the gang-oriented Cholos, viewed school achievement as a sellout to the white world.[66]

26. The Immigration Reform Act of 1965 encouraged the arrival of children of color, mostly from Latin America and Asia, who began their American journey in the inner city, as had immigrant children of the nineteenth century. Here some Southeast Asian kids celebrate Halloween. Photograph by Alice Lucas.

Not that the white world was so available. Esmeralda Santiago moved from Puerto Rico to Brooklyn and entered the eighth grade with no English. "Archie, Veronica, Betty, Reggie, and Jughead," all comic book characters, "were the only American teenagers I'd come to know," she wrote later, although she had a few "American" classmates who "were the presidents of clubs, the organizers of dances, the editors of the school newspaper and yearbook." From the comics she learned about a suburban America inhabited by adolescents whose lives, unlike her own, were lived free of parental domination; they ate hamburgers and fries in soda shops (never at home), dated, and had social lives. "We had no telephone, so unlike Betty and Veronica, I couldn't sit with shapely legs draped over the armrest of an upholstered chair chattering with invisible friends about boys. We had no upholstered chair. I had no friends."[67]

No matter the inner-city conditions, the postindustrial labor market dictated that these immigrant children acquire the necessary academic credentials or be consigned to low-level employment. Indochinese refugees, for example, showed commendable school achievement. The testimony of a Laotian mother suggested the secret: "When I get home, I always ask my children about their homework and ask them to finish doing it. I also direct them to do the house chores.... [My husband and I] don't know how to help them because we don't have enough education.... Their report cards show me they get mostly B's and some A's, with written praise from their teachers.... When they are not doing well in school, my husband and I talk to them seriously. We don't spank our kids.... We express more love than any other expression, to show our kids that we do care for them and so want them to be good. For me, I cry when I see them not doing well, and they are very sad to see me crying and promise to be better."[68]

Korean immigrant parents, on the other hand, mimicked the harsh methods used in their homeland to drive their children toward academic achievement and entrance into prestigious universities where they were expected to become doctors, lawyers, and engineers. Empathy was not valued, evident in a student's recounting of his mother's reaction to his decision to major in history: "She was initially shocked and upset. Then she tried to convince me that I was wrong. And finally she struggled to understand why it had happened. Had she done something wrong?" His father would not communicate with him at all.[69]

College was a luxury available to only a fraction of urban youths, immigrant or native. At the other end of the social scale, somewhere between 1 and 20 percent of inner-city youths were drawn into gangs. Although some liberal observers pointed to positive aspects of such activity, the typical middle-class response was disapproval and fear— unnecessary fear insofar as gang victims, like the perpetrators, were ordinarily adolescent males of like ethnicity. Girl gangs existed, usually younger, less violent, and auxiliary to boy gangs. Group inclusion, in the opinion of one observer, was based on personal characteristics: feelings of social inadequacy, such as school difficulty or low self-esteem, and of boredom; strong attitudes of defiance and aggressiveness; need for status, identity, and/or companionship.[70]

In the early twentieth century, juvenile delinquency was seen as the product of slums and poverty, which destroyed the cultures of newly-urbanized immigrants. The solution was assimilation and Americanization. At midcentury, "delinquency study reflected cultural and social issues that focused on the shifting behavior of youth." The Kennedy and Johnson administrations, for example, were influenced by the idea that a delinquency subculture flourished when lower-class youth were given high expectations without the means to achieve them.[71]

More recently the analytical focus has changed from a social to a psychological perspective, depicting (for example) gang activity as a rite of passage from boyhood to manhood engaged in by those males too rebellious to endure the conventional process of socialization designed to take place in the school and the job market. In the former, "youths encountered demands for subservience and order, frequently issued by female authority from a different class and ethnic background." The latter offered only low-skilled, low-paying jobs where parents, relatives, and older friends were already dead-ended. Where home and school were female-dominated and work demanded unmanly subordination, "the streets were unambiguously and ruthlessly male."[72]

While youthful social mayhem was attributed to the lower orders, domestic violence was apt to be depicted as classless. A new awareness of it, however, has been attributed to the fear of violent crime in the 1950s.[73] Historians have debated whether one feature of domestic violence, child abuse, was a product of contemporary mass society or a continuing American phenomenon.[74] Certainly cruelty to children was nothing new, but a novel sensitivity to it in the late nineteenth century led to the formation of the New York Society for the Prevention of Cruelty to Children (Chapter 5). In 1954, a former director of the NYSPCC conducted a national survey, the first of its kind, on child abuse. Three years later, the Children's Bureau sent out a report recommending that state child welfare departments investigate and take appropriate measures regarding child abuse, the first time the federal government recognized the issue as a public policy matter.[75]

But it was the medical profession, specifically radiologists and pediatricians, which played the major role in scrutinizing child abuse. X-rays told stories that parents failed to divulge, and radiologists were apt to interpret evidence more forthrightly than physicians who knew the parties personally. Yet it was a pediatrician, C. Henry Kempe at the University of Colorado Medical School, who more than anyone else focused attention on child abuse, largely through a well-attended symposium titled "The Battered-Child Syndrome" at the American Academy of Pediatrics convention in 1961 and a follow-up article a year later in the prestigious *Journal of the American Medical Association*, which was accompanied by an editorial estimating that abuse killed more children than leukemia and perhaps even auto accidents. In almost no time, articles appeared in the popular press and programs on television; by 1965, 90 percent of the American public recognized child abuse as a problem. In 1967, there were 9,500 reports of child abuse in the nation; in 1975, almost 300,000; in 1976, 669,000. In 1973, a new Senate subcommittee held hearings on child abuse, and the following year Congress passed the Child Abuse Prevention and Treatment Act. In the heat of this publicity, statistics were misstated; in the intensity of the response, mistakes were made.[76]

One error, no doubt related to the sensational nature of the discovery, was the implication that reputable middle-class parents were as likely to be abusers as lower-class mothers and fathers. Kempe himself had claimed that abusers *could* be "people with good education and stable financial and social background." Defenders of this point of view argued that the middle class concealed abuse while the poor, policed by social welfare agencies, were unable to do so. However, the middle class cannot conceal murder, the ultimate form of domestic violence, yet most family homicides were committed in the lower class. Furthermore, a national survey conducted in 1976 found that lower-class parents were twice as likely to be violent toward their children as middle-class parents. Yet the myth of the classlessness of abuse persisted.[77]

Meanwhile, the 1970 White House Conference on Children had reported a "vast neglect" of America's young, implying that more was at stake than physical violence. During the 1970s, the definition of child maltreatment came to include, in addition to physical abuse, physical neglect (e.g., failure to feed), psychological abuse and neglect (action or inaction which contributes to the emotional disturbance of the child), and sexual abuse (over 90 percent of the incest perpetrators are male and, if in the family, far more often brothers than fathers).[78] This broadening of interpretation was at least partially responsible for a far more serious error than the myth of classlessness: False or at least doubtful accusations of child abuse were made. Such accusations resulted in the removal of children from families where there was only "marginally inadequate child care" (according to the first director of the National Center on Child Abuse and Neglect) and their placement, usually, in foster homes.[79]

Orphanages, which housed children with two, one, or no parents, had been in decline until, in 1958, foster homes housed more children than institutions. Within a decade, 77 percent of dependent children, well over 400,000, were in foster homes (in 1962 AFDC was amended to allow funds to foster families). Yet foster care was subject to plenty of criticism, both from the left, where it was argued that middle-class child protective workers trampled the civil liberties of their powerless lower-class clients, and the right, to whom welfare institutions meant big government and heavy taxes. Conservatives asserted that children belonged in traditional families, and the instability of foster care situations fueled their argument. In 1980 Congress passed the Adoption Assistance and Child Welfare Act; unlike the 1974 Child Abuse and Prevention Treatment Act, it was noninterventionist, especially when the Reagan administration refused to fund it at the promised level. Unfortunately for children who were truly abused, evidence pointed to the conclusion that they were far better off with foster (or adoptive) families than with their biological parents.[80]

Adoption also posed a class issue. Middle-class couples, preponderantly white, wanted to adopt. But the children available were frequently lower-class and black. In the 1960s, white parents adopted about 20,000 black children. Shortly after the Black Power movement emerged, the National Association of Black Social Workers in 1972 declared that African American children should be adopted only by black families; transracial adoptions, which had been favored since around 1950, were labeled as genocidal. In response, most states and almost half of private agencies complied with the NABSW demand. Similarly, white families had adopted American Indian children, and tribal governments interceded to end the process.[81]

Meanwhile, another (but not class-related) issue arose concerning the anonymity of the birth mother to the adopted child. Until World War II, birth mothers were typically married and willing to give up their children for reasons of poverty. During the war, adoption petitions rose dramatically, while the children available were often born out of wedlock. Records were sealed to deal with the shame of illegitimacy and of infertility. In the 1970s adopted children, for psychological reasons of identity, and birth mothers, who felt they had been pressured to give up children and later not allowed to contact them, demanded that records be opened. A few states complied by granting adult adoptees full access, while many states agreed to an open system if all parties (birth parents, adoptive parents, adult adoptees) agreed.[82]

In the 1990s, two more adoption issues made headlines. The first involved a conflict over who had the legal rights to an adopted child: the adoptive parents who had raised the youngster and formed an emotional bond with him/her or the biological parents who decided they wanted their offspring back. Public sentiment appeared to favor the former, but the courts decided for the latter. The second issue was raised over the right of gay couples to adopt, concerning which matter there was no clear legal decision.[83]

Child care, too, was a matter fraught with class distinctions from its very beginnings. Institutional child care was initiated with a nursery set up for working mothers by charitable reformers in late eighteenth-century Philadelphia, followed by an infant school established in early nineteenth-century Boston (initially for the working class, later more inclusive) by educational reformers. Day nurseries proliferated in the later nineteenth century, though parents also turned to kindergartens, orphanages, almshouses, and children's homes. The National Federation of Day Nurseries, founded in 1898 as a philanthropic effort of upper-class policy makers to aid working mothers without government funding, never considered child care more than a temporary matter; though unprogressive, the NFDN managed to dominate the child-care field. But as the number of married women in the workforce climbed (1.9 million to 4.6 million from 1920 to 1940), day nurseries failed to keep pace, while nursery schools were attractive to child welfare experts.[84]

The nursery school model appealed to the New Dealers, partially as a means of employing teachers under the NRA but also due to the alleged educational benefits for children, and the program—now in the hands of the federal government—continued during World War II. On the private side, as represented by the Child Welfare League of America (which absorbed the NFDN in 1942), the position was generally not to offer day care to working mothers despite female employment in the defense industries. In the postwar child care debate, which centered on the question of whether maternal employment was acceptable, the answer was class biased: Federally funded child care was acceptable for working-class and low-income mothers only. Nonpoor parents were forced to find private alternatives, leading to a proliferation of types of child care—in your own or someone else's home, at work, in a child care center. Thus fragmented, child care advocates were unable to unify and press the agenda of universal care, while the New Right built its strength partly on opposition to child care, partly on the demand that welfare recipients, even those with small children, should work.[85]

Not only the New Right but the most prominent advice givers since Benjamin Spock—Penelope Leach and T. Berry Brazelton—have expressed strong reservations about child care. Neither is unsympathetic to the working mother who has no economic choice but to enter the marketplace. Yet both have stressed the critical role that mothers play in the rearing of infants.[86]

The need for care was obvious. From 1960 to 1990, the percentage of mothers with children under six in the labor force doubled from 30 to 60; less than two-fifths of them used child care centers. The Comprehensive Child Developmment Act of 1971, calculated to expand the number of centers and enhance their educational benefits with free care to low-income families and a sliding scale for others, was vetoed by President Richard Nixon as a measure that undermined family togetherness. Opponents of busing to integrate schools saw the same principle of race mixing in the new child care arrangements, and some members of the New Right saw in universalism the thrust toward a "class-less society" which would "Sovietize" American children.[87] During the Reagan years, more funds subsidized child care for moderate- than low-income and poor families, although the Child Care and Development Block Grant signed by President George Bush, while underfunded, targeted mainly low-income families. During the Clinton administration, child care was considered only in the context of welfare reform; no breakthroughs were made.[88]

The American assumption in the twentieth century was that society held no responsibility for children before they began public school at age 5 or 6. The Head Start program was an exception; more typically the family had to provide not only for preschoolers but also for the kids aged 5 to 13 (2–10 million) who faced hours alone before or after classes, since more than two-thirds of the nation's mothers worked outside the home (and contributed over 40 percent of family earnings). Affordability was a major obstacle (at an estimated $3,000 a year for full-time care, child care was the fourth-largest household expense after food, housing, and taxes), but availability was also a problem. A complicating factor was the variety of situations: in-home care (carried out by relatives, babysitters, nannies); family day care home (private residence—the most popular for infants and toddlers); and day care center (larger and more regulated than family day care—most popular for ages 3 to 5). Federal child care subsidies were available through the Child and Dependent Care Tax Credit (available only to taxpayers who itemized deductions) and the Title XX Social Services Block Grant (greatly diminished during the 1980s).[89]

Like child care, special education—the term applied to instructional services for disabled children—was an issue Americans preferred not to face. And, in the opinion of some observers, it was a class issue: "Physical disabilities, sensory handicaps, and chronic health impairments may be twice as common among poor children as among other children. We *believe* this is the case, but the health survey data are ambiguous."[90]

As recently as the 1960s, one out of eight disabled youngsters received *no* education, while half of them (around 4 million) did not receive the special instructional services they needed. The pressure for change came from a court case won by the Pennsylvania Association of Retarded Children in 1971, which ensured that the state would provide access to free public education for every mentally disabled child, followed by a similar victory the following year in the District of Columbia. In 1974, Congress for the first time recognized a disabled child's educational rights; the Education for All Handicapped Children Act of 1975 promised not only "free appropriate education which emphasizes special education and related services designed to meet their unique needs" but also the protection of "the rights of handicapped children and their parents or guardians," the latter being the children's first line of defense.[91]

This dramatic change must be seen, first, in the context of the civil rights movement. Racial discrimination traveled under the disguise of special education. While disabilities stemming from physical or genetic causes are equally distributed among ethnic groups, "mild retardation" or "emotional disturbance" are less clearly grounded. Blacks composed 9 percent of the California school population in 1971, 12 percent of the severely retarded, and 13 percent of the physically disabled—and 27 percent of the "mildly retarded" students. Other states showed similar skewing of the handicap label. While the courts recognized and sought to rectify the racial imbalance in these assessments, they would not go so far as to challenge the basis of the educational establishment's judgment—which was that a disabled child's mental ability and emotional maturity must be measured against able-bodied norms. But the courts did direct schools to tailor each child's program according to his/her needs, and they did accede to "mainstreaming," that is, educating him/her in the company of able-bodied children. State legislatures followed suit.[92]

It had taken a long time to reach mainstreaming. Some of the same men who had been responsible for the common school in the nineteenth century (Chapter 4), given their enlightened interest in learning environments, campaigned also for the establishment of institutions to serve the special needs of deaf, blind, and mentally disabled children. Just as parentless, abandoned, poor, disobedient, and vagrant youngsters were placed in asylums and reformatories (Chapter 5), so disabled children were consigned to and isolated in special institutions, where conventional schooling was brief but industrial training was championed as the way to alleviate the social dependency of the disabled. By the early twentieth century, institutional isolation was being superseded by special segregated classes within the public school system, as social Darwinists and proponents of eugenics demanded a continuing quarantine in the face of pressure for free compulsory education. But as the public attitude toward disability changed about midcentury, so did the stance toward integration of disabled children. Hence, mainstreaming.[93]

Children of the inner city lived not simply in a different socioeconomic class but in a different world from suburban, middle-class youngsters. Poverty was the most evident badge of their difference, and it often stemmed from living in female-headed households. In the 1930s an effort was made by the federal government to support mothers in their homes so they could nurture their young, but by the end of the century women, even those with young children, were being herded into the workforce, surely a policy with no recognition of the value of the attachment bond and its consequences. Furthermore, inner-city children were residents of homes where corporal punishment, if not abuse, was far more common than in the middle-class residence, and violence—often organized by inner-city male adolescents—was replicated in the world immediately outside the household. Schools were not typically friendly to these children, with the obvious exception of the Head Start program. Social services administered to them were no better.

Class was also a regional matter, as rural America in the twentieth century became the poor country cousin of the city, paralleling the decline of inner-urban areas. Although the first two decades of the century were marked by prosperity rare among farmers, urban material standards were much higher and urban institutions and life were judged far richer. Educators and other public figures, but not farmers, formed the short-lived Country Life movement in an attempt to stem a rural decline marked by the exodus of country youth for the city. Education was viewed as critical to revival, with reform of the one-room school as a panacea, but farmers were not convinced. They gave lip service to learning but never forgot the high economic value of working children.[94]

The census of 1920 proclaimed the numerical ascendancy of urban America (more than half the national population now resided in communities of 2,500 or larger) over the countryside. Not only did rural, largely Protestant America wage a losing battle of values against urban, often immigrant America during the 1920s (see Chapter 6) but it was also suffering within. The agricultural sector of the economy continued to shrink, with an attendant loss of resources, as did the farm population, with a consequent decline of local communities. The statistics were telling. In 1940 the rural population was down to 43.5 percent of the national total, while the actual farming population slipped from 60 percent (1920) to 50 percent (1940) of the rural populace. As support for roads, hospitals, and the like depended on taxable income, these services declined, especially during the Depression. Villages evaporated, their social, religious, economic, and educational functions absorbed by the widely separated towns.

School consolidation was part of this process of community disintegration, as 190,000 one-room edifices with 2.8 million students (1920) dwindled to 130,000 single-unit buildings with 1.3 million students (1940). Still, over half of America's school-age children were rural, supported by only 20 percent of the national income. (For rural African American children, the possibility of receiving an education was almost nonexistent.)

By 1970 the rural population was about one-quarter of the national total, though it included 40 percent of the nation's poor. And the farm population was only 18 percent of that quarter. Rural neighborhoods and institutions continued to disappear, despite the federal government's largely unsuccessful efforts to bring economic stability back to the countryside. Young people were strongly inclined to leave, and they did.

The Gale family did better than most. In 1901 young Charles Gale married Chloe Packson; both were the children of small farmers in New Albany, Kansas. Already the church where they married and the grade school they had attended were in trouble, though Charles and Chloe, now resident on the farm that had been his father's, contributed six children to the local population by 1920, all of whom studied in the two-room school of their parents. Other traditional practices—singing in the parlor, for example—persisted, though Charles needed to be a sharp modern businessman to keep his several hundred acres profitable.

By 1925 the three younger children were attending classes in Freedonia, six miles away. Chloe believed her kids should be taught more than reading, writing, and ciphering. The bank, drugstore, lumberyard, hotel, and four of New Albany's five churches had closed, and the school followed suit in 1929. Unlike many farmers, Charles was prosperous enough in the 1920s and 1930s to excuse his children from chores so that they could participate in after-school activities. He was an active advocate of New Deal farm programs, Chloe campaigned to improve the lot of farm wives, and both read widely while encouraging their children's social and academic leanings, the result being several college students.

In 1940 their youngest daughter married Austin Hart, who became a farmer in New Albany, though he came to realize that only commercial tillers of the soil, not small operators like himself, made a good living. He purchased the Gale farm—530 acres, buildings, machinery, and a house—by borrowing on his share of his own father's estate and became a scientific farmer. But New Albany continued to fade; the 4-H program and the Sunday school closed in 1970. Yet most of the five children got professional or college education and returned to the region—one to farming![95]

Most young rural dwellers were not so fortunate as the Gales and Harts. A report issued from the White House Conference on Child Protection and Health in 1930 pointed out that in 1920 8.5 percent of young people between 10 and 15 were gainfully employed, 60 percent on farms. (The remainder worked in the industrial realm, where they could be identified as the children of unskilled and semiskilled workers.)[96] Grace Abbott, former chief of the Children's Bureau, observed in 1938 that until the twentieth century, "little thought was given to the fact that the census returns showed much larger numbers of children were in farmwork rather than other types of employment." Why? Because farmwork was considered not only healthier than city labor but also a family activity. Social welfare movements were thus directed at the urban young. Consequently, "the rural child continued to attend a poor school for fewer months in the year, lacked opportunities for group play, his health needs were neglected, and the social services for those who became dependent or delinquent were entirely inadequate."[97]

At the bottom of the rural social spectrum were the sharecroppers, migrant workers, and mountaineers (or "hillbillies"), for whom school was close to irrelevant. Psychiatrist Robert Coles figured that the children of migrant workers may have attended school only eight days a month, partly due to illness, partly due to lack of clothes, partly due to an attitude that school really did not much matter. Coles explained the situation of Peter, one of those children: "He has left several schools reluctantly, sadly, even bitterly. On the other hand he has also been glad to leave many schools. He feels he has been ignored or scorned. He feels different from other schoolchildren—and has felt that one or another teacher emphasizes those differences, makes them explicit, speaks them out, and in a way makes him feel thoroughly unwanted."[98] One of his teachers requested a birth certificate, but none existed. The family saw no doctor and received no social services. The effect was stunning. "When other children are just beginning to come into their own" between 5 and 10, Coles observed, "migrant children begin to lose interest in the world outside them." They grow up "grimly and decisively fast."[99]

Coles focused on the South. In the North, where farmers until recently (by Abbott's account in 1938) had employed their own sons, little could be done about overwork unless it was so serious as to constitute cruelty. While the mechanization of farming reduced the usefulness of children, there remained specialized areas of agriculture where hand labor was still in demand and "children bent their backs for long hours" and, in addition, were assigned unsanitary living conditions and kept out of school. Out of season they were often on relief.[100] Rural America, poorer than its urban counterpart, featured its own class structure, and children lived their lives accordingly.

27. More children worked on farms than anywhere else before World War II, and their toil continued during postwar prosperity, as shown in Russell Lee's 1947 photograph of a Texas string bean picker and his daughter. Special Collections: Photographic Archives, University of Louisville.

To look at the survivors of a childhood spent in rural poverty, not to mention inner-city deprivation, is to be impressed by their strength and durability, sometimes even their wisdom. But it is undeniable that there are many more victims than survivors along the way, children whose parents (or, at least, whose mothers) struggled unsuccessfully with the consequences of poverty, with inadequate or nonexistent agencies and institutions, with popular hostility or indifference. These children deserved more and, given the wealth of the United States, more was available—but not to them.

The consequences for their autonomy were evident. Parental absence amounted to diminished attachment. It also impinged on competence, when adults were not present to teach (or, as immigrants, taught the lessons of a traditional culture to children who needed to survive in a modern world). Poorly supported schools failed to enrich their students. The horizons of autonomous thought and action were almost always limited.

Epilogue

There are many books about the plight of American children at the onset of the twenty-first century. Some take a long-range view, observing, for example, that the child shaped by biological evolution cannot easily integrate into a society constantly reformed by technological change. Others focus on such topics as health, parental neglect, or poverty and the inequity of government spending.[1] Usually these books lack a historical dimension. Demographers, more than other commentators, provide a vision of basic trends in the recent past. They point to a steady decline in the number of siblings a child has (though children with fewer siblings can boast of higher educational attainments and occupational achievements), as well as in the percentage of two-parent households (with a corresponding decline in income) and in the availability of grandparents. Just as the nineteenth century was increasingly characterized by the absence of the father, employed away from home, so in the late twentieth century the mother is often missing as well, also in the workforce.[2] All of these demographic characteristics, apparently here to stay, seem to tell us that the typical child spends more time without familial contact than ever before.[3] (African American children in slavery and some working-class children in nineteenth-century cities had limited parental contact but spent time with siblings.)

School, at least for the seven- to seventeen-year-olds, supplies company for part of the day, hence the critical importance of peers. The remainder of the child's time alone may be taken up by some sort of electronic activity or, perhaps, spent in the company of a nonparental adult. (In 1984, 24 percent of children aged 5 to 13 were cared for after school by someone other than a parent. Almost a third of these kids took care of themselves.)[4] Child care is more likely to be the situation of the child under 7, however. Neither schools nor child care situations are currently receiving high quality ratings, but given the aging population there are understandable reasons, usually political, why institutions for the young are neglected. Nevertheless, these institutions are by and large not inferior to similar ones in the past.

A substantial percentage of children live in poverty or only slightly above the official poverty line. Contrary to the mythology surrounding welfare, most of these children live in self-supporting, working-poor families. The polarization of wealth in the United States strongly suggests that these children will remain in poverty. To be poor is not to be unloved, but parents struggling to survive have only limited time for their progeny.[5] While it is clear that such a situation would not exist today if we more closely approximated economic equality, living in or close to poverty was a common condition of many children in the past.

Is the United States in a moment of child crisis? "Child crisis" appears applicable; "moment" does not. Regarding the family, "neither historically nor during the industrial era have a majority of children experienced the family stability, economic stability, or homemaking-mother image that was idealized as the typical family system in mid-twentieth-century America." Not since the Depression have a majority of children resided in two-parent families where the father was employed full-time for the whole year and the mother was not working outside the home.[6]

One reason mothers could join the workforce was the large increase in school enrollment and the lengthening of the school day between 1870 and 1940. (Still, since 1940 the percentage of children who had a parent at home full-time has dropped almost as much for infants as for older children. But at-home mothers have doubled the time they devote to child care since the early twentieth century as a result of warnings to attend to the social and mental development of their children.) School achievement has always been a function of parental occupation, family structure, and race, although the advantage of having a well-employed father, both parents in the home, and a white skin has diminished over time in high school—but not yet in college.[7]

Poverty has a different history. The Depression was especially hard on children, while the 1940s and 1950s ushered in much better days: Both economic deprivation and economic inequality were substantially reduced, and the 1960s brought slight additional improvements. All these gains vanished in the 1970s and 1980s; by 1988 the levels of relative poverty and inequality among children returned to those of 1949 or earlier, with 22 percent of white and 53 percent of black children (the situation of Hispanics resembled that of blacks) in relative poverty. Blacks, who had experienced relatively little economic improvement from the Civil War to the Depression, shared in the post–World War II economic boom, but did not see the racial gap in relative poverty close until the 1960s and 1970s, when it still remained large. Two-thirds of black children *never* reached a middle-class standard of living.[8]

Children in the beginning years of the twenty-first century face a crisis, but it is not momentary. The menace to their well-being has existed as long as we know. It is built into the economic system.[9] Major relief has come only in times of prosperity, and then mitigation is not distributed equally but by class, as well as race and ethnicity—and to a lesser extent region and gender. The political system reflects the economic one; adult matters take primacy. Relief from this bleak state of affairs has come from the occasional intercession of child-savers. And, of course, there are child advocates today.[10] But given the evidence of the past and the political strength of seniors in the present, predicting a bright future for all children is unjustified.

Surely the autonomy of children today is constantly compromised, at one end of the socioeconomic scale by poverty, at the other end by parental/academic pressure to succeed, and at almost every point by peer coercion to conform. Thus, the combination of factors limiting autonomy is different for children in the present than in the past, but the restrictions on freedom of action have existed in most cultures, the American Indians being something of an exception (though conformity was certainly a social expectation among them).

Child rearing among American Indians demonstrates the power of protracted and intimate contact between the infant/toddler and a caregiver in planting the seeds of autonomy, as well as the utility of community in directing its young members toward shared social goals. Protracted contact between American Indians and European Americans, however, ultimately undermined both autonomy and community.

European American children in the seventeenth century were subject to devastating parental loss (Chesapeake) or debilitating parental control (New England). By the eighteenth century, parental survival was no longer so critical an issue. Some parents continued the practice of inflexible control, others were indulgent toward the young except when it came to corporal punishment, and a third group operated somewhere between the extremes, moderating control but maintaining strong discipline and, thus, fostering the autonomy that was given voice in the American Revolution.

Autonomy for European Americans, that is, certainly not for their slaves. African American parents in the eighteenth and early nineteenth centuries were around their children too infrequently to control them, and when the two generations were together, children were not indulged but treated harshly, perhaps to prepare them for a future of forced labor. There was, however, a carefree quality to the years before age 10, when responsibilities were minimal and play, often with European American age peers, was dominant. But these circumstances, followed by a life of slavery, were essentially irrelevant to autonomy.

Meanwhile, in the industrializing, urbanizing regions of the United States in the nineteenth century, class formation set the stage for changes in child rearing among European Americans. In the middle class, an absent father ceded family governance to an ever-present mother, whose task was lightened by the decline in number of children in the household and whose sensitivity to the emotional needs of her off-spring was superior to that of her spouse. Under these conditions, autonomy became more possible, although unwavering obedience was expected of the young, who now received more adult attention than ever before, both at home and in school. Conditions in the working class made sensitivity to the needs of children virtually impossible; the young were expected to join the workforce as soon as they were able. Individual autonomy could not be encouraged when mutual dependence was necessary to the survival of the household. True, younger children were often unsupervised because their parents were at work. Middle-class reformers, appalled at the circumstances of these youngsters, interceded—not to augment the autonomy of the young but to subject them to bourgeois morals. The state followed in the train of these reformers, ultimately to the material benefit of working-class children.

In the twentieth century, the children of suburban privilege followed the pattern set by the urban middle class of the nineteenth: As the wealth of the family grew, its size shrank, thus releasing more material and human resources to its children, who remained inhabitants of childhood longer than ever. By the middle of the century, many previous members of the working class rose to the middle. Autonomy could flourish under these conditions, but longer schooling perpetuated dependence, and the unequal distribution of wealth had by the end of the century often sent both parents to work, depriving the young of needed nurturing. Still, these circumstances were far superior to those of the children of the inner city, as well as much of rural America, where the pattern of the nineteenth-century working class prevailed: poverty, family instability, corporal punishment. The state continued its intervention, impotent though it was to alter substantially domestic conditions that undermined autonomy.

A Note on Sources

Despite the enthusiasm for Philippe Aries's *L'Enfant et la Vie Familiale sous l'Ancien Regime* (1960), published in English as *Centuries of Childhood: A Social History of Family Life* (1962), the field of childhood history until recently has had only limited appeal for American historians. Aries's assertion that no concept of childhood existed before the fifteenth or sixteenth century, that young and old mixed without age distinction, was exciting news but failed to create a vital area of research.

Edmund S. Morgan, a highly respected scholar, published *Virginians at Home: Family Life in the Eighteenth Century* (1952) before the appearance of Aries's book, and he rewrote *The Puritan Family: Religion and Domestic Relations in Seventeenth-Century New England* (rev. ed., 1966) with more attention to the young. In 1970 John Demos issued *A Little Commonwealth: Family Life in Plymouth Colony*, paying attention to infancy and early childhood, stages of life which Aries and Morgan ignored, by introducing the developmental ideas of psychoanalyst Erik Erikson to his study. This book was a promising start and remains a major contribution to the history of American childhood. It is a model of what can be accomplished, drawing on archaeology (material culture) as well as psychology to aid in explaining the rearing of a Pilgrim child.

The barely born field was infused with controversy when in 1974 Lloyd deMause launched his *History of Childhood Quarterly: A Journal of Psychohistory* and edited *The History of Childhood*, two of whose ten chapters concerned America.[1] Highly critical of the historical profession for its neglect of childhood, deMause established his own vantage point with the assertion that the "further back in history one goes, the lower the level of child care, and the more likely children are to be killed, abandoned, beaten, terrorized, and sexually abused." The explanation for the improvement of care with time, he argued, lay in "the ability of successive generations of parents to regress to the psychic age of their children and work through the anxieties of that age in a better manner the second time they encounter them than they did during their own childhood[s],"[2] a process that occurred "independent of social and technological change."

Historians, not kindly disposed toward progressive theories of history and unconvinced about psychoanalysis in the service of Clio, were skeptical of deMause's forward march from the past, disdainful of his exclusion of material circumstances from the historical process, and offended by (or scornful of) his appropriation of the label "psychohistory" at a time when this subfield deeply divided the historical profession. Consequently, to write about the history of childhood was to enter an arena where lines had been drawn. For those disposed to the domestic, family history was a far more neutral venture.

Nevertheless, there emerged studies of childhood which were provocative, and none more so than two works by Philip J. Greven, *The Protestant Temperament: Patterns of Child-Rearing, Religious Experience, and the Self in Early America* (1977) and *Spare the Child: The Religious Roots of Punishment and the Psychological Impact of Physical Abuse* (1990). Demonstrating a firm command of both the historical and psychological literature, Greven set out to portray the emotional lives of early European Americans through the lens of childhood experience, and as he became aware of the pervasiveness of corporal punishment and its shaping effect on personality, he traced it through the American past.

That is, the European American past. Strong corroboration for the determinative role of physical force in child rearing was provided by Carl H. Nightingale in *On the Edge: A History of Poor Black Children and Their American Dreams* (1993). Violence in the household and on the street, as well as the psychic connection between the two, is a powerful (but not singular) theme of Nightingale's study, in which he is a participant observer of inner-city life in late twentieth-century Philadelphia.

A different sort of observation forms the basis for Glen H. Elder, Jr.'s *Children of the Great Depression: Social Change in Life Experience* (1974), which draws upon the data gathered from people at various points in their lives to demonstrate the effect of a major social phenomenon that affected all of them.[3] Of course, longitudinal studies are relatively recent. But as Greven observes, "Historians have the unique advantage of studying people whose lives have been completed, being able to track them in many cases from birth to death. We therefore know, as few others can, what the outcomes of various types of upbringing actually were."[4]

We can know if we can locate the sources, usually literary. Harvey J. Graff, in *Conflicting Paths: Growing Up in America* (1995), has presented a complex array of stories—about boys following traditional paths, deviating from the old routes, carving out wholly new trails, as well as girls finding their ways—based on over 500 first-person accounts of growing up from the mid-eighteenth to the early twentieth century.

Yet one of the great contributions to the writing of childhood history has been innovation in the gathering and use of demographic data, as evidenced in Demos's *A Little Commonwealth*. Considering the implications of child spacing in a family, Demos is able to speculate intelligently on weaning and sibling rivalry. Joseph Kett, in *Rites of Passage: Adolescence in America, 1790 to the Present* (1977), utilizes certain types of demographic information (school attendance, movement from rural to urban areas) against the backdrop of modernization to discuss the lengthening of childhood. Demography in the hands of such skilled historians as Daniel Scott Smith and Robert V. Wells has contributed tremendously to our knowledge of the history of childhood.[5]

Yet a third source (literary remains and quantitative data being the first two) for understanding the past is the surviving artifact, used to great effect by Karin Calvert in *Children in the House: The Material Culture of Early Childhood, 1600–1900* (1992). Looking at portraits of the young, for example, Calvert treats such matters as the nature and duration of childhood, as well as the emerging importance of the nuclear family.

Several historians, notably John Demos and Philip J. Greven (see above), have effectively interpreted the sources on childhood from a psychological vantage point. Of course, there is no single perspective, since psychologists, like historians, write within the context of their times. Freud, a citizen of the age of industrialization, assumed "as other natural sciences have led us to expect, that in mental life some sort of energy is at work." This was the energy which propelled a child to seek physically pleasurable experience and, hence, individuals (primarily mothers) who would provide it. Latter-day Freudians, whose context was no longer the inner-directed character of production but the other-directed character of consumption, attributed at least equal motivational importance to the infant's proclivity simply to relate to others. (Thus, the title of Erik Erikson's classic is *Childhood and Society*.) John Bowlby, although acknowledging Freud's leadership, abandoned the Viennese psychic energy model altogether for an understanding of behavior, human and animal, based on Darwin: the survival of the species depends on the attachment of the young to the old for protection.[6]

During the past three decades, the cutting edge of psychological research has focused on cognitive rather than emotional development, a perspective that derives from the early twentieth-century work of Jean Piaget and Lev Vygotsky. Contrary to both Freud and the behaviorists, "Piaget saw that learning was innate, [while] Vygotsky saw that culture was natural." In this view babies are seen as omnivorous learners powered by brains analogous to computers, though more adaptable and more complex. Parents serve as tools for children to solve the problem of knowledge on the road to becoming "decent, independent adults,"[7] a goal shared with attachment theory.

Historians have and will continue to make their own choices regarding whether and how best to draw upon the various psychological approaches. Meanwhile, psychiatrist Robert Coles has provided an abundance of literature on childhood based on his discussions with children as well as interpretations of their drawings, not to mention Coles's ever-present sensitivity to the cultural milieu.[8] Social scientists Frank J. Sulloway and Judith Rich Harris have taken fresh looks at the family and argued that birth order and peer group influence have played greater roles in determining child development and adult behavior than we have previously believed.[9]

In addition to a variety of sources and methodologies useful for narrating the history of American childhood, there exists a major collection of institutional records—Robert H. Bremner et al., eds., *Childhood and Youth in America: A Documentary History,* 3 vols. (1970–74), which was preceded by Grace Abbott, *The Child and the State,* 2 vols. (Chicago, 1938)—and a volume of bibliographical essays—Joseph M. Hawes and N. Ray Hiner, eds., *American Childhood: A Research Guide and Historical Handbook* (1985)—to aid the historian. Finally, a fair amount of visual material has been handily collected, much of it in catalogs of museum exhibitions on childhood (mainly concerning upper-class European Americans).[10]

Notes

1. American Indian Childhood

1. Leo W. Simmons and Don C. Talayesva, eds., *Sun Chief: The Autobiography of a Hopi Indian* (New Haven, Conn., 1942).

2. A concise description (including excellent maps) of the first Americans and the natural environment they faced appears in Jacob E. Cooke, ed., *Encyclopedia of the North American Colonies*, 3 vols. (New York, 1993), I, 3–45.

3. A recently uncovered settlement in south-central Chile has been dated at about 13,000 years ago. Tom Dillehay, *Monte Verde: A Late Pleistocene Settlement in Chile* (Washington, D.C., 1997). For evidence of even earlier settlement, see Michael Parfit, "Hunt for the First Americans," *National Geographic* 198, no. 6 (December 2000): 41–67.

4. The number of assigned culture areas has varied from 7 to 13, according to William W. Newcomb, Jr., *North American Indians: An Anthropological Perspective* (Pacific Palisades, Calif., 1974), 21.

5. Robert V. Wells, *Revolutions in Americans' Lives: A Demographic Perspective on the History of Americans, Their Families, and Their Society* (Westport, Conn., 1982), 10–11.

6. Ibid., 31.

7. An excellent guide to European observations on the domestic life of the natives in the Northeast is James Axtell, ed., *The Indian Peoples of Eastern America: A Documentary History of the Sexes* (New York, 1981), which cites the most useful primary sources; wherever possible, I will make reference to Axtell rather than the originals. It can be supplemented by Bruce Trigger, *The Huron Farmers of the North* (New York, 1969) and Helen C. Rountree, *The Powhattan Indians of Virginia: Their Traditional Culture* (Norman, Okla., 1989).

8. A kinship group, limited to twenty-five people, was the basic unit of society. The tribe was composed of about five hundred people, the smallest congregation possible without violating the taboo against incest. But it appears that the smaller groups had to belong to networks of 4,000 to 5,000 people to maintain a reasonable balance of the sexes. Harold E. Driver, *Indians of North America*, 2nd ed. (Chicago, 1969); Gary B. Nash, *Red, White, and Black: The Peoples of Early North America*, 3rd ed. (Englewood Cliffs, N.J., 1992), 9–17. On community size, William W. Newcomb cites sources telling of twenty-three Delaware gatherings in New Jersey, ranging in size from fourteen to six hundred persons. *The Culture and Acculturation of the Delaware Indians* (Ann Arbor, Mich., 1956), 24. See also A. J. Jaffe, *The First Immigrants from Asia: A Population History of the North American Indians* (New York, 1992), 76.

9. For example, though he emphasizes variety, Driver generalizes about

birth, infancy, and puberty as well as education. *Indians of North America*, 365–73, 378–95. See also John U. Terrell and Donna M. Terrell, *Indian Women of the Western Morning* (New York, 1974), 157–75.

10. Axtell, *Indian Peoples*, 3, 8, 10; Elisabeth Tooker, *An Ethnography of the Huron Indians, 1615–1649* (Washington, D.C., 1964), 127.

11. Axtell, *Indian Peoples*, 11, 15, 22, 26; Tooker, *Ethnography*, 122–23; J. Franklin Jameson, ed., *Narratives of New Netherland, 1609–1664* (New York, 1909), 174; John R. Swanton, *The Indians of the Southeastern United States* (Washington, D.C., 1946), 711–13; Pierre de Charlevoix, *Journal of a Voyage to North America*, 2 vols. (orig. ed. in French, 1744; Ann Arbor, Mich., 1966), II, 84.

12. M. Inez Hilger, *Chippewa Child Life and Its Cultural Background* (Washington, D.C., 1951), 5–7. See also Tooker, *Ethnography*, 123; Trigger, *Huron*, 64–65, for confirmation by contemporary anthropologists.

13. Axtell, *Indian Peoples*, 9 (Micmacs), 11 (Gaspians, who also pierced); Rountree, *Powhatan*, 94; Swanton, *Southeastern*, 711–12.

14. Axtell, *Indian Peoples*, 7.

15. Ibid., 10, 15, 24, 26; Tooker, *Ethnology*, 123; Swanton, *Southeastern*, 711. On infanticide, see Driver, *Indians*, 367. The French entrepreneur Nicholas Denys thought that there was "much mortality" among the Micmacs because the genitals of children were exposed to the weather in the cradleboards. Axtell, *Indian Peoples*, 9. On family size, see Axtell, *Indian Peoples*, 25; Trigger, *Huron*, 64.

16. Axtell, *Indian Peoples*, 6; Rountree, *Powhatan*, 79–80; Tooker, *Ethnography*, 4–46, 123; Kenton, *Indians*, 447–48, 454; Swanton, *Southeastern*, 671–74; Emma H. Blair, *The Indian Tribes of the Upper Mississippi Valley and Region of the Great Lakes*, 2 vols. (Cleveland, Ohio, 1911), II, 167–69, 210–11; Trigger, *Huron*, 103. See also George A. Pettitt, *Primitive Education in North America* (Berkeley, 1946), chap. 6, "The Educational Function of Personal Names."

17. Axtell, *Indian Peoples*, 5, 16, 22; Jameson, *Narratives*, 70, 108, 128; Swanton, *Southeastern*, 709, 719; Blair, *Indian Tribes*, II, 164; Nicholas Denys, *Description and Natural History of the Coasts of North America* (New York, 1968; orig. pub. in English, 1908), 404. Fondness for the young did not prevent some Indians, the Hurons at any rate, from exchanging children with other tribes as "evidence of trust and goodwill and also to provide hostages." Bruce G. Trigger, *The Children of Aataentsic: A History of the Huron People to 1660*, 2 vols. (London, 1976), I, 64.

18. Axtell, *Indian Peoples*, 11–12.

19. Ibid., 6; Charlevoix, *Journal*, II, 73.

20. Axtell, *Indian Peoples*, 9, 15, 24, 26; John Heckewelder, *History, Manners, and Customs of the Indian Nations Who Once Inhabited Pennsylvania and the Neighboring States* (1876; New York, 1971), 221–22; Tooker, *Ethnography*, 123; Swanton, *Southeastern*, 711; Charlevoix, *Journal*, II, 79, 178. Most estimates of weaning range from 24 to 48 months, though Charlevoix observes that "we sometimes see children of six or seven years which still suck their mothers." In the mid-twentieth century Erik Erikson reported a Sioux mother nursing her eight-year-old son. *Childhood and Society*, 2nd ed. (New York, 1963), 136.

21. Swanton, *Southeastern*, 562–63; Axtell, *Indian Peoples*, 13. See also Axtell, *Indian Peoples*, 6, 26, 29–30; Kenton, *Indians*, II, 119–20; Charlevoix, *Journal*, II, 79, 109; Tooker, *Ethnography*, 123–24; Rountree, *Powhattan*, 94.

22. Robert Beverley, *The History and Present State of Virginia* (1705; Chapel Hill, N.C., 1947), 171–73.

23. Axtell, *Indian Peoples*, 15.

24. Ibid., 33.

25. Trigger, *Huron*, 65; Axtell, *Indian Peoples*, 18, 24, 33–34, 39; Jameson, *Narratives*, 73; Tooker, *Ethnography*, 124; Swanton, *Southeastern*, 715–16; Blair, *Indian Tribes*, II, 165. For other examples of corporal punishment, though not among Indians of the Northeast or Southeast, see Pettitt, *Primitive Education*, 6–7.

26. The care of Indian children conforms to the model for secure attachment: The mother figure remains accessible during the early years. The success of attachment is judged by a child's ability to explore a strange situation with his parent(s) as a secure base, as an Indian child aged three or four was expected to do. John Bowlby, *Attachment and Loss*, 3 vols. (London, 1969–80), I, 203–4, 338.

27. Ibid., 36, also 41–42, 64–67; Swanton, *Southeastern*, 715; Rountree, *Powhattan*, 78; Blair, *Indian Tribes*, II, 165, 212.

28. Trigger, *Aataentsic*, 47–48; Trigger, *Huron*, 65.

29. Axtell, *Indian Peoples*, 25, 34, 39.

30. Pettitt, *Primitive Education*, 8–9, 11–13. Regarding the issue of family protection, Pettitt argues that punishment, though depicted as existing for the good of the recipient, still must be administered from the outside, most frequently by the mother's brother.

31. Axtell, *Indian Peoples*, 34.

32. James Axtell, *The Invasion Within: The Contest of Cultures in Colonial North America* (New York, 1985), 16.

33. Philip Greven, *Spare the Child: The Religious Roots of Punishment and the Psychological Impact of Physical Abuse* (New York, 1991), 135–36.

34. Heckewelder, *History*, 113–17.

35. Pettitt, *Primitive Education*, 151–60.

36. Axtell, *Indian Peoples*, 57; see also 61–63, 67–69.

37. Ibid., 48–49; see also 45, 50–51; Rountree, *Powhatan*, 80–84.

38. Axtell, *Indian Peoples*, 53.

39. Pettitt, *Primitive Education*, 89.

40. Axtell, *Indian Peoples*, 74–75, 84–87, 91, 94; Trigger, *Huron*, 66; Rountree, *Powhatan*, 90; Swanton, *Southeastern*, 703, 706–8; Driver, *Indians*, 223–24. Male friendship was a different matter from a male/female relationship, however. See Axtell, *Indian Peoples*, 39–40, 42.

41. Ramon A. Gutierrez, *When Jesus Came, the Corn Mothers Went Away: Marriage, Sexuality, and Power in New Mexico, 1500–1846* (Stanford, Calif., 1991), 8–18, 26–33.

42. Ibid., 74–80, 92–93.

43. Wayne Dennis, *The Hopi Child* (New York, 1940), 29–86.

44. Dorothy Eggan, "Instruction and Affect in Hopi Cultural Continuity," in John Middleton, ed., *From Child to Adult* (Garden City, N.Y., 1970), 116. Eggan asserts that resistance to cultural change among the Hopi was remarkably consistent until World War II brought drastic changes (112).

45. *Hopi: Songs of the Fourth World* (1983), a film created by Pat Ferrero.

46. Hilger, *Chippewa Child Life*.

47. Erikson, *Childhood and Society*, 114–24.

48. Ibid., 131.

49. Ibid., 154–55, 161. Erikson's point of view on the gap between home training and schooling was hardly new. A Quaker Indian agent in the late nineteenth century wrote home to the Associated Executive Committee on Indian Affairs: "What they [the children] learn from their books during the day is half lost during the night *lounging in the old wigwam.*" Quoted in Joseph E. Illick, "Some of Our Best Indians Are Friends...," *Western Historical Quarterly* 2 (1971): 290.

50. James J. Rawls, *Chief Red Fox Is Dead: A History of Native American Indians Since 1945* (New York, 1996), 13–20.

51. Ibid., 35–50. See also Alan L. Sorkin, *The Urban American Indian* (Lexington, Mass., 1978).

52. Rawls, *Chief Red Fox,* 78–90.

53. Ibid., 70–73, 88, 98–102. In "Factors and Events Leading to the Passage of the Indian Child Welfare Act," in Eve P. Smith and Lisa A. Merkel-Holgín, eds., *A History of Child Welfare* (New Brunswick, N.J., 1996), 257–75, Marc Mannes points out that in most of the states with large Indian populations, "roughly 25% to 35% of Indian young people had been separated from their families, and that Indian children were much more likely to experience out-of-home placement than non-Indian children" (260).

2. European American Childhood

1. Robert Middlekauff, *The Mathers: Three Generations of Puritan Intellectuals, 1596–1728* (New York, 1971), 10–17, 80–83, 191–94, 201–2; N. Ray Hiner, "Cotton Mather and His Children," in Barbara Finkelstein, ed., *Regulated Children, Liberated Children: Education in Psychohistorical Perspective* (New York, 1979), 24–43.

2. Peter Laslett, *The World We Have Lost* (New York, 1965), 1–21. The so-called grand level and the clear divisions within English society are discussed on pages 22–52.

3. Ibid., 53–54; Bernard Bailyn, *The Peopling of British North America* (New York, 1986), 20.

4. Laslett, *World We Have Lost,* 54–80.

5. Ibid., 107.

6. Joseph E. Illick, "Child-Rearing in Seventeenth-Century England and America," in Lloyd deMause, ed., *The History of Childhood* (New York, 1974), 304. See also James Axtell, *The School upon a Hill: Education and Society in Colonial New England* (New Haven, Conn., 1974), esp. 54–95.

7. Illick, "Child-Rearing," 304–7. The figures are even higher in Lawrence Stone, *The Family, Sex, and Marriage in England, 1500–1800* (New York, 1977), 68–70. Childbirth can be studied in Richard W. Wertz and Dorothy C. Wertz, *Lying-In: A History of Childbirth in America* (New York, 1977) and Judith Walzer Leavitt, *Brought to Bed: Childbearing in America, 1750 to 1950* (New York, 1986).

8. The quote is from François Mauriceau's *The Diseases of Women with Child … With Fit Remedies for the Several Indispositions of New-Born Babes,* in Illick, "Child-Rearing," 307.

9. Ibid., 307–8.

10. R. V. Schnucker, "The English Puritans and Pregnancy, Delivery, and Breast-Feeding," *History of Childhood Quarterly* 1 (1973/74): 637–58.

11. Illick, "Child-Rearing," 308–11.

12. Ibid., 310–12; Stone, *Family,* 105–14.

13. Illick, "Child-Rearing," 312; Stone, *Family,* 161.

14. Illick, "Child-Rearing," 312, 314.

15. Ibid., 337. See also Stone, *Family,* 163–66.

16. Illick, "Child-Rearing," 320–21; Laslett, *World We Have Lost,* 14.

17. Illick, "Child-Rearing," 312–15.

18. Illick, "Child-Rearing", 318–320. A thoughtful interpretation of Locke's

Some Thoughts Concerning Education appears in Daniel Calhoun, *The Intelligence of a People* (Princeton, N.J., 1973), 139–44.

19. Captain John Smith, "A Description of New England, " in R. H. Pearce, *Colonial American Writing*, 2nd ed. (New York, 1969), 13, 17; William Bradford, *Of Plymouth Plantation*, ed. S. E. Morison (New York, 1953), 24–25.

20. "The Humble Request," as quoted in Illick, "Child-Rearing," 324.

21. Regional origins are discussed in D. H. Fischer's *Albion's Seed: Four British Folkways in America* (New York, 1989), 31–36, 240–46. On the Chesapeake, see W. F. Craven, *White, Red, and Black: The Seventeenth-Century Virginian* (Charlottesville, Va., 1971), 1–37; James Horn, "Adapting to the New World: A Comparative Study of Local Society in England and Maryland, 1650–1700," in L. G. Carr et al., eds., *Colonial Chesapeake Society* (Chapel Hill, N.C., 1988), 133–75. Virginia also demonstrated its heritage through "an English sense of family, of kith and kin, and of society as an ordered array of interdependent families committed to the common good." Darrett B. and Anita H. Rutman, *A Place in Time: Middlesex County, Virginia, 1650–1750* (New York, 1984), 51. Among the family and community studies tying New England to England are S. C. Powell, *Puritan Village: The Formation of a New England Town* (New York, 1963); K. A. Lockridge, *A New England Town, the First Hundred Years: Dedham, Massachusetts, 1636–1736* (New York, 1970); P. J. Greven, Jr., *Four Generations: Population, Land, and Family in Colonial Andover, Massachusetts* (Ithaca, N.Y., 1970); John Demos, *A Little Commonwealth: Family Life in Plymouth Colony* (New York, 1970).

22. Darrett B. and Anita H. Rutman, "'Now-Wives and Sons-in-Law': Parental Death in a Seventeenth-Century Virginia County," in Thad W. Tate and David Ammerman, eds., *The Chesapeake in the Seventeenth Century* (Chapel Hill, N.C., 1979), 167. On nuclear families coming to New England, see T. H. Breen and Stephen Foster, "Moving to the New World: The Character of Early Massachusetts Immigration," *William and Mary Quarterly*, 3rd ser., 30 (1973): 194.

23. Rutman and Rutman, "'Now-Wives and Sons-in-Law,'" 169. A regional comparison and further citations appear in Ross W. Beales, Jr., "The Child in Seventeenth-Century America," in Joseph M. Hawes and N. Ray Hiner, *American Childhood: A Research Guide and Historical Handbook* (Westport, Conn., 1985), 16.

24. Irene W. D. Hecht, "The Virginia Muster of 1624/5 as a Source for Demographic History," *William and Mary Quarterly*, 3rd ser., 30 (1973): 84; Hecht makes clear that Virginia's demographic pattern does not reflect England's (87) nor resemble New England's (88–91).

25. Laurel Thatcher Ulrich, *Good Wives: Image and Reality in the Lives of Women in Northern New England, 1650–1750* (New York, 1982), 126–41; Demos, *A Little Commonwealth*, 66; Lorena S. Walsh, "'Till Death Us Do Part': Marriage and Family in Seventeenth-Century Maryland," in Tate and Ammerman, *Chesapeake*, 141; Lois Green Carr and Lorena S. Walsh, "The Planter's Wife: The Experience of White Women in Seventeenth-Century Maryland," *William and Mary Quarterly*, 3rd ser., 34 (1977): 554.

26. Beales, "Child in Seventeenth-Century America," 26–27; Illick, "Child-Rearing," 324–25; Fischer, *Albion's Seed*, 93–97, 306–10; and especially Daniel Scott Smith, "Child-Naming Patterns and Family Structure Change: Hingham, Massachusets, 1640–1880," *Newberry Papers in Family and Community History*, nos. 75–76 (Chicago, 1977).

27. Axtell, *School upon a Hill*, is excellent upon this issue, tying the training into naming, reliance on the family, and the instruction and literacy of children. The church, Axtell reminds us, "was the locus of the deep layer of common

values shared by New Englanders, the physical center that gave point and structure to their various lives" (49).

28. Karen Calvert, *Children in the House: The Material Culture of Early Childhood, 1600–1900* (Boston, 1992), 19–25. In *A Little Commonwealth,* 132–33, John Demos makes the case against the persistence of swaddling.

29. Walsh, "'Till Death Us Do Part,'" 141–42; Demos, *A Little Commonwealth,* 133.

30. Robert V. Wells, *Revolutions in Americans' Lives: A Demographic Perspective on the History of Americans, Their Families, and Their Society* (Westport, Conn., 1982), 3. Wells (30) estimates that life expectancy at birth after 1650 for whites was between 35 and 45 (50 or more in New England, as low as 20 in the South). These statistics indicate a very young population; the median age was 16 in the eighteenth century. See Wells's chart of age and sex composition from 1625 to 1970 (80–81).

31. Charles R. King, *Children's Health in America* (New York, 1993), 5.

32. Walsh, "'Till Death Us Do Part,'" 142–43; Rutman and Rutman, *A Place in Time,* 114; Bowlby, *Attachment and Loss,* III, 295–310. Bowlby makes clear that not every child who loses a parent is impaired (310, 318). He makes no pretense of knowing why some individuals recover from experiences of separation and loss while others do not (II, 5). Since the Chesapeake population was largely replenished by immigration rather than natural increase during the seventeenth century, it becomes academic to speculate about whether these grown-up children were neurotic adults.

33. Rutman and Rutman, *A Place in Time,* 119. The issue of children and death is dealt with more realistically in Gerald F. Moran and Maris A. Vinovskis, "The Puritan Family and Religion: A Critical Reappraisal," *William and Mary Quarterly,* 3rd ser., 39 (1982): 52–54.

34. Demos, *Little Commonwealth,* 134–39; Fischer, *Albion's Seed,* 97–101.

35. Bowlby, *Attachment and Loss,* II, 23; see also 208, 210.

36. Quoted in William S. Simmons, "Cultural Bias in the New England Puritans' Perception of Indians," *William and Mary Quarterly,* 3rd ser., 38 (1981): 62, 71.

37. Elizabeth Pleck, *Domestic Tyranny: The Making of Social Policy against Family Violence from Colonial Times to the Present* (New York, 1987), 25–29. John Demos disagrees; see "Child Abuse in Context: An Historian's Perspective," in *Past, Present, and Personal* (New York, 1986), 68–88.

38. Quoted in Beales, "The Child in Seventeenth-Century America," 31.

39. Karin Calvert, *Children in the House: The Material Culture of Early Childhood, 1600–1900* (Boston, 1992), 48–52. See also Bernard Mergen, *Play and Playthings: A Reference Guide* (Westport, Conn., 1982), 16, for what might qualify as a toy.

40. Karin Calvert, "Children in American Family Portraiture, 1670–1810," *William and Mary Quarterly,* 3rd ser., 39 (1982): 87–88. See also Alice Morse Earle, *Child Life in Colonial Days* (New York, 1899); Ross W. Beales, Jr., "In Search of the Historical Child: Miniature Adulthood and Youth in Colonial England," *American Quarterly* 27 (1975): 379–91.

41. E. S. Morgan, *The Puritan Family: Religion and Domestic Relations in Seventeenth-Century New England,* 2nd ed. (New York, 1966).

42. Edmund Morgan advances both possibilities in *The Puritan Family,* 77–78. For other explanations see Beales, "The Child in Seventeenth-Century America," 34–35. From the perspective of attachment theory, however, the issue would not be parental motivation but, rather, the effect of the separation on the child, since attachment is considered a dominant force throughout the latency period. For example, Samuel Sewall's 13-year-old daughter wept for fear of

being abandoned when her father took her to a new home, and his son cried at leaving as well. Bowlby, *Attachment and Loss*, I, 207. Sewall's *Diary* is cited in Fisher, *Albion's Seed*, 101–2.

43. Wells, *Revolutions*, 53. Wells also notes that "a sense of oneself as distinct from others must have been hard to develop and preserve."

44. Roger Thompson, *Sex in Middlesex: Popular Mores in a Massachusetts County, 1649–1699* (Amherst, Mass., 1986), 92; Mary Ann Mason, *From Father's Property to Children's Rights: The History of Child Custody in the United States* (New York, 1994), xiii. Bastards, orphans, and impoverished children were usually "put out" to households for labor, relieving the community of the burden of support (24–35, 46). Morgan, *Puritan Family*, 87–108. Bernard Bailyn points out that masters increasingly put literacy instruction and other nonvocational matters in the hands of teachers. *Education in the Forming of American Society* (Chapel Hill, N.C., 1960), 32. See also Robert M. Bremner et al., eds., *Children and Youth in America: A Documentary History*, 3 vols. (Cambridge, Mass., 1970–74), I, 72–102; Lawrence A. Cremin, *American Education: The Colonial Experience, 1607–1783* (New York, 1970). A broad cultural approach to the education of the child is the theme of James Axtell's eminently readable *School upon a Hill: Education and Society in Colonial New England* (New Haven, Conn., 1974)

45. Roger Thompson, "Adolescent Culture in Colonial Massachusetts," *Journal of Family History* 13 (summer 1984): 127–44.

46. Constance Schulz, "Children and Childhood in the Eighteenth Century," in Hiner and Hawes, *American Childhood*, 57–109; John Walzer, "A Period of Ambivalence: Eighteenth-Century American Childhood," in deMause, *History of Childhood*, 351–82; Arlene W. Scadron, "The Formative Years: Childhood and Child Rearing in Eighteenth Century Anglo-American Culture," Ph.D. diss., University of California, Berkeley, 1979. In *Quakers and the American Family* (New York, 1988), Barry Levy alludes to child rearing without discussing it.

47. Philip Greven, *The Protestant Temperament: Patterns of Child Rearing, Religious Experience, and the Self in Early America* (New York, 1977), in which the labels *evangelical, moderate,* and *genteel* are used. Michael Zuckerman, in "William Byrd's Family," *Perspectives in American History* 12 (1979): 255–311, and Jan Lewis, in *The Pursuit of Happiness: Family and Values in Jefferson's Virginia* (Cambridge, 1983), 30–39, argue that the Southern genteel family was not affectionate; Daniel Blake Smith, in *Inside the Big House: Planter Life in Eighteenth-Century Chesapeake Society* (Ithaca, N.Y., 1980), esp. chaps. 1 and 3, argues that it was.

48. Beverly P. Smaby, *The Transformation of Moravian Bethlehem: From Communal Mission to Family Economy* (Philadelphia, 1988), 145.

49. The Quaker family, like the Puritan, was hierarchical, but mothers—"spiritualized women"—played a larger role in the latter. J. William Frost, *The Quaker Family in Colonial America* (New York, 1973), 31–35, 64–92; Barry Levy, *Quakers and the American Family* (New York, 1988), 75–78, 98, 130, 144–51, 224.

50. Ibid., 147–48; Frost, *Quaker Family*, 135; Greven, *Four Generations*, chap. 9; N. Ray Hiner, "Adolescence in Eighteenth-Century America," *History of Childhood Quarterly* 3 (1975): 253–80.

51. Brenda Stevenson, *Life in Black and White: Family and Community in the Slave South* (New York, 1996), 112–13.

52. Calvert, "Children in American Family Portraiture, 1670–1810," 87–113.

53. N. Ray Hiner, "Adolescence in Eighteenth-Century America," *History of Childhood Quarterly: The Journal of Psychohistory* 3 (fall 1975): 253–80.

54. Ibid.; Greven, *Protestant Temperament*, 60–61, 65, 66, 74–76, 80, 94, 103, 111–12.

55. Daniel Scott Smith and Michael S. Hindus, "Premarital Pregnancy in America, 1640–1971: An Overview and Interpretation," *Journal of Interdisciplinary History* 6 (1978): 113–37.

56. Smith, *Great House*, chaps. 2, 3. Smith sees paternal influence over sons declining (113–25), though he admits that "deference and duty remained integral to the psychological well-being of most sons" (117). Regarding daughters, see Anne Firor Scott, *The Southern Lady: From Pedestal to Politics, 1830–1930* (Chicago, 1970).

57. "Severity of upbringing, corporal punishment, and subordination *increase* attachment, albeit an anxious or even insecure one. Beyond common sense we know little at present about the durability and reversibility of 'normal' anxious attachment." Personal communication from Aubrey Metcalf, M.D., January 31, 1996.

58. Benjamin Franklin, *Autobiography* (New York, 1950), 12–29.

59. L. H. Butterfield, ed., *Diary and Autobiography of John Adams*, 4 vols. (Cambridge, 1964), III, 253–63.

60. Greven, *Protestant Temperament*, 339–41. Other scholars drawing upon family experience to help explain the American Revolution include Winthrop D. Jordan, "Familial Politics: Thomas Paine and the Killing of the King, 1776," *Journal of American History* 60 (1973): 294–308, which focuses on Freud's ideas about the Oedipus complex; Jay Fliegelman, *Prodigals and Pilgrims: The American Revolution Against Patriarchal Authority, 1750–1800* (Cambridge, 1982); Edwin G. Burrows and Michael Wallace, "The American Revolution: The Ideology and Psychology of National Liberation," *Perspectives in American History* 6 (1972): 255–94. For an examination of the role of mother, see Joseph E. Illick, "John Quincy Adams: The Maternal Influence," *Journal of Psychohistory* 4 (1976–77): 185–95; David F. Musto, "The Youth of John Quincy Adams," *Proceedings of the American Philosophical Society* 113 (1969): 269–82; Ruth H. Bloch, "American Feminine Ideals in Transition: The Rise of the Moral Mother, 1785–1815," *Feminist Studies* 4 (1978): 101–26.

61. Wells, *Revolutions*, 54–55. Wells also notes that "early [European] Americans from all the colonies were remarkably consistent in the values they expressed in their letters, diaries, wills, legal codes, divorce proceedings, children's literature, newspapers, magazines, court cases regarding illegitimacy, sermons, church records, or advice manuals for young husbands or young wives," although values do not always reflect reality. Ibid., 56.

62. Ibid., 32–40.

63. James Axtell has pointed out that few if any natives became civilized Englishmen, but white captives were so strongly drawn to the native way of life that few wished to return to "civilization." See "The White Indians of Colonial America," *William and Mary Quarterly*, 3rd ser., 32 (1975): 55–88.

64. Alexis de Tocqueville, *Democracy in America* (New York, 1966), 585. Though Tocqueville emphasizes male independence, he notes elsewhere that "the same social impetus which brings nearer to the same level father and son, master and servant, and generally every inferior to every superior does raise the status of women and should make them more and more nearly the equal of men" (600).

65. Mary P. Ryan, *Cradle of the Middle Class: The Family in Oneida County, New York, 1790–1865* (Cambridge, 1981), 18–59.

66. John Mack Faragher, *Sugar Creek: Life on the Illinois Prairie* (New Haven, Conn., 1986), 87–88, 93, 118. Settlers often came to Sugar Creek with kin and established more family ties through multiple intermarriages with other kin groups (55–60, 151). Faragher poses an interesting comparison between these families and those of twentieth-century Kickapoo Indians (114–16).

67. Ibid., 95, 100. John Mack Faragher, *Women and Men on the Overland Trail* (New Haven, Conn., 1979), 58–59, 88–89, 123; Carol Fairbanks and Sara Brooks Sundberg, *Farm Women on the Prairie Frontier* (Metuchen, N.J., 1983), 56–57; Elliott West, *Growing Up with the Country: Childhood on the Far Western Frontier* (Albuquerque, N.Mex., 1989), 73–94; Elizabeth Hampsten, "From a Children's Point of View," paper delivered at PCB/AHA Conference, San Francisco State University, August 13, 1988.

68. Bertram Wyatt-Brown, *Southern Honor: Ethics and Behavior in the Old South* (New York, 1982), 117–74.

69. Hal S. Barron, *Those Who Stayed Behind: Rural Society in Nineteenth-Century New England* (Cambridge, 1984), 8; see also 55, 94.

3. African American Childhood

1. William S. McFeely, *Frederick Douglass* (New York, 1991), 3–73; an explanation of Douglass's three autobiographies appears on 7–8.

2. These three paragraphs are derived from Donald R. Wright, *African Americans in the Colonial Era: From African Origins Through the American Revolution* (Arlington Heights, Ill., 1990). See also Matt Schaffer, *Mandinko: The Ethnography of a West African Holy Land* (New York, 1980); C. C. Robertson and M. A. Klein, "Women's Importance in African Slave Systems," in C. C. Robertson and M. A. Klein, eds., *Women and Slavery in Africa* (Madison, Wisc., 1983), 3–25; H. S. Klein, "African Women in the Atlantic Slave Trade," in ibid., 29–38; John Thornton, "Sexual Demography: The Impact of the Slave Trade on Family Structure," in ibid., 39–48; G. I. Jones, ed., "The Early Travels of Olaudah Equiano [Gustavus Vasa]," in Philip D. Curtin, ed., *Africa Remembered* (Madison, Wisc., 1967), 60–98. Contemporary accounts of child rearing include Margaret Read's *Children of Their Fathers: Growing Up among the Ngoni of Malawi* (New York, 1968) and R. D. Whittemore's "Child Caregiving and Socialization to the Mandinka Way: Toward an Ethnography of Childhood" (Ph.D. diss., UCLA, 1989).

3. Until the publication by Melville Herskovits of *The Myth of the Negro Past* (New York, 1941), the prevalent belief among European Americans was that the African American had no past and, therefore, no survivals could exist. Sterling Stuckey, in *Slave Culture: Nationalist Theory and the Foundations of Black America* (New York, 1987), maintains that "the depths of African culture in America have been greatly underestimated" (ix).

4. Elizabeth Anne Kuznesof, "Brazil," in Joseph M. Hawes and N. Ray Hiner, eds., *Children in Historical and Comparative Perspective* (Westport, Conn., 1991), 151. Also William Bosman, *A New and Accurate Description of the Coast of New Guinea* (1704; New York, 1987), 122–23, 208; R. E. Ellison, "Marriage and Child-Birth Among the Kanuri," *Africa* 9 (1936): 533–34; and Schaffer, *Mandinko*, 71, where it is observed that the "infant's naming ceremony of today is virtually identical to this one described … 180 years ago." Herskovits, *Myth*, 188–94.

5. Cheryll Ann Cody, "Naming, Kinship, and Estate Dispersal: Notes on Slave Family Life on a South Carolina Plantation, 1786–1833," *William and Mary*

Quarterly, 3rd ser., 39 (1982): 202; Cody, "There Was No 'Absolom' on the Ball Plantations: Slave-Naming Practices in the South Carolina Low Country, 1720–1865," *American Historical Review* 92 (1987): 563–96; Herbert G. Gutman, *The Black Family in Slavery and Freedom, 1750–1925* (New York, 1976), 185–204; Peter Wood, *Black Majority: Negroes in Colonial South Carolina from 1670 Through the Stono Rebellion* (New York, 1974), 181–86; Philip D. Morgan, "Slave Life in Piedmont Virginia, 1720–1800," in Lois Green Carr et al., eds., *Colonial Chesapeake Society* (Chapel Hill, N.C., 1988), 452.

6. Kuznesof, "Brazil," 151; Bosman, *Coast of Guinea*, 121; Russell R. Menard, "The Maryland Slave Population, 1658–1730: A Demographic Profile of Blacks in Four Counties," *William and Mary Quarterly*, 3rd ser., 32 (1975): 41.

7. Menard, 38–49. Herbert S. Klein and Stanley L. Engerman, "Fertility Differentials Between Slaves in the United States and the West Indies: A Note on Lactation Practices and Their Possible Implications," *William and Mary Quarterly*, 3rd. ser., 35 (1978): 358; John Campbell, "Work, Pregnancy, and Infant Mortality among Southern Slaves," *Journal of Interdisciplinary History* 14 (1983/84): 793–812; L. H. Owens, *This Species of Property: Slave Life and Culture in the Old South* (New York, 1976), 40. In *Time on the Cross: The Economics of American Negro Slavery* (Boston, 1974), Robert Fogel and Stanley Engerman applaud health care for pregnant slave women and state that nursing mothers were kept on a light work schedule (122–23). Richard Dunn observes that on the Jamaican plantation of Mesopotamia, women with five or more children were allowed to stay home and raise them. "Caribbean Versus Old South Slavery," paper delivered at the University of Minnesota, April 29, 1994, 21.

8. Kuznesof, "Brazil," 151; Rev. Charles T. Dooley, "Child-Training Among the Wanguru. I. Physical Education," *Primitive Man* 7 (April 1934): 24–26.

9. Campbell, "Work, Pregnancy," 793–812; Brenda E. Stevenson, *Life in Black and White: Family and Community in the Slave South* (New York, 1996), 195; Owens, *This Species*, 40–41.

10. Kenneth F. Kiple and Virginia Himmelsteib King, *Another Dimension to the Black Diaspora: Diet, Disease, and Racism* (Cambridge, 1981), 96–116; Todd L. Savitt, *Medicine and Slavery: The Diseases and Health Care of Blacks in Antebellum Virginia* (Urbana, Ill., 1978), 120–29; Richard Dunn, "Caribbean versus Old South Slavery," 15; Richard Steckel, "A Dreadful Childhood: The Excess Mortality of American Slaves," *Social Science History* 10 (1986): 791. Cf. Fogel and Engerman, *Time on the Cross*, 124.

11. Eugene D. Genovese, *Roll, Jordan, Roll: The World the Slaves Made* (New York, 1974), 502; Paul Bohannan and Philip Curtin, *Africa and Africans,* rev. ed. (Garden City, N.Y., 1971), 115.

12. R. D. Whittemore and Elizabeth Beverly, "Trust in the Mandinka Way: The Cultural Context of Sibling Care," in P. G. Zukow, ed., *Sibling Interaction Across Cultures* (New York, 1989), 26–53. Photo in Schaffer, *Mandinko, 100*. See also Zukow, *Sibling Interaction,* chaps. 3 and 4.

13. Owens, *This Species*, 41–42, argues the case of child neglect while Fogel and Engerman, *Time on the Cross*, 206–7, present the other side.

14. Ira Berlin, in "Time, Space, and the Evolution of Afro-American Society on British Mainland North America," *American Historical Review* 85 (1980): 44–78, describes many different living situations, varying considerably by region and including households where there were but one or two slaves. Jean Butenhoff Lee, in "The Problem of Slave Community in the Eighteenth-Century Chesapeake," *William and Mary Quarterly*, 3rd ser., 43 (1986): 333–61, observes that 45

percent of the slaves in Charles County, Maryland, lived in groups of ten or fewer. Obviously the issue of attachment would be different in these situations than on plantations.

Changes in African American ways of life during the late eighteenth century are the subject of essays by Gary B. Nash, Richard S. Dunn, Philip D. Morgan, and Allan Kulikoff in Ira Berlin and Ronald Hoffman, eds., *Slavery and Freedom in the Age of the American Revolution* (Charlottesville, Va., 1983).

15. J. W. C. Pennington, *The Fugitive Blacksmith* (London, 1850), 2, as quoted in Owens, *This Species*, 201.

16. "The situational feature of special interest to us in this work is, of course, being alone. Probably nothing increases the likelihood that fear will be aroused more than that." John Bowlby, *Attachment and Loss*, 3 vols. (London, 1969–80), II, 118. See also 142–43, 148, for the evolutionary explanation of the importance of companionship; 178–81 on fear.

17. Lester Alston, "Children as Chattel," in Elliott West and Paula Petrik, eds., *Small Worlds: Children and Adolescents in America, 1850–1950* (Lawrence, Kans., 1992), 210–15.

18. Wilma King, *Stolen Childhood: Slave Youth in Nineteenth-Century America* (Bloomington, Ill., 1995), 71; Marie Jenkins Schwartz, *Born to Bondage: Growing Up Enslaved in the Antebellum South* (Cambridge, 2000), 77–82. See also Mary Beth Norton et al., "The Afro-American Family in the Age of Revolution," in Berlin and Hoffman, eds., *Slavery and Freedom*, 180; John Blassingame, *The Slave Community: Plantation Life in the Antebellum South*, 2nd ed. (New York, 1979), 178.

19. Allan Kulikoff, "The Beginnings of the Afro-American Family in Maryland," in C. Aubrey Land et al., *Law, Society, and Politics in Early Maryland* (Baltimore, 1977), 176–82. The argument that most slaves lived in nuclear households and sustained monogamous marriages is challenged in Brenda E. Stevenson, "Black Family Structure in Colonial and Antebellum Virginia: Amending the Revisionist Perspective," in M. Belinda Tucker and Claudia Mitchell-Kerna, eds., *The Decline in Marriage Among African Americans* (New York, 1995), 27–56. On the contemporary African family, see A. R. Radcliffe-Brown and Daryll Forde, *African Systems of Kinship and Marriage* (London, 1950). On the extended family, see Cody, "Kinship and Estate Dispersal," 193. On vulnerability, see Stevenson, *Life in Black and White*, 179, 206–25; Lee, "The Problem of Slave Community," 361; Richard S. Dunn, "A Tale of Two Plantations: Slave Life at Mesopotamia and Mount Airy in Virginia," *William and Mary Quarterly*, 3rd ser., 34 (1977): 32–65.

Frederick Douglass, drawing on the authority of his own early years in bondage in early nineteenth-century Maryland, always denied the compatibility of slavery with the family. *My Bondage and My Freedom* (New York, 1855), chap. 3. In *Rituals of Blood: Consequences of Slavery in Two American Centuries* (New York, 1999), sociologist Orlando Patterson terms the idea of a stable slave family not only an "academic absurdity" but an "intellectual disgrace."

20. Genovese, *Roll, Jordan, Roll*, 505–6; David K. Wiggins, "The Play of Slave Children in the Plantation Communities of the Old South, 1820–1860," *Journal of Sports History* 7, no. 2 (1980): 21–39. Bernard Mergen, *Play and Playthings: A Reference Guide* (Westport, Conn., 1982), strongly disputes the contention that slave children relieved anxieties and fears through play and thus more easily withstood bondage (42–43, 53 n. 1). Kuznesof says that in Africa "corporal punishment for children was rare"; see "Brazil," 151. But in Whittemore, "Child Caregiving," 173, 230, there are references to corporal punishment. And

Herskovits views whipping as a survival from Africa, where it was and is "the outstanding method of correction." *Myth of the Negro Past,* 196. Genovese emphasizes beating as life preparation. *Roll, Jordan, Roll,* 509–12. Stevenson has evidence that white children were not whipped in front of blacks. *Life in Black and White,* 110.

21. Mergen, *Play,* 31, 39–41, 45. Dooley, "Child-Training," 26–31, treats games played by East African children today. C. M. Eastman's "NZW Swahili child's worldview," *Ethos* 14, no. 2 (summer 1986): 144–73, compares play in western and nonwestern societies. On reading and the petting of children, see Blassingame, *Slave Community,* 185; Genovese, *Roll, Jordan, Roll,* 512, 515–19; Wiggins, "Play of Slave Children," 25, 30–36. Though educating slaves was outlawed in some states, white owners might teach slaves to read the Bible, and of course house slaves and urban slaves might become literate simply by their proximity to the written word. And some ex-slaves claimed they were able to teach themselves. Janet Cornelius, "'We Slipped and Learned to Read': Slave Accounts of the Literacy Process, 1830–1865," *Phylon* 44 (1983): 171–85.

In *Deep like the Rivers: Education in the Slave Quarter Community, 1831–1865* (New York, 1968), Thomas Webber paints a benign picture of early African American life, arguing that "few slave children seem to have realized the significance of their slave status until their slave training began in earnest" between the ages of 10 and 14 (3–21).

22. Richard H. Steckel, "A Peculiar Population: The Nutrition, Health, and Mortality of American Slaves from Childhood to Maturity," *Journal of Economic History* 46 (1986): 721–41. Fogel and Engerman judge slave diet to have been "quite substantial" (*Time on the Cross,* 113), while L. H. Owens assesses it as wholly inadequate (*This Species,* 50–69). In *Medicine and Slavery,* Todd L. Savitt, a medical student before he became a historian, questions the use of evidence by Fogel and Engerman as well as Owens on the matter of diet (86–87, nn. 8, 9). Savitt argues for the substantiality of diet (96). However, Steckel's work is the most convincing.

23. Alston sees this fact as possibly misleading, since children always had to perform *some* tasks, and thus "they may not have experienced changes in the work they did as mileposts in their lives." "Children as Chattel," 226–27.

24. On examining the records of a South Carolina planter, Cody found that no children under 10 were separated from their parents, few children between 10 and 19 were separated, but at the end of the 20–29 age span, only 40 percent of men were still with their mothers; daughters were twice as likely to stay with mothers. "Naming, Kinship, and Estate Dispersal," 207–8. Other evidence of keeping a family together appears in Daniel C. Littlefield, *Rice and Slaves* (Baton Rouge, La., 1981), 71. To the contrary, see Morgan, "Slave Life," 448–49.

25. Charles T. Dooley, "Child-Training Among the Wanguru. III. Moral Education," *Primitive Man* 9 (January 1936): 6; G. M. Culwick, "New Ways for Old in the Treatment of Adolescent African Girls," *Africa* 12 (1939), 425–27. On the circumcision ceremonies for boys and girls, see Schaffer, *Mandinko,* 95–101.

26. Owens, *This Species,* 44–46.

27. Gutman, *Black Family,* 402–12.

28. Leon F. Litwack, *Trouble in Mind: Black Southerners in the Age of Jim Crow* (New York, 1998), 3–76. Also John Dittmer, *Black Georgia in the Progressive Era, 1900–1920* (Urbana, 1977); Charles S. Johnson, *Growing Up in the Black Belt: Negro Youth in the Rural South* (Washington, D.C., 1941).

29. Litwack, *Trouble,* 8.

30. Donald G. Nieman, ed., *African Americans and Education in the South, 1865–1900* (New York, 1994), xi.

31. Booker T. Washington, *Up from Slavery* (1901; New York, 1965), 37.

32. Richard Wright, *Black Boy: A Record of Childhood and Youth* (New York, 1945). Half of this autobiography was expurgated to please the Book-of-the-Month Club, remaining unpublished until 1977. See Louis Menand, "The Hammer and the Nail," *New Yorker,* July 20, 1992, 79–84.

33. C. Peter Ripley, "The Black Family in Transition: Louisiana, 1860–1865," *Journal of Southern History* 41 (1975): 369–80; Robert H. Abzug, "The Black Family During Reconstruction," in Nathan Huggins, ed., *Key Issues in the Afro-American Experience* (New York, 1971), 26–41; Leon Litwack, *Been in the Storm So Long: The Aftermath of Slavery* (New York, 1979), 229–47.

34. Gutman, *Black Family*, 443–50; Litwack, *Trouble*, 350–51, 420–22. For a good sense of rural family life, see Theodore Rosengarten, ed., *All God's Dangers: The Life of Nate Shaw* (New York, 1974).

35. Virginia Heyer Young, "Family and Childhood in a Southern Negro Community," *American Anthropologist* 72 (1970): 269–88.

36. *New York Times,* September 15, 1998.

37. Webber, *Deep like the Rivers*, 27–42.

38. Ibid., 157–250. That blacks accepted or rejected white values, attitudes, and understandings is not an issue with a single answer. Note the debate over slave personality, concisely summarized in Owens, *This Species*, 238, n. 8. Kenneth Stampp, in *The Peculiar Institution: Slavery in the Ante-Bellum South* (New York, 1956), made the case for extensive role playing. Stanley Elkins, in *Slavery: A Problem in American Institutional and Intellectual Life* (Chicago, 1959), argued that slaves became the role they played. Stampp conceded that some slaves became the role but most did not; see "Rebels and Sambos: The Search for the Negro's Personality in Slavery," *Journal of Southern History* 37 (1971): 367–92.

39. George M. Fredrickson, *The Black Image in the White Mind: The Debate on Afro-American Character and Destiny, 1817–1914* (New York, 1971), 43. This observation is born out in Winthrop D. Jordan, *White over Black: American Attitudes Toward the Negro, 1550–1812* (Baltimore, 1969). Europeans were concerned with issues such as complexion, religion, behavior (especially perceived sexuality), always viewing the Africans as alien but not depicting them as children.

40. Fredrickson, *Black Image*, 43–197.

41. Litwack, *Been in the Storm So Long*, 191–92.

42. Ibid., 198–282.

43. Actually, the first film about African Americans in which whites appear in blackface was *The Pickaninnies Doing a Dance* (1894). James R. Nesteby, *Black Images in American Films, 1896–1954* (Washington, D.C., 1982), 14. And despite the popularity of *The Birth of a Nation*, there was simultaneously a strong undercurrent of criticism, causing Hollywood to refrain from casting Negroes in bad guy roles until *Sweet Sweetback's Baadasssss Son* (1971), save for the release of *Free and Equal* in the mid-1920s. Donald Bogle, *Toms, Coons, Mulattoes, Mammies, and Bucks,* 3rd ed. (New York, 1994), 16, 24–25.

44. Fredrickson, *Black Image*, 287, 295–96. A year before *The Southerner* was published, Jack Johnson became the world's first black heavyweight champion. The film of him kayoing white boxer Tommy Burns was burned to prevent race riots. Bogle, *Toms*, 17.

45. On Harriet Beecher Stowe's novel, as well as other pre–Civil War writings

on slave childhood, see J. E. Illick, "African Americans: Childhood in Slavery, Childlike in Freedom—and Paul Robeson as Child and Parent," in William Pencak, ed., *Paul Robeson* (Jefferson, N.C., 2001).

46. Maybe the enormously popular radio show *Amos 'n Andy* would fit this interpretation. For a different point of view, see Gerald Nachman, *Raised on Radio* (New York, 1998), 272–95.

47. Catherine Clinton, *The Plantation Mistress: Woman's World in the Old South* (New York, 1982), 202.

48. Leon Litwack suggests that such memories were prompted by white repugnance at the assertiveness of the now-freed blacks. Conversation with author, January 13, 1999.

49. Genovese, *Roll, Jordan, Roll*, 360–61.

50. For an interpretation that Jews assimilated by appearing blackfaced in films, see Michael Rogin, *Blackface, White Noise: Jewish Immigrants in the Hollywood Melting Pot* (Berkeley, Calif., 1996).

51. Herskovits, *Myth*, I, 293.

52. Owens, *This Species of Property*, 238 n. 8.

53. Richard Kluger, *Simple Justice: The History of* Brown v. Board of Education *and Black America's Struggle for Equality* (New York, 1975).

54. Robert Coles, *Children of Crisis: A Study of Courage and Fear* (Boston, 1967), 319, 321, 337.

55. Ibid., 48–49, 76–82.

56. Ibid., 323, 331.

4. Urban Middle-Class Childhood

1. Thomas Mellon, *Thomas Mellon and His Times* (Pittsburgh, 1994), 33, 48.

2. Richard D. Brown defines a "modern personality syndrome" and sees its full flowering as a consequence of the American Revolution. *Modernization: The Transformation of American Life, 1600–1865* (New York, 1976), esp. 95, 101. David Riesman discusses "social character" (that part of personality "shared among significant social groups") and attributes an "inner-directed character" to the age that emerged with the Renaissance and Reformation. *The Lonely Crowd: A Study of the Changing American Character* (New Haven, Conn., 1950). David Landes depicts modernization in terms of many ingredients, but at its heart lay "technological maturity and the industrialization that goes with it"—which would locate modernization in nineteenth-century America. *The Unbound Prometheus: Technological Change and Industrial Development in Western Europe from 1750 to the Present* (Cambridge, 1970), 7. Robert V. Wells dates the advent of the contemporary world from demographic developments that were becoming evident in 1770. *Revolutions in Americans' Lives: A Demographic Perspective on the History of Americans, Their Families, and Their Society* (Westport, Conn., 1982), esp. 44–45 and chap. 5.

3. Wells, *Revolutions*, 157.

4. Joseph F. Kett, *Rites of Passage: Adolescence in America, 1790 to the Present* (New York, 1977), 38.

5. Philip J. Greven, *Four Generations: Population, Land, and Family in Colonial Andover, Massachusetts* (Ithaca, N.Y., 1970), chap. 9.

Mary P. Ryan characterizes the change in family as "a shift from patriarchal authority to domestic affection" and observes that the social functions of the rural family were in the urban setting "redistributed along a jagged border between family and society." *Cradle of the Middle Class: The Family in Oneida County, New York, 1790–1865* (Cambridge, 1981), 231, 235.

See Linda K. Kerber, *Women of the Republic: Intellect and Ideology in Revolutionary America* (Chapel Hill, N.C., 1980), 11, 199–200; Ruth H. Bloch, "American Feminine Ideals in Transition: The Rise of the Moral Mother, 1785–1815, " *Feminist Studies* 4 (June 1978): 109. See also Sylvia D. Hoffert, *Private Matters: American Attitudes Toward Childbearing and Infant Nurture in the Urban North, 1800–1860* (Urbana, Ill., 1989).

6. Karin Calvert, *Children in the House: The Material Culture of Early Childhood, 1600–1900* (Boston, 1992), 87–94.

7. Bloch, "American Feminine Ideals," 112; Irvin G. Wylie, *The Self-Made Man in America: The Myth of Rags to Riches* (New York, 1954), 29.

8. Bloch, "American Feminine Ideals," 116. See also Jan Lewis, "Mother's Love: The Construction of an Emotion in Nineteenth-Century America," in Rima D. Apple and Janet Golden, eds., *Mothers and Motherhood* (Columbus, Ohio, 1997), 52–71. The altered perception of the child is evident in Philip J. Greven's *Child-Rearing Concepts, 1628–1861* (Itaska, Ill., 1973)

See Nancy Cott, "Notes Toward an Interpretation of Antebellum Childrearing," *Psychohistory Review* 4 (spring 1978): 4–20; Anne L. Kuhn, *The Mother's Role in Childhood Education: New England Concepts, 1830–1860* (New Haven, Conn., 1947).

9. Mary Ann Mason, *From Father's Property to Children's Rights: The History of Child Custody in the United States* (New York, 1994), 1–83.

10. See, e.g., Elizabeth Pleck, *Domestic Tyranny: The Making of American Social Policy Against Family Violence from Colonial Times to the Present* (New York, 1987), appendix A: "Patterns of Childhood Punishment"; William G. McLoughlin, "Evangelical Childrearing in the Age of Jackson: Francis Wayland's Views on When and How to Subdue the Willfulness of Children," *Journal of Social History* 8 (1975): 20–43; Charles Strickland, "A Transcendentalist Father: The Child-Rearing Practices of Bronson Alcott," *History of Childhood Quarterly* 1 (1973/74): 4–61. Alcott recognized his daughter Anna's attachment to her mother as well as the cause of her bad behavior when younger sister Louisa occupied so much of Mrs. Alcott's time. Anna felt deserted by her mother, although she did have an attendant. Once Anna was readmitted to her parents' bedroom, Alcott noted the striking change in her temper and behavior, as if in response to her renewed attachment.

11. Wells, *Revolutions*, 91–100; Kett, *Rites*, 115. See also Daniel Scott Smith, "Family Limitation, Sexual Control, and Domestic Feminism in Victorian America," in Mary S. Hartman and Lois Banner, eds., *Clio's Consciousness Raised* (New York, 1974), 119–36. Smith prefers "domestic feminism" to "voluntary motherhood" as a descriptive term.

12. Catherine M. Scholten, "'On the Importance of the Obstetrick Art': Changing Customs of Childbirth in America, 1760 to 1825," *William and Mary Quarterly*, 3rd ser., 34 (1977): 426–45; Calvert, *Children*, 88–90; Hoffert, *Private Matters*, 61–105.

13. Wells, *Revolutions*, 153.

14. Richard Sennett, "Middle-Class Families and Urban Violence: The Experience of a Chicago Community in the Nineteenth Century," in Stephan Thernstrom and Richard Sennett, eds., *Nineteenth-Century Cities: Essays in the New Urban History* (New Haven, Conn., 1969), 386–420; Christopher Lasch, *Haven in a Heartless World: The Family Beseiged* (New York, 1977); Calvert, *Children in the House*, 106.

15. Carl Degler's explanation of why the nineteenth century was the "century of the child" is based not on the psychodynamics of the vulnerable family and its innocent children in the hostile city but rather on the new role of women in the family. See *At Odds: Women and the Family in America from the Revolution to the Present* (New York, 1980), 73–85. See also Bloch, "American Feminine Ideals," 10–11; Charles R. King, *Children's Health in America* (New York, 1993), 33–37. The complexity of the nursing situation is captured in Janet Golden, "The New Motherhood and the New View of Wet Nurses, 1780–1865," in Apple and Golden, *Mothers and Motherhood,* 72–89. Swaddling had had the virtue of protecting infants against the cold; it now was argued that babies accustomed to cold would be healthier. Even cold baths were recommended. Calvert, *Children,* 55–70.

16. Faye E. Dudden, *Serving Women: Household Service in Nineteenth-Century America* (Middletown, Conn., 1983), 147–54.

17. Heman Herman as quoted in Cott, "Antebellum Childrearing," 10.

18. But for the continuation of corporal punishment in the nineteenth century, see Degler, *At Odds,* 86–90, as well as Philip J. Greven, *Spare the Child: The Religious Roots of Punishment and the Psychological Impact of Physical Abuse* (New York, 1991). Hoffert, *Private Matters,* 142–92, is a good source for mothers' (and, to a lesser degree, fathers') feelings about infants, including the matter of death. It is her opinion that parents' "fear of losing their babies did not effectively diminish the degree of affection they felt for them" (158).

19. A point made in Robert L. Griswold, *Fatherhood in America: A History* (New York, 1993), 19.

20. In the developmental scheme of Erik Erikson, children between the ages of four and six are torn between initiative and guilt; no gender distinctions are made. See *Childhood and Society* (New York, 1950), chap. 7. Lillian Rubin does make gender distinctions (and deals with the subject of male romance), but she introduces them before the age of four. The internalization of mother in a pre-Oedipal stage of development has different consequences for girls and boys when they seek their gender identity. Without a father figure to identify with, the boy achieves his masculinity by unconsciously repressing his identity with his mother; he thus becomes hostile toward women generally. The girl may maintain her identification with her mother and simply add her father to her mental world, thus having a richer and more complex inner life. Lillian Rubin, *Intimate Strangers: Men and Women Together* (New York, 1983), chap. 3. See also Cott, "Antebellum Childrearing," 15–17; Bloch, "Feminine Ideals," 120.

21. Peter N. Stearns and Timothy Haggerty, "The Role of Fear: Transitions in American Emotional Standards for Children, 1850–1950," *American Historical Review* 96 (1991): 65–74.

22. Calvert, *Children,* 97–110.

23. Ibid., 110–19; Gary Cross, *Kids' Stuff: Toys and the Changing World of American Childhood* (Cambridge, 1997), 23. Portraiture between 1830 and 1870 puts toys into the hands of two-thirds of the boys but only one-fifth of the girls. Cross, *Kids' Stuff,* 21.

24. Zona Gale, *When I Was a Little Girl* (New York, 1925), quoted in Bernard Mergen, "Toys and the Culture of Childhood," in Elliott West and Paula Petrik, eds., *Small Worlds: Children and Adolescents in America, 1850–1950* (Lawrence, Kans., 1992), 96.

25. Peter N. Stearns, "Girls, Boys, and Emotions: Redefinitions and Historical Change," *Journal of American History* 80 (1993–94): 36–53.

26. Bernard Mergen, *Play and Playthings. A Reference Guide* (Westport, Conn., 1982), 57–77.

27. Cross, *Kids' Stuff,* 21–32; Macleod, *Age of the Child,* 65–69.

28. Cross, *Kids' Stuff,* 32–49.

29. E. Anthony Rotundo, *American Manhood: Transformations in Masculinity from the Revolution to the Modern Era* (New York, 1993), 3–5, 31–55. When Rotundo alludes to "a kind of autonomy he had not enjoyed in early childhood," he is not speaking in a Bowlbian sense but, rather, suggesting that the urban middle-class boy had the opportunity to draw on the confidence he achieved in early childhood and to act freely. On sports, see Macleod, *Age of the Child,* 120–28.

30. Rotundo, *American Manhood,* 56–108. The word "homosexual" had not even popular usage before the late 1880s. Michael S. Kimmel, ed., *Changing Men* (Newbury Park, Calif., 1987), 280.

31. King, *Children's Health,* 61–68, 95–117 (esp. 72–93).

32. Robert H. Bremner et al., eds., *Children and Youth in America,* 3 vols. (Cambridge, 1970–74), I, 758–60; II, 811–12. Bremner devotes I, pt. 2, sect. 7 and II, pt. 7 to child health. See also Degler, *At Odds,* 101–3.

33. Wells, *Revolutions,* 124–40; Priscilla F. Clement, *Growing Pains: Children in the Industrial Age, 1850–1890* (New York, 1997), 36–50, 74–80; Macleod, *Age of the Child,* 18–26, 120–38. Macleod observes that "America's [fertility decline] was not triggered by decreasing child mortality making fewer children a safe bet. American child mortality did not decrease until long after fertility began to fall, and mortality rates do not explain group differences in fertility" (ibid., 11).

34. Karin Calvert, "To Be a Child: An Analysis of the Artifacts of Childhood" (Ph.D. diss., University of Pennsylvania, 1984), 198–249; Clement, *Growing Pains,* 153–54.

35. Bernard Wishy, *The Child and the Republic: The Dawn of Modern American Child Nurture* (Philadelphia, 1968), chap. 6. See also Daniel T. Rogers, "Socializing Middle-Class Children: Institutions, Fables, and Work Values in Nineteenth-Century America," *Journal of Social History* 14 (spring 1980): 354–67; Anne Scott McLeod, *A Moral Tale* (Hamden, Conn., 1975) and *American Childhood* (Athens, Ga., 1994); R. Gordon Kelly, *Mother Was a Lady* (Westport, Conn., 1974).

Elizabeth Francis observes that children's books until the mid-eighteenth century must be categorized as "catechism, primer, textbook, juvenile elegy, advice book, sermon, and moralized 'token' or example, genres that admitted narratives to their structures only for purposes of instruction," but that in the late eighteenth and early nineteenth centuries informative, patriotic, and even imaginative literature emerged, still with a strong moralistic tone. She depicts *Little Women* as an "intellectual watershed" in writing for the young because it reconciles "earthly and heavenly concerns." See Francis, "American Children's Literature, 1646–1880," in Joseph M. Hawes and N. Ray Hiner, eds., *American Childhood: A Research and Historical Handbook* (Westport, Conn., 1985), 185–233.

36. Bremner, *Children and Youth,* I, 72–102.

37. Ibid., 185–261.

38. Carl F. Kaestle, *Pillars of the Republic: Common Schools and American Society, 1780–1860* (New York, 1983), chap. 3.

39. Ibid., chap. 2. Kaestle points out that there was little difference between these rural district schools in 1780 and 1830. See also David B. Tyack, *The One Best System: A History of American Urban Education* (Cambridge, 1974), pt. 1.

40. Kaestle, *Pillars,* 64.

41. Ibid., chap. 4.

42. Ibid., 70–71, 106; Tyack, *One Best System*, 30–32, 40–45; Priscilla F. Clement, "The City and the Child, 1860–1885," in Hawes and Hiner, *American Childhood*, 241–43.

43. Clement, "The City and the Child," 238–39 (referring to Carl F. Kaestle and Maris A. Vinovskis, *Education and Social Change in Nineteenth-Century Massachusetts* [New York, 1980], 37, 82–83, 85), 242. See also Clement, *Growing Pains*, 81–91.

44. Lawrence A. Cremin, *American Education: The National Experience, 1783–1876* (New York, 1980), 58, 66–70; Cremin, *American Education: The Metropolitan Experience, 1876–1980* (New York, 1988), 87–89; Paul Boyer, *Urban Masses and Moral Order in America, 1820–1920* (Cambridge, 1978), 34–53. On Sunday schools in the early twentieth century, see Macleod, *Age of the Child*, 132–34.

45. Kett, *Rites*, 115.

46. Joseph F. Kett, "History of Age Grouping in America," in President's Science Advisory Committee, *Youth: Transition to Adulthood* (Chicago, 1974), 8–29.

47. Ibid., 144, 172.

48. Ibid., 173–204, 223–24; Boyer, *Urban Masses*, 108–20.

49. Kett, *Rites*, 11–37, 86–93, 111–43, 204–11.

50. G. Stanley Hall, *Adolescence: Its Psychology and Its Relations to Physiology, Anthropology, Sociology, Sex, Crime, Religion, and Education*, 2 vols. (New York, 1904); Dorothy Ross, *G. Stanley Hall: The Psychologist as Prophet* (Chicago, 1972), 309–40.

51. Sally Allen McNall, "American Children's Literature, 1880–Present," in Hawes and Hiner, *American Childhood*, 377–87.

52. Clement, *Growing Pains*, 44–50; David I. Macleod, *Building Character in the American Boy: The Boy Scouts, YMCA, and Their Forerunners, 1870–1920* (Madison, Wisc., 1983), 153–54.

53. The project, which was initiated in the early 1890s, was too amorphous to yield useful results. Elizabeth M. R. Lomax, *Science and Patterns of Child Care* (San Francisco, 1978), 18, 35.

54. Ross, *G. Stanley Hall*, 114–24, 316, 319; Bremner, *Children*, II, pt. 2, 1383ff.

55. Clement, "The City and the Child," 245–46.

56. Documentation of kindergarten as an Americanizing institution appears in Bremner, *Children*, II, 1459–62. For the early twentieth century, see Macleod, *Age of the Child*, 71–74. See also Michael S. Shapiro, *Child's Garden: The Kindergarten Movement from Froebel to Dewey* (University Park, Pa., 1983).

57. Bremner, *Children*, II, pt. 2, 1119, 1124.

58. Macleod, *Age of the Child*, 75–100. Intelligence testing of school children did not begin until after (and as a consequence of) World War I. Paul Davis Chapman, *Schools as Sorters: Lewis M. Terman, Applied Psychology, and the Intelligence Testing Movement, 1890–1930* (New York, 1988).

59. Bremner, *Children*, II, pt. 2, 1392–95; Reed Ueda, *Avenues to Adulthood: The Origins of the High School and Social Mobility in an American Suburb* (Cambridge, 1987), especially chap. 5. The reproduction of social inequality in the schools is examined into the early twentieth century in Ronald D. Cohen, "Child-Saving and Progressivism," in Hawes and Hiner, *American Childhood*, 281–87, where intelligence, especially IQ, is also treated (289–90), and in the mid-twentieth century in Joseph E. Illick, *At Liberty: The Story of a Community and a Generation: The Bethlehem, Pennsylvania, High School Class of 1952* (Knoxville, Tenn., 1989), chap. 4.

60. Kett, "History of Age Grouping in America"; Dom Cavallo, "Adolescent Peer Group Morality: Its Origins and Functions in the United States," *Psychohistory Review* 6(fall-winter, 1978–79): 88–101; Ueda, *Avenues*, chap. 6.

5. Urban Working-Class Childhood

1. This portrait is derived from Billy G. Smith, *The "Lower Sort": Philadelphia's Laboring People, 1750–1800* (Ithaca, N.Y., 1990).

2. See, e.g., Carl and Jessica Bridenbaugh, *Rebels and Gentlemen: Philadelphia in the Age of Franklin* (New York, 1942).

3. Robert H. Bremner et al., eds., *Children and Youth in America: A Documentary History*, 3 vols. (Cambridge, Mass., 1970–74), I, 145–49.

4. Anthony F. C. Wallace, *Rockdale* (New York, 1978), 484.

5. Ibid., 180–83, 326–37.

6. Steven Mintz and Susan Kellogg, *Domestic Revolutions: A Social History of American Family Life* (New York, 1988), 87–91; Alexander Keyssar, *Out of Work: The First Century of Unemployment in Massachusetts* (Cambridge, 1986), 416–17, n. 35; Susan A. Glenn, *Daughters of the Shtetl: Life and Labor in the Immigrant Generation* (Ithaca, N.Y., 1990); David I. Macleod, *The Age of the Child: Children in America, 1890–1920* (New York, 1998), 6–10.

7. Wallace, *Rockdale*, 58–61, 64–67; Mintz and Kellogg, *Domestic Revolutions*, 84, 94–95. (Mintz and Kellogg rely on figures from Margaret F. Byington, *Homestead: The Households of a Mill Town* [New York, 1910], a graphic portrait of industrial life, including photos of children); Stephan Thernstrom, *Poverty and Progress: Social Mobility in a Nineteenth-Century City* (Cambridge, Mass., 1964), esp. 84–90, 106.

8. Robert Wells, *Revolutions in Americans' Lives* (Westport, Conn., 1982), 100–110. Wells also points to the huge internal migration; the 2.5 million mostly rural Americans who lived near the Atlantic Ocean in 1770 expanded to 100 million predominantly urbanites spread across North America by 1920 (110–24).

9. Oscar Handlin, *The Uprooted* (New York, 1951), 227–58; John Bodnar, *The Transplanted* (Bloomington, Ill., 1985), 57–84, 184–205; Mintz and Kellogg, *Domestic Revolutions*, 86–87. See also Selma Cantor Berrol, *Growing Up: American Immigrant Children in America Then and Now* (New York, 1995).

10. Stephan Thernstrom, ed., *Harvard Encyclopedia of American Ethnic Groups* (Cambridge, Mass., 1980), 405–25; Kathleen N. Conzen, *Immigrant Milwaukee, 1836–1860* (Cambridge, Mass., 1976), 50–61.

11. Hasia R. Diner, *Erin's Daughters in America: Irish Immigrant Women in the Nineteenth Century* (Baltimore, 1983), 3–4.

12. Ibid., 4–69; Thernstrom, *American Ethnic Groups*, 524–40; Charles H. Mindel et al., eds., *Ethnic Families in America*, 3rd ed. (New York, 1988), 45–56.

13. Diner, *Erin's Daughters*, 70–105.

14. Thernstrom, *American Ethnic Groups*, 545–56; Mindel, *Ethnic Families*, 109–12; John Bodnar et al., *Lives of Their Own: Blacks, Italians, and Poles in Pittsburgh, 1900–1960* (Urbana, Ill., 1982), 89–112; Virginia Yans-McLaughlin, *Family and Community: Italian Immigrants in Buffalo, 1880–1930* (Ithaca, N.Y., 1977). Yans-McLaughlin denies that immigration produced discontinuity in newcomers' lives, arguing that humans desire and therefore create continuity, in the case of Italians through the family. As she states it: "Tradition interpenetrates and facilitates social change" (22). On childhood as a stage of life, see 254.

15. Thernstrom, *American Ethnic Groups*, 787–98; Mindel, *Ethnic Families*, 17–40; Caroline Golab, "The Impact of the Industrial Experience on the Immigrant Family: The Huddled Masses Reconsidered," in R. L. Ehrlich, ed., *Immigrants in Industrial America, 1850–1920* (Charlottesville, Va., 1977), 1–32; John J. Bukowczyk, *Polish Americans and Their History* (Pittsburgh, 1996), 58–79; Paul

Wrobel, *Our Way: Family, Parish, and Neighborhood in a Polish-American Community* (Notre Dame, Ind., 1979), 77–86; Robert F. Hill, *Exploring the Dimensions of Ethnicity* (New York, 1980), 126–30, 206–10; Bodnar et al., *Lives of Their Own*, 89–112.

The Poles were the largest of many Slavic groups—Czechs, Slovaks, Ukranians, and Russians in the north, Croats, Serbs, and Slovenes in the south—who emigrated to the United States. I am using the Poles as a model of the others.

16. Thernstrom, *American Ethnic Groups*, 571–83; Glenn, *Daughters of the Shtetl*, 1–11, 16, 23, 48–49, 64–87, 125, 163–65; Sydney S. Weinberg, *The World of Our Mothers: The Lives of Jewish Immigrant Women* (Chapel Hill, N.C., 1988), 25–40, 105, 112–13, 118, 160–63, 173, 187, 192, 196, 259–60; Mary Antin, *The Promised Land* (Boston, 1912), 186.

17. Priscilla F. Clement, *Growing Pains: Children in the Industrial Age, 1850–1890* (New York, 1997), 54–62, 113–14, 131–49.

18. Mary E. Odem, *Delinquent Daughters: Protecting and Policing Adolescent Female Sexuality in the United States, 1885–1920* (Chapel Hill, N.C., 1995), 38–62.

19. Ibid., 71–74, 114–15, 184; Herbert Gutman, *The Black Family in Slavery and Freedom, 1750–1925* (New York, 1977), 432–52.

20. David Rothman, *The Discovery of Asylum: Social Order and Disorder in the New Republic* (Boston, 1971), introduction.

21. In addition to Rothman, see Joseph M. Hawes, *Children in Urban Society: Juvenile Delinquency in Nineteenth-Century America* (New York, 1971); Robert M. Mennel, *Thorns and Thistles: Juvenile Delinquents in the United States, 1825–1940* (Hanover, N.H., 1973); LeRoy Ashby, *Saving the Waifs: Reformers and Dependent Children, 1890–1917* (Philadelphia, 1984) and *Endangered Children: Dependency, Neglect, and Abuse in American History* (New York, 1997). See Steven L. Schlossman, *Love and the American Delinquent: The Theory and Practice of "Progressive" Juvenile Justice, 1825–1920* (Chicago, 1977), 219, n. 4, for differences of interpretation among these and other secondary accounts.

22. See W. J. Rorabaugh, *The Craft Apprentice: From Franklin to the Machine Age in America* (New York, 1986).

23. Boyer, *Urban Masses*, 34–53.

24. Schlossman, *Love*, 8–14. The challenge was *People v. Turner* (1870) in Illinois.

25. In 1900 less than a fifth of children in orphanages had lost both parents. David I. Macleod, *The Age of the Child: Children in America, 1890–1920* (New York, 1998), 17.

26. Boyer suggests that the asylum and the Sunday school shared important characteristics. *Urban Masses*, 95.

27. Rothman, *Discovery*, 260. Also, the lower-class, immigrant population of the institutions must have allowed middle-class citizens to rationalize the harsh treatment of inmates.

28. Schlossman, *Love*, 42–49; Boyer, *Urban Masses*, 82, 94–107. See also Marilyn Irvin Holt, *The Orphan Trains: Placing Out in America* (Lincoln, Nebr., 1992); Stephen O'Connor, *Orphan Trains: The Story of Charles Loring Brace and the Children He Saved and Failed* (Boston, 2001).

29. Rothman, *Discovery*, 260–87.

30. Bremner, *Children*, II, 502–99; Ronald D. Cohen, "Child-Saving and Progressivism, 1885–1915," in Joseph M. Hawes and N. Ray Hiner, eds., *American Childhood: A Research Guide and Historical Handbook* (Westport, Conn., 1985), 273–81; Anthony M. Platt, *The Child Savers: The Invention of Delinquency* (Chicago, 1977); Schlossman, *Love*, 66–78, 126–36; David Rothman, *Conscience and Convenience: The Asylum and Its Alternatives in Progressive America* (Boston, 1980),

205–12. Insofar as some of these interpretations are contradictory, Rothman's observation is well kept in mind: "In juvenile justice particularly, the ease with which proponents moved from one message to another, from the promise to uplift to the threat to coerce, testified to their ultimate confidence in the moral social superiority of the American system. There was no conflict between the helping power and the policing power because both sought to adjust the youthful deviant to an environment that provided optimal conditions for promoting his own well-being" (225).

31. Schlossman, *Love,* 136–88. The most renowned of the juvenile court judges, Ben Lindsey of Denver, appears to have been an exception to this generalization, but he is usually cited as *the* example of how well the courts operated.

32. Rothman, *Conscience,* 208, 222–30; Molly Ladd-Taylor, *Mother-Work: Women, Child Welfare, and the State, 1890–1930* (Urbana, Ill., 1994), 43–73.

33. Mary Ann Mason, *From Father's Property to Children's Rights: The History of Child Custody in the United States* (New York, 1994), 82, 86.

34. Ibid., 100–103; Elizabeth Pleck, *Domestic Tyranny: The Making of American Social Policy Against Family Violence from Colonial Times to the Present* (New York, 1987), 69–87; Linda Gordon, *Heroes of Their Own Lives: The Politics and History of Family Violence, Boston, 1880–1960* (New York, 1988).

35. Carl F. Kaestle, *Pillars of the Republic: Common Schools and American Society, 1780–1860* (New York, 1983), 66–72, 234–35 n. 3; Ira Katznelson and Margaret Wier, *Schooling for All: Class, Race, and the Decline of the Democratic Ideal* (New York, 1985).

36. David B. Tyack, "Ways of Seeing: An Essay on the History of Compulsory Schooling," *Harvard Educational Review* 46 (1976): 359–63; Priscilla F. Clement, "The City and the Child, 1860–1885," in Hawes and Hiner, *American Childhood,* 240–42, 247–48.

37. Clement, "The City and The Child," 247; Tyack, "Ways of Seeing," 364–73; Joseph M. Hawes, *Children Between the Wars: American Childhood, 1920–1940* (New York, 1997), 36–39.

38. Clement, "The City and the Child," 373–87; Paul C. Violas, *The Training of the Urban Working Class* (New York, 1978), 124.

39. Bremner, *Children,* II, 601–4, 611–34, 641–49, 703–5, 712–16; Jeremy P. Felt, *Hostages of Fortune: Child Labor Reform in New York State* (Syracuse, N.Y., 1965).

40. Jane Addams, *Twenty Years at Hull-House* (New York, 1910), 20–21 (1960 ed.).

41. David Nasaw, *Children of the City: At Work and at Play* (Garden City, 1985). I am unconvinced. See my critical review in the *New Leader,* August 12–26, 1985, 18–19. The case for using reports by contemporary middle-class social investigators, abetted where possible by working-class sources, as a way of viewing the work situations of young women (in the six to eight years between their early departures from school until their marriages) is made by Leslie Woodcock Tentler in *Wage-Earning Women: Industrial Work and Family Life in the United States, 1900–1930* (New York, 1979), 5–7.

42. Jacob Riis, *The Children of the Poor* (New York, 1892), 101.

43. Ibid., 39.

44. Ibid., 85–114; Grace Abbott, *The Child and the State,* 2 vols. (Chicago, 1938), I, 358–404, 598–636; Bremner, *Children,* II, 611–34.

45. David M. Katzman, *Seven Days a Week: Women and Domestic Service in Industrializing America* (Urbana, Ill., 1981), 155–67.

46. Marvin Lazerson, *Origins of the Urban School: Public Education in Massachusetts, 1870–1915* (Cambridge, 1971), xiv, 199–200.

47. Ibid., 36–73.

48. Byington, *Homestead,* 145–47. See Charles R. King, *Child Health in America* (New York, 1993), 50–54. King labels children's hospitals, "the most important legacy of the child-saving movement," 61–68. See also Jacob A. Riis, *How the Other Half Lives: Studies Among the Tenements of New York* (New York, 1890).

49. Dominick Cavallo, *Muscles and Morals: Organized Playgrounds and Urban Reform, 1880–1920* (Philadelphia, 1981), 2.

50. Ibid., 22.

51. Kriste Lindenmeyer, *"A Right to Childhood": The U. S. Children's Bureau and Child Welfare, 1912–46* (Urbana, Ill., 1997), 1, 24–30. See also Ladd–Taylor, *Mother-Work,* 74–103.

52. Lindenmeyer, "A Right to Childhood," 27–51.

53. Ibid., 62–63.

54. Ibid., 108–38.

55. Ibid., 76–107; Bremner, *Children,* II, 1003–25; Ladd-Taylor, *Mother-Work,* 17–26.

56. Ibid., II, 564–76, 1050–57; Margo Horn, *Before It's Too Late: The Child Guidance Movement in the United States, 1922–1945* (Philadelphia, 1989). Elizabeth Pleck suggests that psychoanalysis "furnished new ideas that undercut the moral outrage that family violence reform needs to flourish." *Domestic Tyranny,* 146.

57. Lindenmeyer, *"A Right to Childhood,"* 139–62. As a consequence of studying fatherless children, the Bureau went so far as to advocate mothers' pensions.

58. Ibid., 163–98; Bremner, *Children,* III, 519–38; Leroy Ashby, "Partial Promises and Semi-Visible Youths: The Depression and World War II," in Hawes and Hiner, *American Childhood,* 489–501.

59. Mintz and Kellogg, *Domestic Revolutions,* 133–49.

60. Glen H. Elder, Jr., *Children of the Great Depression* (Chicago, 1974), 32.

61. Cf. Robert L. Griswold, *Fatherhood in America: A History* (New York, 1993), 42–51.

62. Elder, *Children,* 62, 71, 78–80, 85, 88, 91, 93, 100, 102, 110–12, 114. See also John A. Clausen, *American Lives: Looking Back at the Children of the Great Depression* (New York, 1993), which argues that, while the impact of economic privation should not be ignored, a lot more was important in shaping the children who lived through the Depression. See also Ruth S. Cavan and Katherine H. Ranck, *The Family and the Depression: A Study of One Hundred Chicago Families* (Chicago, 1938).

63. Elder, *Children,* 151–75; William Tuttle, *"Daddy's Gone to War": The Second World War in the Lives of America's Children* (New York, 1993), 30–31, 45, 48.

64. Lindermeyer, *"A Right to Childhood,"* 202–47.

65. Quoted from *Parents' Magazine* in Terry Strathman, "From the Quotidian to the Utopian: Child-Rearing Literature in America, 1926–1946," *Berkeley Journal of Sociology* 19 (1984), 25.

66. Anzia Yezierska, *Children of Loneliness: Stories of Immigrant Life in America* (New York, 1923), 21.

6. Suburban Childhood

1. Four places with a population of 1 million or more accounted for less than 10 percent of the total population. *Abstract of the Fourteenth Census of the United*

States, 1920 (Washington, D.C., 1923), 75; Robert Wells, *Revolutions in Americans' Lives* (Westport, Conn., 1982), 219.

2. Looking at 29 metropolitan districts in 1920, one-quarter of the inhabitants lived outside the central cities. *Abstract of Fourteenth Census*, 87.

3. Kenneth T. Jackson, *Crabgrass Frontier: The Suburbanization of the United States* (New York, 1985), 103–230; see also Gwendolyn Wright, *Building the Dream: A Social History of Housing in America* (New York, 1981), 240–61.

4. David Riesman, *The Lonely Crowd: A Study in the Changing American Character,* abr. ed. (Garden City, N.Y., 1953), 42.

5. Roughly 35 percent of workers were in the service sector in 1920, as compared to 31.5 percent in 1910. *Abstract of Fourteenth Census*, 481–96. By 1929 it was 40 percent, in 1947 it reached 46 percent, and by 1976, 61 percent. Thomas M. Stanback, Jr., *Understanding the Service Economy* (Baltimore, 1979), 1.

6. Mrs. Max West, *Infant Care,* U.S. Children's Bureau, Publication no. 8 (Washington, D.C., 1914).

7. John B. Watson, *Behaviorism* (New York, 1924) and *Psychological Care of Infant and Child* (New York, 1928). Early in the century, Watson had attributed behavior to a combination of innate instincts and acquired habits, not unlike some of his fellow scientists, but by the 1920s he was committed to an exclusively environmental explanation. Elizabeth M. R. Lomax, *Science and Patterns of Child Care* (San Francisco, 1975), 109–29; Terry Strathman, "From the Quotidian to the Utopian: Child Rearing Literature in America, 1926–1946," *Berkeley Journal of Sociology* 29 (1984): 1–34; Celia B. Stendler, "Sixty Years of Child Training Practices," *Journal of Pediatrics* 36 (Jan.-June, 1950): 122–34; Clark E. Vincent, "Trends in Infant Care Ideas," *Child Development* 22, no. 3 (Sept. 1951): 199–209; Martha Wolfenstein, "Fun Morality: An Analysis of Recent American Child-Rearing Literature," in Margaret Mead and Martha Wolfenstein, eds., *Childhood in Contemporary Cultures* (Chicago, 1955), 168–78.

8. Lomax, *Science,* 6–44. Hall was president and professor of psychology at Clark University, which granted about one-quarter of all American doctorates in psychology in the 1920s, not to mention an honorary degree to Sigmund Freud in 1909, when the Viennese analyst was hardly acknowledged by American experimental psychologists.

9. Cravens, "Child-Saving," 415–88; Joseph M. Hawes, *Children Between the Wars: American Childhood, 1920–1940* (New York, 1997), 65–85. Commentaries by some of the participants can be found in Milton J. E. Senn, "Insights on the Child Development Movement in the United States," *Monographs of the Society for Research in Child Development,* ser. no. 161, 40 (August 1975).

10. Lucille C. Birnbaum, "Behaviorism in the 1920s," *American Quarterly* 7 (spring, 1955): 15–30.

11. Quoted in ibid., 12. Gesell, a student of Hall, believed (like his teacher) that the mind was innate—and also that most children could live up to their hereditary potential.

12. Gary Cross, *Kids' Stuff: Toys and the Changing World of American Childhood* (Cambridge, Mass., 1997), 51, 82–120.

13. Paula Fass, *The Damned and the Beautiful: American Youth in the 1920s* (New York, 1977), 55–57, 86–87; Robert L. Griswold, *Fatherhood in America: A History* (New York, 1993), 88–142.

14. Peter N. Stearns and Timothy Haggerty, "The Role of Fear: Transitions in American Emotional Standards for Children, 1850–1950," *American Historical Review* 96 (1991): 74–94.

15. Peter N. Stearns, "Girls, Boys, and Emotions: Redefinitions and Historical Change," *Journal of American History* 80 (1993–94): 54–74.

16. Peter N. Stearns, "Consumerism and Childhood: New Targets for American Emotions," in Peter N. Stearns and Jan Lewis, eds., *An Emotional History of the United States* (New York, 1998), 396–413.

17. Fass, *Damned*, 120–21.

18. Ibid., 53–71; Peter Uhlenberg, "Death and the Family," *Journal of Family History* 5 (1980): 313–20; Steven Mintz and Susan Kellogg, *Domestic Revolutions: A Social History of American Family Life* (New York, 1988), 107–31; Wells, *Revolutions*, 92, 96–100.

19. Fass, *Damned*, 3–9.

20. For example, an article in *Harper's* in 1920 accused the mothers of wild young people of being "indulgent and permissive, allowing their children to dominate the household." Quoted in Fass, *Damned*, 37.

21. Strathman notes that Watson "gave pride of place to the nineteenth-century ideal of the entrepreneur—the self-controlled, self-determining individual that [David] Riesman would come to call the 'inner-directed' personality." "From the Quotidian," 6–8, 21.

22. Hawes, *Children Between the Wars*, 122.

23. Glen H. Elder, Jr., *Children of the Great Depression: Social Change in Life Experience* (Chicago, 1974), 36. Robert Griswold observes that "the men most likely to weather unemployment and retain the love and respect of their children exhibited the 'modern' traits that composed the new fatherhood ... love, nurture, and admiration" (*Fatherhood*, 145). These were more often the characteristics of middle-class than working-class fathers.

24. Strathman, "From the Quotidian," 24–27.

25. William M. Tuttle, Jr., *"Daddy's Gone to War": The Second World War in the Lives of America's Children* (New York, 1993), 33, 226–28.

26. Griswold, *Fatherhood*, 176–82.

27. A version of this remembrance appeared in *New Leader*, February 8, 1971, 21.

28. Kenneth C. Davis, in *Two-Bit Culture: The Paperbacking of America* (Boston, 1984), 3, discusses the sales of *Baby and Child Care*. On *Infant Care*, see R. H. Bremner, "Families, Children, and the State," in R. H. Bremner and G. W. Reichard, eds., *Reshaping America: Society and Institutions, 1945–1960* (Columbus, Ohio, 1982), 11–12; Lawrence Cremin, *American Education: The Metropolitan Experience, 1876–1980* (New York, 1988), 287–88.

29. Spock, *Baby and Child Care*, 3.

30. Ibid., 42.

31. Sydney A. Halpern, *American Pediatrics: The Social Dynamics of Professionalism, 1880–1980* (Berkeley, Calif., 1988), 82.

32. Jacobi's successor at Columbia was L. Emmett Holt, author of *The Care and Feeding of Children* (New York, 1894); see Harold E. Harrison, "The History of Pediatrics in the United States," in *General Pediatrics*, 2–4. I have also been the beneficiary of information from Myron Genel, M.D., professor of pediatrics at Yale Medical School, and Morris A. Wessel, M.D., professor emeritus at Yale Medical School.

33. American Academy of Pediatrics, Committee for the Study of Child Health Services and Pediatric Education, *Child Health Services and Pediatric Education* (New York, 1949) as quoted in Robert H. Bremner et al., *Children and Youth in America: A Documentary History*, 3 vols. (Cambridge, Mass., 1974), III, 1283–88. On Truman, see Bremner, "Families, Children, and the State," 19.

34. AAP, *Lengthening Shadows: A Report of the Council on Pediatric Practice of the American Academy of Pediatrics* (Evanston, Ill., 1971) as quoted in Bremner, *Children*, III, 1313–17. See also Elliott West, *Growing Up in Twentieth-Century America*, (Westport, Conn., 1996), 226–31.

35. Lynn Z. Bloom, *Doctor Spock: Biography of a Conservative Radical* (Indianapolis, 1972), 32.

36. According to Ann Hulbert: "This wasn't an about face: he [Spock] was simply changing emphases, spelling out what he had earlier felt went without saying, or had merely mentioned in passing." *New Yorker,* June 20, 1996, 87. Third (1968), fourth (1976), and fifth (1985) editions appeared, the latter being a collaboration with Michael B. Rothenberg (see the *New York Times*, March 1, 1985; also March 5, 1992). I am quoting from the second edition.

37. Spock, *Baby and Child Care*, 4.

38. Ibid., 6–10.

39. Ibid., 324–27, 333–34.

40. Landon Y. Jones, *Great Expectations: America and the Baby Boom Generation* (New York, 1980), 25. Richard Easterlin renders a different interpretation of the baby boom, arguing that the decision to reproduce is largely the product of a couple's "relative income," that is, the ratio between earnings potential (very high in the prosperous baby boom years, 1946–60) and material aspirations (quite restrained, given the Depression experience of potential parents in the late 1940s and the 1950s). See *Birth and Fortune: The Impact of Numbers on Personal Welfare*, rev. ed. (Chicago, 1987), chap. 3.

41. Jones, *Great Expectations*, 1. Jones argues that "no single generation has had more impact on us.... The baby boom is, and will continue to be, the decisive generation in our history." Campbell Gipson, in "The Four Baby Booms," *American Demographics* 15 (November 1993): 36–40, follows that generation through its life stages. In *Declining Fortunes: The Withering of the American Dream* (New York, 1993), Katherine S. Newman looks not only at the conflicts between the affluent postwar parents and their adult progeny who are faced with economic struggle but also at the political division within the generation of baby boomers.

42. Jones, *Great Expectations*, 29–30, 59.

43. Charles E. Strickland and Andrew M. Ambrose, "The Baby Boom, Prosperity, and the Changing Worlds of Children, 1945–1963," in Hawes and Hiner, *American Childhood*, 536–38, 561–62; Mintz and Kellogg, *Domestic Revolutions*, 178–79. See also Elaine May, *Homeward Bound: American Families in the Cold War Era* (New York, 1988); Stephanie Coontz, *The Way We Never Were: American Families and the Nostalgia Trap* (New York, 1992); John R. Gillis, *A World of Their Own Making: Myth, Ritual, and the Quest for Family Values* (New York, 1996).

44. Ibid., 63–64. It is not evident why Spock believed so strongly in breast-feeding, since the issue of how best to obtain milk was by no means scientifically settled. See Clark E. Vincent, "Trends in Infant Care Ideas," *Child Development* 22 (September 1951): 197–203; Bettye M. Caldwell, "The Effects of Infant Care," in L. W. Hoffman and M. L. Hoffman, eds., *Review of Child Development Research* (Chicago, 1964), I, 19–41.

45. Lomax, *Science*, 67. Lomax observes that "psychoanalytic theories of child development had their greatest impact in the United States between 1940 and 1960" (73), using as an example the work of Erik Erikson (75). In my opinion, Erikson represents the conversion of Freudianism from an inner-directed to an other-directed perspective. Selma Fraiberg's *The Magic Years* (New York, 1959) is a more orthodox Freudian child-rearing manual.

46. A. Michael Sulman, "The Humanization of the American Child: Benjamin Spock as a Popularizer of Psychoanalytic Thought," *Journal of the History of the Behavioral Sciences* 9 (1973): 258–65; William G. Bach, "The Influence of Psychoanalytic Thought on Benjamin Spock's *Baby and Child Care*," ibid., 10 (1974): 91–94; *Who's Who in America*, 47th ed. (1992–93), XII, 92–93.

Freudian concepts are also evident in some of Spock's observations on parents. He advised that it was normal and permissible for mothers to harbor mixed feelings toward pregnancy or to react differently from one pregnancy to another. Mothers might come to love their babies only gradually or feel differently about one child than another. Fathers could have unexpected or even unwanted emotions toward a pregnant wife or a newborn child. Spock, *Baby and Child Care*, 10–23.

47. Mintz and Kellogg, *Domestic Revolutions*, 182–86; Paul S. Boyer et al., *The Enduring Vision*, 2nd ed., 2 vols. (Lexington, Mass., 1993), II, 973.

48. David Potter, *People of Plenty: Economic Abundance and the American Character* (Chicago, 1954), 193–208.

49. Ibid., 205.

50. Dictionaries, originally composed during the age of production, define both independence and autonomy in terms of inner-directedness, i.e., in terms of self. David Riesman has a more contextual definition: Autonomy is, of course, not unthinking adjustment to or rejection of the culture but, rather, an ability to transcend the culture and decide whether or not to conform. *The Lonely Crowd: A Study of the Changing American Character*, abr. ed. (New Haven, Conn., 1961), 239–49.

51. Robert Sklar, *Movie-Made America* (New York, 1975); Lary May, *Screening Out the Past: The Birth of Mass Culture and the Motion Picture Industry* (New York, 1980); Gerald Nachman, *Raised on Radio* (New York, 1998).

52. Statistics on households with television, multiple-set ownership, and time spent viewing can be found in Margaret S. Andreasen, "Evolution in the Family's Use of Television: Normative Data from Industry and Academe," in Jennings Bryant, ed., *Television and the American Family* (Hillsdale, N.J., 1990). See also Lynn Spiegel, *Make Room for TV: Television and the Family Ideal in Postwar America* (Chicago, 1992); J. E. Illick, "Kids and TV," *Connect for Kids Weekly*, September 20, 1999.

53. Wilbur Schramm et al., *Television in the Lives of Our Children* (Stanford, Calif., 1960), 12; John Condry, "Thief of Time, Unfaithful Servant: Television and the American Child," *Daedalus*, 122 (winter 1993): 259–78.

54. William Melody, *Children's Television* (New York, 1973) discusses the early years of kids' TV, while Edward L. Palmer, *Children in the Cradle of Television* (Lexington, Mass., 1987), focuses on the federal government's response. See also Douglas Cater and Stephen Strickland, *TV Violence and the Child: The Evolution and Fate of the Surgeon General's Report* (New York, 1975) and Edward L. Palmer and Aimee Dorr, eds., *Children and the Faces of Television: Teaching, Violence, Selling* (New York, 1980). Books attacking TV included Jerry Mander, *Four Arguments for the Elimination of Television* (New York, 1978); Marie Winn, *The Plug-in Drug* (New York, 1977; revised 1985); and Neil Postman, *The Disappearance of Childhood* (New York, 1982). Action for Children's Television was the most prominent of lobbying groups.

55. Edward L. Palmer, *Television and America's Children: A Crisis of Neglect* (New York, 1988).

56. See the National Institute of Mental Health's *Television and Behavior: Ten*

Years of Scientific Progress and Implications for the Eighties, 2 vols. (Rockville, Md., 1982). An industry response can be found in *Children's Television: The Art, the Business and How It Works* (Chicago, 1987) by Cy Schneider, who marketed the Barbie Doll and later led Nickelodean cable TV; he had only contempt for the reformers.

57. *New York Times,* March 4 and 8, 1993.

58. For the affimative on both questions, see Bernard Mergen, *Play and Playthings* (Westport, Conn., 1982); Mary and Herbert Knapp, *One Potato, Two Potato. . . : The Secret Education of Children* (New York, 1976).

59. Cross, *Kids' Stuff,* 121–87. For an account of a parents' group challenging the merchandising behavior of network TV, see Edward L. Palmer, *Children in the Cradle of Television* (Lexington, Mass., 1987), 31–34. See also William Melody, *Children's Television: The Economics of Exploitation* (New Haven, Conn., 1973), which comes as close as any book to being a history of the early years of kids' TV.

60. Charles Hamm, "Changing Patterns in Society and Music: The U.S. Since World War II," in Charles Hamm et al., eds., *Contemporary Music and Music Cultures* (Englewood Cliffs, N.J., 1975), 35–70.

61. James Gilbert, *A Cycle of Outrage: America's Reaction to the Juvenile Delinquent in the 1950s* (New York, 1986), 3–14. On the power of comics, see Jules Feiffer, *The Great Comic Book Heroes* (New York, 1965); J. E. Illick, "Big, Bad 'Mad,'" *New Leader,* October 27, 1969, 18–19. A half-century of *Mad* is now available on CD-ROM.

The matter of the generation gap, a term not yet used in the 1950s, is also related to the alienation of elite youth, a phenomenon which saw serious writers such as Paul Goodman and Kenneth Keniston siding with youth. Strickland and Ambrose, "Baby Boom," 566–68.

62. Arlene Skolnick, *Embattled Paradise: The American Family in an Age of Uncertainty* (New York, 1991), 84–90; John D'Emilio and Estelle B. Freedman, *Intimate Matters: A History of Sexuality in America* (New York, 1988), 302–8.

63. Gilbert, *Cycle of Outrage,* 5, 18–19.

64. Cremin, *American Education,* 230–36; Mintz and Kellogg, *Domestic Revolutions,* chap. 7, note 26. Robert L. Hampel points out that since retention and graduation rates were lower in black, rural, and poor areas, the rise in numbers of students must refer to white urban and suburban youth. *The Last Little Citadel: American High Schools Since 1940* (Boston, 1986), 1–22. See also Hawes, *Children Between the Wars,* 33–35; Fass, *Damned,* 210–11.

65. John Dewey and Evelyn Dewey, *Schools of Tomorrow* (New York, 1919), 303–16.

66. Hampel, *Last Little Citadel,* 1–22; J. E. Illick, *At Liberty: The Story of a Community and a Generation: The Bethlehem, Pennsylvania, High School Class of 1952* (Knoxville, Tenn., 1989).

67. Gilbert, *Cycle,* 17; Strickland and Ambrose, "The Baby Boom," 552–57. See also Ronald Lora, "Education: Schools as Crucible in Cold War America," in Bremner and Reichard, *Reshaping America,* 223–60; James S. Coleman, *The Adolescent Society: The Social Life of the Teenager and Its Impact on Education* (New York, 1961). Coleman investigated 10 high schools, different in size and community base, and found an adolescent culture segregated from the rest of American society.

68. Hampel, *Citadel,* 65–77.

69. The persistence of these problems is evident in Janet E. Gans et al., *America's Adolescents: How Healthy Are They?* (Chicago, 1990).

70. Ellen Greenberger and Laurence Steinberg, *When Teenagers Work: The Psychological and Social Costs of Adolescent Employment* (New York, 1986).

71. "A central theme of this book concerns what we judge to be a reduced integration of American adults into the social structure." Joseph Veroff et al., *The Inner American: A Self-Portrait from 1957 to 1976* (New York, 1981), 14–17. See also Skolnick, *Embattled Paradise*, 11–18.

72. Strickland and Ambrose, "Changing Worlds," 565.

73. Todd Gitlin, *The Sixties: Years of Hope, Days of Rage* (New York, 1987), 19–20, 107–8.

74. William L. O'Neill, *Coming Apart: An Informal History of America in the 1960s* (Chicago, 1971), 252–67. An alternative to O'Neill's skeptical view is furnished by Theodore Roszak in *The Making of a Counter Culture* (Garden City, N.Y., 1969). See also Kenneth Keniston, *The Uncommitted: Alienated Youth in American Society* (New York, 1965), strongly psychological with a focus on white middle-class youth; *Young Radicals: Notes on Committed Youth* (New York, 1968), which begins with a gathering called the Vietnam Summer of 1967 and moves on to a consideration of the New Left; and *Youth and Dissent: The Rise of a New Opposition* (New York, 1971).

75. Hampal, *Citadel*, 87–102. As the classroom atmosphere became more relaxed, parents began complaining that national test scores were declining. Ibid., 142–44.

76. Skolnick, *Embattled Paradise*, 5–8, 144–49, 201–6.

77. Frank F. Furstenberg, Jr. and Andrew J. Cherlin, *Divided Families: What Happens to Children When Parents Part* (Cambridge, Mass., 1991), 5–6. See also Andrew J. Cherlin, *Marriage Divorce Remarriage* (Cambridge, Mass., 1981).

78. Furstenberg and Cherlin, *Divided Families*, 6.

79. Joseph Veroff et al., *The Inner American: A Self-Portrait from 1957 to 1976* (New York, 1981), 14.

80. Judith Wallerstein and Joan Kelley, *Surviving the Breakup: How Children and Parents Cope with Divorce* (New York, 1980); Judith Wallerstein and Sandra Blakeslee, *Second Chances: Men, Women, and Children a Decade After Divorce* (New York, 1989); and Judith Wallerstein, Sandra Blakeslee, and Julia Lewis, *The Unexpected Legacy of Divorce: A 25-Year Landmark Study* (New York, 2000). See also E. Mark Cummings and Patrick Davies, *Children and Marital Conflict* (New York, 1994).

Regarding the emotional consequences of divorce, Douvan notes that there are only "small studies and limited samples" ("Age of Narcissism," 592). In 1991 Furstenberg and Cherlin were describing evidence regarding children's emotional response as "mixed," "limited," and "thin" (*Divided Families*, 73, 75, 76). A brief discussion of the debate appears in Sara McLanahan and Gary Sandefur, *Growing Up with a Single Parent* (Cambridge, 1994), 12–17.

81. Mary Ann Mason, *From Father's Property to Children's Rights: The History of Child Custody in the United States* (New York, 1994), 121–23, 149; Mason, *The Custody Wars* (New York, 1999), 2–3, 14–17, 21, 40. Mason also deals with the triumph of biologism, the awarding of custody on the basis of biological ties even in the face of strong emotional bonding to foster or adoptive parents. See also Lenore J. Weitzman, *The Divorce Revolution: The Unexpected Social and Economic Consequences for Women and Children in America* (New York, 1985), 262–322. A somewhat more sympathetic view of fathers appears in Griswold, *Fatherhood*, 219–39. But there is no doubting that fathers were withdrawing from their children's lives.

82. Victor R. Fuchs and Diane M. Reklis, "America's Children: Economic Perspectives and Policy Options," *Science* 255 (1992): 42 (Table 1), 43.

83. Kevin Phillips, *Boiling Point* (New York, 1993), 36 (and note table 1, p. 28). The long view on the 1980s begins with the social leveling that took place during the New Deal and continued with the expansion of the middle class after World War II and the effort to ameliorate poverty in the 1960s.

The economic policies of the 1970s and after are best described in Kevin Phillips, *The Politics of Rich and Poor: Wealth and the American Electorate in the Reagan Aftermath* (New York, 1990). For alternative explanations, see Frank Levy, *Dollars and Dreams. The Changing American Income Distribution* (New York, 1987), which focuses on cyclical change; Bennett Harrison and Barry Bluestone, *The Great U-Turn: Corporate Restructuring and the Polarizing of America* (New York, 1988), which emphasizes the private sector's response to globalism; Donald L. Bartlett and James B. Steele, *America: What Went Wrong?* (Kansas City, Kans., 1992), which claims the government has forgotten the middle class.

84. Fuchs and Reklis, "America's Children," 42.

85. Kingsley Davis, "Demographic Changes and the Future of Childhood," in L. L. Empey, ed., *The Future of Childhood and Juvenile Justice* (Charlottesville, Va., 1979), 112–37. Davis sees another barrier in family disorganization, the consequence of divorce and illegitimacy.

86. Fuchs and Reklis, "America's Children," 41–46. The focus here is more on the material than the cultural (e.g., effect of divorce) analysis of family issues, and the solution is found in government economic intervention.

87. Elliott A. Medrich et al., *The Serious Business of Growing Up: A Study of Children's Lives Outside School* (Berkeley, Calif., 1982). This study, based on a survey of 20 neighborhoods in Oakland, California, found that class differences hardly existed regarding use of time.

88. The suggestion of McLanahan, *Single Parent*, 153. In the Medrich study, children devoted less than an hour a day to organized activities.

89. Lawrence A. Cremin, *American Education: The Metropolitan Experience, 1876–1980* (New York, 1988), 645.

90. Hampel, *Last Little Citadel*, 143–44; Robert Bly, *The Sibling Society* (Reading, Mass., 1996), 6.

91. Larry Cuban, *How Teachers Taught: Constancy and Change in American Classrooms, 1890–1990*, 2nd ed. (New York, 1993). Of course, it would be accurate to say that students lacked respect for their teachers. Coleman, *Adolescent Society*, 5.

92. Arthur G. Powell et al., *The Shopping Mall High School: Winners and Losers in the Educational Marketplace* (Boston, 1985), 2.

After the Sputnik launching, when high schools were being damned for inadequacies in the teaching of math and science, Harvard president James Conant published *The American High School Today* (New York, 1959), advocating the comprehensive high school.

In *The Rise and Fall of the American Teenager* (New York, 1999), Thomas Hine depicts his subjects as the victims of high schools, as well as old-fashioned psychological thinking about adolescents. Hine, Powell et al., and Bly agree that teenagers need more enlightened leadership from their seniors.

93. Theodore R. Sizer, *Horace's Compromise: The Dilemma of the American High School* (Boston, 1992), x–xiii; Cuban, *How Teachers Taught*, 276–82. Cuban makes the case that the possibilities for reform are far greater in the lower grades, especially elementary schools where so little attention is paid to policy making, than the upper, where complaisance reigns: "Were policymakers deeply interested in

pursuing forms of schooling that aimed at cultivating the intellectual, social, and economic powers of individual children while creating democratic communities in schools, they would see that current classroom organization discourages students from learning from one another, limits the growth of independent reasoning and problem solving, restricts opportunities for student decision-making at the classroom and school level, and largely ignores the contributions that the community can make to the students and that students can make to the community" (278).

94. Dorothy Ross, *G. Stanley Hall: The Psychologist as Prophet* (Chicago, 1972), 325–33.

95. Colman, *Adolescent Society*, 2–4.

7. Inner-City and Rural Childhoods

1. Brent Staples, *Parallel Time: Growing Up in Black and White* (New York, 1994).

2. The myth of classlessness is pursued in Benjamin DeMott, *The Imperial Middle: Why Americans Can't Think Straight About Class* (New Haven, Conn., 1990).

3. Michael Harrington, *The Other America: Poverty in the United States* (New York, 1962), 49–50, 182–83.

4. William Issel points out, "Midway through the 1930s some 61 million Americans, making up 51 percent of the population, were poor, but in 1960 only 21 percent, or 39 million people were poor." *Social Change in the United States, 1945–1983* (New York, 1985), 140.

5. Harrington, *The Other America*, 4–6, and chaps. 3, 4, and 6. In *America's Struggle Against Poverty, 1900–1985*, rev. ed. (Cambridge, Mass., 1994), James T. Patterson observes, "When Americans 'rediscovered' poverty in the early 1960s, social scientists were appalled to realize how little they knew about it" (78). Patterson wrote that when he began his study (his book was first published in 1981) of poverty and welfare, "no historian had yet published a broad demographic history of the poor, a social history of poor people, or a synthetic study of the changing causes of poverty in the United State" (viii). See also James T. Patterson, "Poverty and Welfare in America, 1945–1960," in R. H. Bremner and G. W. Reichard, eds., *Reshaping America: Society and Institutions, 1945–1960* (Columbus, Ohio, 1982), 193–221.

Donald J. Henandez, *America's Children: Resources from Family, Government, and the Economy* (New York, 1993), 235–36, 245, fig. 7.1: "Children by Relative Income Levels, 1939–1988," and table 7.1, 246–47. See also Alvin L. Schorr, *Poor Kids* (New York, 1966), 11.

6. Elliott West, *Growing Up in Twentieth-Century America* (Westport, Conn., 1996), 314–21.

7. Walter I. Trattner, *From Poor Law to Welfare State: A History of Social Welfare in America*, 4th ed. (New York, 1989), 200–203; Patterson, *America's Struggle Against Poverty*, 67–71.

8. Early in the century Charles F. Weller wrote about the nation's capital: "Resourceful people live for years in attractive residences on the avenues without knowing or affecting in the slightest degree the life of the alley hovels just behind them." *Neglected Neighbors* (Philadelphia, 1909), 9, quoted in James Borchert, *Alley Life in Washington: Family, Community, Religion, and Folklife in the City, 1850–1970* (Urbana, Ill., 1980), 2.

9. R. H. Bremner, "Families, Children, and the State," in Bremner and Reichard, *Reshaping*, 22; Patterson, *America's Struggle Against Poverty*, 84–91.

10. Robert S. Lynd and Helen Merrell Lynd, *Middletown. A Study in Modern American Culture* (New York, 1929), esp. chap. 11. The Lynds' follow-up investigation, *Middletown in Transition: A Study in Cultural Conflicts* (New York, 1937), also showed minimal class difference regarding child rearing. Almost half a century later, Muncie was again surveyed; class differences had diminished, and there were still small contrasts in child-rearing practices. Theodore Caplow et al., *Middletown Families: Fifty Years of Change and Continuity* (Minneapolis, 1982), esp. chap. 7.

11. John E. Anderson, *The Young Child in the Home: A Survey of Three Thousand American Families* (New York, 1936), 23. Included in the survey were 202 black families with 321 children (3,779 white children were surveyed). The average black family was thought to resemble most the family of the white laboring class (269).

12. E. W. Burgess, *The Adolescent in the Family: A Study of Personality Development in the Home Environment* (New York, 1934), 112, 114. In his study of the effects of economic hardship on children, Glen H. Elder, Jr. occasionally introduced the class element, but he found deprivation a more dominant factor than class. See *Children of the Great Depression: Social Change in Life Experience* (Chicago, 1974), esp. 55, 87–97, 110–11, 124, 137.

13. Arguing that lower-class parents were more permissive were Martha C. Ericson, "Social Status and Child-Rearing Practices," in T. M. Newcomb and E. L. Hartley, eds., *Readings in Social Psychology* (New York, 1947), 494–501, and A. Davis and R. J. Havighurst, "Social Class and Color Differences in Child Rearing," *American Sociological Review* 11 (December 1946): 698–710. (Davis and Havighurst noted that class differences held regardless of race.) Finding that middle-class parents were more permissive were E. E. Maccoby et al., "Methods of Child-Rearing in Two Social Classes," in W. Martin and C. Stendler, eds., *Readings in Child Development* (New York, 1954), 380–96, and R. R. Sears et al., *Patterns of Child Rearing* (Evanston, Ill., 1957). (Note that this latter viewpoint is a product of the 1950s.) Pointing out that insignificant differences existed between classes were D. R. Miller and G. E. Swanson in *The Changing American Parent: A Study in the Detroit Area* (New York, 1958), esp. chap. 5. In stressing the growing divergence between entrepreneurial labor (small organizations where risk taking and competition could provide upward mobility) and bureaucratic work (large organizations with specialized positions offering job security), these two authors did see entrepreneurial middle-class parents to be the more controlling. One investigator observed that the standards of family evaluation were themselves middle-class; see C. S. Chilman, "Child-Rearing and Family Relationship Patterns of the Very Poor," *Welfare in Review* 2 (January 1965): 9–18.

14. Urie Bronfenbrenner, "Socialization and Social Class Through Time and Space," in Eleanor E. Maccoby et al., eds., *Readings in Social Psychology*, 3rd ed. (New York, 1958), 400–425; the effect of child-rearing literature is explicitly acknowledged.

15. Robert L. Griswold, *Fatherhood: A History* (New York, 1993), 187, 194, 208, 211–13, 252–54.

16. Charles E. Strickland and Andrew M. Ambrose, "The Baby Boom, Prosperity, and the Changing Worlds of Children, 1945–1963," in Joseph M. Hawes and N. Ray Hiner, eds., *American Childhood: A Research and Historical Handbook* (Westport, Conn., 1985), 550–51. But as Strickland and Ambrose observe, scholars judged black child-rearing methods from a special perspective: African Americans were seen as culturally deprived.

17. Richard Kluger, *Simple Justice: The History of* Brown v. Board of Education *and Black America's Struggle for Equality* (New York, 1975), 407–10.

18. Kluger, *Simple Justice*, 700–710.

19. Robert H. Mnookin, *In the Interest of Children. Advocacy, Law Reform, and Public Policy* (New York, 1985), 4–10. Mnookin and his fellow authors, looking at a variety of cases, wonder whether test-case litigation is a sensible way to promote the welfare of children.

20. Taylor Branch, *Parting the Waters: America in the King Years, 1954–1963* (New York, 1988) and *Pillar of Fire: America in the King Years, 1963–1965* (New York, 1998); Doug McAdam, *Freedom Summer* (New York, 1988); Howell Raines, *My Soul Is Rested: Movement Days in the Deep South Remembered* (New York, 1977); David Halberstam, *The Children* (New York, 1998); *Eyes on the Prize: America's Civil Rights Years*, 6 videotapes (Alexandria, Va., 1986); *Eyes on the Prize: America at the Racial Crossroads*, 8 videotapes (Alexandria, Va., 1990).

21. See J. Anthony Lukas, *Common Ground: A Turbulent Decade in the Lives of Three American Families* (New York, 1986).

22. Sheldon H. Danziger and Daniel H. Weinberg, eds., *Fighting Poverty: What Works and What Doesn't* (Cambridge, 1986), 1. Federal antipoverty programs have received bad reviews from the left; see Francis Fox Piven and Richard A. Cloward, *Regulating the Poor: The Functions of Public Welfare* (New York, 1971; 2nd ed., 1993), xv. W. Norton Grubb and Marvin Lazerson, *Broken Promises: How Americans Fail Their Children* (New York, 1982), 48; Michael B. Katz, *In the Shadow of the Poorhouse: A Social History of Welfare in America* (New York, 1986), 251. But none of these accounts refutes James Patterson, who points out: "Save for the World War II years that ended the Depression, no comparable period in American history witnessed such progress in diminishing poverty as did the 1960s and early 1970s" (162). The percentage of poor declined from 22 in 1959 to 11 in 1973 (160).

23. The statement was made by Sargent Shriver, head of the Office of Economic Opportunity. Edward Zigler and Sally J. Styfco, eds., *Head Start and Beyond: A National Plan for Extended Childhood Intervention* (New Haven, Conn., 1993), 3. Adam Yarmolinsky, one of John Kennedy's chief planners, later denied that the war on poverty was a "help-the-blacks program. . . . We said, 'Most poor people are not black, and most black people are not poor.'" Patterson, *Poverty*, 134.

24. Ibid., 146.

25. Ibid., 1–95. Johnson's statement is on 73.

26. Philip Greven, *The Protestant Temperament: Patterns of Child-Rearing, Religious Experience, and the Self in Early America* (New York, 1977), 39–40.

27. Dobson iterated his contempt for Benjamin Spock until he met and talked with him; apparently he had never read him. *Dare to Discipline* (Wheaton, Ill., 1970), 14–15; *The Strong-Willed Child* (Wheaton, Ill., 1978), 121–30.

28. Elizabeth M. R. Lomax, *Science and Patterns of Child Care* (San Francisco, 1975), 153–63. See also Genevieve Clapp, *Child Study Research: Current Perspectives and Applications* (Lexington, Mass., 1988), 13–16.

29. Later, when Kagen observed infants in Guatemala who received minimal maternal stimulation, he was unsurprised to discover that by age 10 they were alert and lively, able to remember and to analyze (1973). Lomax, *Science*, 90–92.

30. Ibid., 76–80. See also Ann M. Clarke and A. D. B. Clarke, *Early Experience: Myth and Evidence* (New York, 1976), 8–11. While Bowlby's statement sounds exaggerated, it would be silly to treat it as part of a conspiracy. But that is exactly what Diane E. Eyer does in *Mother-Infant Bonding: A Scientific Fiction* (New Haven, Conn., 1992), 1.

31. Lomax, *Science*, 88–90, 189–91; Clapp, *Child Study*, 2.

32. Bowlby, for example, drew on the idea of a critical period in his 1951 report to the United Nations on the importance of attachment. Lomax, *Science*, 170–79.

33. Ibid., 183–93.

34. Ibid., 196–97; Clapp, *Child Study*, 16–23; Clarke and Clarke, *Early Experience*, sec. 2–5. The most recent challenge to the importance of early experience is Judith Rich Harris's *The Nurture Assumption: Why Children Turn Out the Way They Do* (New York, 1998), which argues that a child's personality is formed not by his/her parents but by his/her peers.

35. Zigler and Styfco, *Head Start*, 8–13.

36. Grubb and Lazerson, *Broken Promises*, 167; Sar A. Levitan and Robert Taggert III, *The Job Crisis of Black Youth* (New York, 1971), 3–4.

37. Richard B. Freeman and Harry J. Holzer, eds., *The Black Youth Employment Crisis* (Chicago, 1986), 3.

38. LeRoy Ashby, *Endangered Children: Dependency, Neglect, and Abuse in American History* (New York, 1997), 127–31; Katz, *In the Shadow*, 252–54; Lester A. Sobel, *Welfare and the Poor* (New York, 1977).

39. Whether or not the conditions of poverty and welfare created a special group of people, an underclass, was a matter of debate. Ken Auletta, *The Underclass* (New York, 1982), argues that it did; this book contains little about children, unfortunately.

40. Ashby, *Endangered Children*, 131–32; Patterson, *Poverty*, 164–65.

41. Patterson points out that, although whites became more tolerant of blacks in the 1960s, attitudes about illegitimacy, female-headed families, and the movement of people of color into poor areas of large cities caused whites to think of blacks in terms of welfare. And indeed, though whites composed almost 70 percent of America's poor, the incidence of poverty among nonwhites (41 percent) was far higher than among whites (12 percent). *Poverty*, 110, 158.

42. Ibid., 166–67, 181–83; Grubb and Lazerson, *Broken Promises*, 192–95; "U.S. Welfare System Dies as State Programs Emerge," *New York Times*, June 30, 1997.

43. Katz, *In the Shadow*, 252–53, 257.

44. Moynihan, *The Negro Family: The Case for National Action* (Washington, D.C., 1965), 5–6, reprinted in Lee Rainwater and W. L. Yancey, eds., *The Moynihan Report and the Politics of Controversy* (Cambridge, Mass., 1967), 41–124, which assesses Moynihan's strategy and reprints reactions from the White House, intellectuals, and civil rights leaders. See also the brief discussions in Griswold, *Fatherhood*, 213–17, and Auletta, *Underclass*, 261–63, 268.

On African American families, see Eleanor Engram, *Science, Myth, Reality: The Black Family in One-Half Century of Research* (Westport, Conn., 1982); Charles V. Willie, *Black and White Families: A Study in Complementarity* (Bayside, N.Y., 1985); Richard A. Davis, *The Black Family in a Changing Black Community* (New York, 1993); Donna L. Franklin, *Ensuring Inequality: The Structural Transformation of the African American Family* (New York, 1997).

45. Herbert G. Gutman, *The Black Family in Slavery and Freedom, 1750–1925* (New York, 1976), xix, 432–60. See also Nicolas Lemann, *The Promised Land: The Great Black Migration and How It Changed America* (New York, 1991).

46. William Julius Wilson, *The Truly Disadvantaged: The Inner City, the Underclass, and Public Policy* (Chicago, 1987), 149.

47. Between 1960 and 1976 the number of black workers who held white-collar jobs doubled from one-sixth to one-third of the black workforce. Wilson,

Truly Disadvantaged, 7–8. See also Thomas J. Sugrue, *The Origins of the Urban Crisis: Race and Inequality in Postwar Detroit* (Princeton, N.J., 1996).

48. M. Belinda Tucker and Claudia Mitchell-Kernan, "Trends in African American Family Formation," in M. Belinda Tucker and Claudia Mitchell-Kernan, eds., *The Decline in Marriage Among African Americans* (New York, 1995), 21; Wilson, *Truly Disadvantaged,* 73. The government attempted to put a floor under income while opening the door to jobs through self-help. Patterson, *America's Struggle Against Poverty,* 185–98. Many factors explained joblessness; see Thomas M. Stanback Jr. et al., *Services: The New Economy* (Totowa, N.J., 1981), 71, 78–79.

49. See, for example, Kingsley Davis, "Demographic Changes and the Future of Childhood," in L. L. Empey, ed., *The Future of Childhood and Juvenile Justice* (Charlottesville, Va., 1979), 112–37. "If the black family was disorganized when Patrick Moynihan . . . wrote about it a few years ago," Davis wrote, "it is even more disorganized now." The consequences, he thought, were lawbreaking, suicide, drugs, and the like.

50. Carol B. Stack, *All Our Kin: Strategies for Survival in a Black Community* (New York, 1974). See also Nancy Tanner, "Matrifocality in Indonesia and Africa and Among Black Americans," in M. Z. Rosaldo and Louise Lamphere, eds., *Women, Culture, and Society* (Stanford, Calif., 1974), 129–56; Elijah Anderson, *Streetwise: Race, Class, and Change in an Urban Community* (Chicago, 1990), 112–37; Borchert, *Alley Life in Washington,* xii.

51. Andrew J. Cherlin and Frank F. Furstenberg, Jr., *The New American Grandparent: A Life in the Family, a Place Apart* (New York, 1986), 16, 127–31. Despite the title of their book and the obvious demographic fact that today grandparents live longer, Cherlin and Furstenberg find only modest changes in the role of grandparents over the past century. They point to racial but no class differences in grandparenting. See also Griswold, *Fatherhood,* 234.

52. *On the Edge: A History of Poor Black Children and Their American Dreams* (New York, 1993), 15–40, 79–107. Nightingale's story focuses on boys rather than girls; the latter are more the concern of Leon Dash in *When Children Want Children: The Urban Crisis of Teenage Childbearing* (New York, 1989). Griswold, *Fatherhood,* 239–42, discusses teenage fathers. See also Barry Silverstein and Ronald Krate, *Children of the Dark Ghetto: A Developmental Psychology* (New York, 1975).

53. Alex Kotlowitz, *There Are No Children Here: The Story of Two Boys Growing Up in the Other America* (New York, 1991).

54. Jonathan Kozol, *Savage Inequalities: Children in America's Schools* (New York, 1991), 40–82.

55. *Black Child Care* (New York, 1975), 11–12; reissued in 1992 as *Raising Black Children,* essentially the same book, Poussaint's disclaimers notwithstanding (*New York Times,* June 10, 1993).

A survey conducted in the 1960s showed that while 77 percent of white middle-class (and 48 percent of white working-class) mothers had read Dr. Spock, only 32 percent of black middle-class (and 12 percent of black working-class) mothers had read it. See Strickland and Ambrose, "The Baby Boom," in Hawes and Hiner, *American Childhood,* 550.

56. Comer and Poissant, *Raising Black Children,* 54. This caution bore comparison with the contemporaneous advice rendered by James Dobson, founder of the Christian Right organization Focus on the Family, who believed that the cardinal rule of child rearing should be submission of the child's will to the parent's, hence: "Two or three stinging strokes on the legs or bottom with a

switch are usually sufficient to emphasize the point: 'You must obey me.'" James Dobson, *The Strong-Willed Child* (Wheaton, Ill., 1978), 53–54.

57. Comer and Poussaint, *Black Child Care*, 61–65. Borrowing from Dr. Spock, one of the last sentences in both editions is "Relax and enjoy your children."

58. See his *Beyond Black and White* (New York, 1972), *Maggie's American Dream* (New York, 1988), and *Waiting for a Miracle* (New York, 1997).

59. Kozol, *Savage Inequalities*.

60. M. E. Goodman and Alma Beman, "Child's-Eye-Views of Life in an Urban Barrio," in N. N. Wagner and M. J. Haug, eds., *Chicanos: Social and Psychological Perspectives* (St. Louis, 1971), 109–19; Ellen Lewin, *Mothers and Children: Latin American Immigrants in San Francisco* (New York, 1980), 89–176; Angela L. Carrasquilla, *Hispanic Children and Youth in the United States* (New York, 1991), 89–130; Alejandro Garcia, "The Changing Demographic Face of Hispanics in the U.S.," in Marta Sotomayor, ed., *Empowering Hispanic Families: A Critical Issue for the '90s* (Milwaukee, Wisc., 1991), 21–38; Neil Fligstein and R. M. Fernandez, "Hispanics and Education," in Pastora San Juan Cafferty and W. C. McCready, eds., *Hispanics in the United States: A New Social Agenda* (New Brunswick, N.J., 1985), 113–46.

61. *Pan Asian Child Rearing Practices: Filipino, Japanese, Korean, Samoan, Vietnamese* (San Diego, Calif., 1982); Richard T. Sollenberger, "Chinese American Child-Rearing Practices and Juvenile Delinquency," *Journal of Social Psychology* 74 (1968): 13–23; Susan Matoba Adler, "Social, Historical, Political, and Cultural Settings of Japanese American Motherhood, 1940–1990: The Tradition of *Amae, Gambare,* and *Gaman* in the American Midwest," in Rima D. Apple and Janet Golden, eds., *Mothering and Motherhood* (Columbus, Ohio, 1997), 351–61.

62. Maxine Hong Kingston, *The Woman Warrior* (New York, 1977), 163–65.

63. The use of the terms "Hispanic," "Latino," and "Chicano" is discussed in Carrasquillo, *Hispanic Children*, 3. The 1990 Census counted 13.5 million Mexican Americans (mainly in California and Texas), 2.7 million Puerto Ricans (in or around New York City), 1 million Cuban Americans (primarily in Florida), and 5 million "other Hispanics" (the original residents of New Mexico and Central Americans in California), all in all 10.2 percent of the national population and predicted to replace African Americans as the largest minority by 2010.

Less than 4 percent of the U.S. population but the fastest-growing minority group, Asian Americans include the Chinese (1.6 million), Filipinos (1.4 million), Indian, Japanese, Korean (each 1 million), and Vietnamese (0.6 million), according to the 1990 Census.

64. Marcelo M. Suarez-Orozco, *Central American Refugees and U.S. High Schools* (Stanford, 1989); Jeremy Hein, *From Vietnam, Laos, and Cambodia: A Refugee Experience in the United States* (New York, 1995); Frederick L. Ahearn, Jr. and Jean L. Athey, eds., *Refugee Children* (Baltimore, 1991).

65. Alejandro Portes and Ruben G. Rumbaut, *Immigrant America: A Portrait,* 2nd ed. (Berkeley, Calif., 1966), ix, xxiii, 6–8; Alejandro Portes, ed., *The New Second Generation* (New York, 1996); Ruben G. Rumbaut and Wayne A. Cornelius, eds., *California's Immigrant Children* (San Diego, Calif., 1995); Selma Cantor Berrol, *Growing Up American: Immigrant Children in America Then and Now* (New York, 1995).

66. Portes and Rumbaut, *Immigrant America*, 245–53. See also, James Diego Vigil, *Personas Mexicanas: Chicano High Schoolers in a Changing Los Angeles* (Fort Worth, Tex., 1997); Carola and Marcelo Suarez-Orozco, *Transformations: Immigration, Family Life, and Achievement Motivation Among Latino Adolescents* (Stanford, Calif., 1995).

67. Esmeralda Santiago, *Almost a Woman* (Reading, Mass., 1998), 26–27.

68. Nathan Caplan et al., *The Boat People and Achievement in America: A Study of Family Life, Hard Work, and Cultural Values* (Ann Arbor, Mich., 1989), 70–75, 111–14. See also Portes and Rumbaut, *Immigrant America*, 243–44. A less optimistic portrait of the Indochinese young is drawn in Hein, *From Vietnam, Laos, and Cambodia*, esp. 121–28.

69. Pyong Gap Min, *Changes and Conflicts: Korean Immigrant Families in New York* (Boston, 1998), 66–72.

70. Malcolm W. Klein, *The American Street Gang: Its Nature, Prevalence, and Control* (New York, 1995), 72–76, 82–85, 105–12. See also James Diego Vigil, *Barrio Gangs: Street Life and Identity in Southern California* (Austin, Tex., 1988). Sanyika Shakur, a.k.a. Monster Kody Scott, *Monster: The Autobiography of an L.A. Gang Member* (New York, 1994), provides a graphic account of gang activity.

71. Gilbert, *Outrage*, 128, 139.

72. Eric C. Schneider, "Performing Masculinity: Streetgangs in Postwar New York," paper delivered at childhood conference, Benton Foundation, Washington, D.C., August 6, 2000, based on the author's *Vampires, Dragons, and Egyptian Kings: Youth Gangs in Postwar New York* (Princeton, N.J., 1999). The movement from social to psychological interpretation is dealt with concisely in Mercer L. Sullivan, *"Getting Paid": Youth Crime and Work in the Inner City* (Ithaca, N.Y., 1989), 3–8. A recent psychological interpretation is James Garbarino, *Lost Boys: Why Our Sons Turn Violent and How We Can Save Them* (New York, 1999).

73. Elizabeth Pleck, *Domestic Tyranny: The Making of American Social Policy Against Family Violence from Colonial Times to the Present* (New York, 1987), 164.

74. In "Child Abuse in Context: An Historical Perspective," in his book *Past, Present, and Personal* (New York, 1986), 68–88, John Demos takes the former view, while Philip Greven, in *Spare the Child: The Religious Roots of Punishment and the Psychological Impact of Physical Abuse* (New York, 1991), takes the latter. See also Murray A. Straus, *Beating the Devil Out of Them: Corporal Punishment in American Families* (New York, 1994).

75. Pleck, *Domestic Tyranny*, 164–66.

76. Ibid., 166–81; Ashby, *Endangered Children*, 132–37; Ray E. Helfer and C. Henry Kempe, eds., *The Battered Child* (Chicago, 1968).

77. Pleck, *Domestic Tyranny*, 171–72; Ashby, *Endangered Children*, 146–47, 179–81.

78. Ashby, *Endangered Children*, 136–37; Robert T. Ammerman and Michael Hersen, eds., *Children at Risk* (New York, 1990), 24–27; Griswold, *Fatherhood*, 255.

79. Ashby, *Endangered Children*, 137.

80. Ibid., 137–41. For outrageous examples of child abuse, of continuing battles over child protective services, and of the introduction of *sexual* abuse into the controversy in the 1980s, see ibid., 160–67. Ashby concludes: "By commanding so much attention, the horrific incidents and sensational trials ultimately overshadowed the underlying poverty and other devastating social ills that jeopardized millions of American children. And given the shifting political mood of the late twentieth century, there was little chance that those ills would receive much consideration." Some of the political players in the move to restore orphanages gave weight to Ashby's gloomy conclusion. Ibid., 175–78.

81. Ibid., 141–46, 168–70. Andrew Billingsly, in *Children of the Storm: Black Children and American Child Welfare* (New York, 1972), argued that racism pervaded child welfare services.

82. E. Wayne Carp, *Family Matters: Secrecy and Disclosure in the History of Adoption* (Cambridge, Mass., 1998).

83. Ashby, *Endangered Children*, 170–73.

84. Sonya Michel, *Children's Interests/Mothers' Rights* (New Haven, Conn., 1999), 1–117, argues that the deeply held belief that mothers should remain in the home undermined universal child care. An older study is Margaret O'Brien Steinfels, *Who's Minding the Children?* (New York, 1973).

85. Michel, *Children's Interests*, 118–235.

86. Penelope Leach, *Your Baby and Child* (New York, 1977), *Babyhood* (New York, 1976), *The First Six Months* (New York, 1986), *Children First* (New York, 1994); Gwen Kinkead, "Penelope Leach," *New York Times*, April 10, 1994; T. Berry Brazelton, *Infants and Mothers* (New York, 1959), *Toddlers and Parents* (New York, 1974), *On Becoming a Family* (New York, 1981), *Working and Caring* (New York, 1984), Fred Clement, "Dr. Spock's Successor," *Princeton Alumni Weekly*, January 28, 1987.

87. Michel, *Children's Interests*, 236–51.

88. Ibid., 252–80.

89. Edward F. Zigler and Mary E. Lang, *Child Care Choice: Balancing the Needs of Children, Families, and Society* (New York, 1991), 1–26, 45–53.

90. John Gliedman and William Roth, *The Unexpected Minority: Handicapped Children in America* (New York, 1980), 5.

91. Ibid., 173–76.

92. Ibid., 176–82.

93. Margaret A. Winzer, *The History of Special Education: From Isolation to Integration* (Washington, D.C., 1993), 77–224, 251–385.

94. David B. Danbom, *Born in the Country: A History of Rural America* (Baltimore, 1995), 161–72; William L. Bowers, *The Country Life Movement in America, 1900–1920* (Port Washington, N.Y., 1974).

95. John G. Clark et al., *Three Generations in Twentieth-Century America: Family, Community, and Nation* (Homewood, Ill., 1977), 9–13, 51–54, 62–65, 78, 187–91, 294–99, 392–97, 463–67.

96. Martha van Renssalaer et al., *The Home and the Child* (New York, 1931), 141–43.

97. Grace Abbott, *The Child and the State*, 2 vols. (Chicago, 1938), I, 564–65.

98. Robert Coles, *Migrants, Sharecroppers, Mountaineers* (Boston, 1971), 71.

99. Ibid., 83, 90, 103.

100. Abbott, *Child and the State*, I, 565–69.

Epilogue

1. In *When the Bough Breaks: The Cost of Neglecting Our Children* (New York, 1991), economist Sylvia Ann Hewlett argues that children suffer a resource deficit (e.g., in 1989 the federal government spent 11 times as much on each senior over 65 as on each child under 18) and a time deficit (which she attributes, erroneously I think, to self-indulgent parents). In *American Childhood: Risks and Realities* (New Brunswick, N.J., 1995), epidemiologist Dona Schneider discusses health risks (e.g., two-thirds of deaths between ages 1 and 19 are caused by injuries, often preventable), education risks, and economic and social risks (poverty, child care, working teens, crime, abuse and neglect). In *Today's Children: Creating a Future for a Generation in Crisis* (New York, 1992), David A. Hamburg, after comparing the gradualness of biological evolution to the speed of technological change, focuses on early childhood (prenatal and preventative health

care, importance of attachment, child care) and early adolescence, a stage longer (in evolutionary terms) and socially more dangerous than ever; this well-informed and thoughtful book emphasizes the need for social support of the young. Hamburg was president of the Carnegie Corporation (437 Madison Avenue, New York, NY 10022) when it issued *Starting Points: Meeting the Needs of Our Youngest Children* (New York, 1994). In *The Vulnerable Child: What Really Hurts America's Children and What We Can Do About It* (Reading, Mass., 1996), Richard Weissbourd adds a personal interview dimension to a discussion of the problems which all observers seem to agree upon. In *Succeeding Generations: On the Effects of Investments in Our Children* (New York, 1994), Robert Haveman and Barbara Wolfe assert that "one of the most useful ways of understanding the level of children's success and attainment in our society is by viewing children as human capital" (241), a perspective that allows them to conduct a careful and revealing study. Some other examples: "America's Childhood," *Daedalus* 122 (winter 1993), which contains essays, often thoughtful, several on the difficult topic of education, from a variety of perspectives; "Who Cares About the Kids?" *Utne Reader* 57 (May/June 1993); "What Grown-Ups Don't Understand: A Special Issue on Childhood in America," *New York Times Magazine*, October 8, 1995.

2. Almost one-third of today's infants are born to unmarried mothers, and almost half the children born to married parents are predicted to experience divorce. Sara McLanahan and Gary Sandefur, *Growing Up with a Single Parent* (Cambridge, Mass.,1994), 2. How do the facts of women in the workforce and mothers independently running households affect the rearing of children, especially daughters? Since the rising divorce rate has been accompanied by a steep incline in the number of mothers who never married, the question seems even more urgent.

3. Donald J. Hernandez, *America's Children. Resources from Family, Government, and the Economy* (New York, 1993). See also Federal Interagency Forum on Child and Family Statistics, *America's Children: Key National Indicators of Well-Being* (Washington, D.C., 1998).

4. Hernandez, *America's Children*, 149.

5. Ibid., 12. Greg J. Duncan and Jeanne Brooks-Gunn, eds., *Consequences of Growing Up Poor* (New York, 1997), a volume in which several dozen demographers, developmental psychologists, economists, educationists, psychiatrists, social workers, and sociologists analyze virtually every aspect of poverty's effect on children. In *Succeeding Generations: On the Effects of Investments in Children* (New York, 1994), economists Robert Haveman and Barbara Wolfe analyze factors that contribute to the economic success of children, including family and neighborhood characteristics, schooling, teenage pregnancy and welfare receipt, and economic inactivity.

6. Hernandez, *America's Children*, 107, 135.

7. Ibid., 146, 150, 165, 190

8. Ibid., 235, 248, 261–64.

9. A comprehensive recent summary of these matters appears in Reynolds Farley, ed., *State of the Union*, 2 vols. (New York, 1995), where 18 demographers, economists, sociologists, and urban planners discuss employment and income, education, housing and living arrangements, immigration, and diversity, all of which directly or indirectly affect children. See also Reynolds Farley, *The New American Reality: Who We Are, How We Got Here, Where We Are Going* (New York, 1996), a follow-up to *State of the Union* which treats race, gender, sex, the economy, the family, immigrants, and internal migration. But the author does not

have children in mind when he states unequivocally: "We are better off now than in the past" (334).

10. The most prominent of these is the Children's Defense Fund (25 E Street NW, Washington, DC 20001), which publishes *The State of America's Children Yearbook*. See "On Mounting Effective Child Advocacy," *Proceedings of the American Philosophical Society* 119, no. 6 (December 1975): 470–78, by Marian Wright Edelman, founder and director of CDF. See also "An Interview with Marian Wright Edelman," *Harvard Educational Review* 44 (1974): 53–73; Hillary Rodham (then with CDF), "Children Under the Law," ibid. 43 (1973): 487–514.

In 1993 the American Bar Association's Presidential Working Group on the Unmet Legal Needs of Children and Their Families published *America's Children at Risk: A National Agenda for Legal Action*. Also by lawyers: Thomas A. Nazario, *In Defense of Children: Understanding the Rights, Needs, and Interests of the Child* (New York, 1988), which contains information not only on children's legal rights but also on medical care, education, and social services; and Robert H. Mnookin, *Child, Family, and State: Problems and Materials on Children and the Law* (Boston, 1978), which focuses on legal precedents that have decided children's issues.

The Committee for Economic Development (477 Madison Avenue, New York, NY 10022) publishes occasional reports, e.g., *Investing in Our Children: Business and the Public Schools* (1985); *Children in Need: Investment Strategies for the Educationally Disadvantaged* (1987). The Columbia University School of Public Health issues a newsletter, *National Center for Children in Poverty*, three times a year. The Benton Foundation (1634 Eye Street NW, Washington, DC 20006) publishes a weekly newspaper, *Connect for Kids: Guidance for Grown-Ups* (www.connectforkids.org).

A Note on Sources

1. One of these chapters was mine. My assessment of deMause's work, "Does the History of Childhood Have a Future?" appears in the *Journal of Psychohistory* 13 (1985–86): 159–72.

2. In "Looking for Waldo: Reflections on the History of Children and Childhood," a thoughtful and judicious paper presented at the History of Childhood in America Conference, Washington, D.C., August 5, 2000, N. Ray Hiner and Joseph M. Hawes cited Therese Benedict's observation that parents can move backward as well as forward in response to their experience with children (note 14).

3. John Snarey's *How Fathers Care for the Next Generation: A Four-Decade Study* (Cambridge, Mass., 1993) is also a longitudinal approach.

4. "The Self Shaped and Misshaped: *The Protestant Temperament* Reconsidered," in Ronald Hoffman et al., eds., *Through a Glass Darkly: Reflections on Personal Identity in Early America* (Chapel Hill, N.C., 1997).

5. Daniel Scott Smith, "The Demographic History of Colonial New England," *Journal of Economic History* 32 (March 1972): 165–83; "Parental Power and Marriage Patterns: An Analysis of Historical Trends in Hingham, Massachusetts," *Journal of Marriage and the Family* 35 (August 1973): 419–28; "Family Limitation, Sexual Control, and Domestic Feminism in Victorian America," *Feminist Studies* 1 (winter-spring 1973): 40–57; (with M. Hingus), "Premarital Pregnancy in America, 1640–1971: An Overview and Interpretation," *Journal of*

Interdisciplinary History 5 (spring 1975): 537–70; "Child-Naming Practices as Cultural and Familial Indicators," *Local Population Studies* 32 (spring 1984): 17–27; "Early Fertility Decline in America: A Problem in Family History," *Journal of Family History* 12 (April 1987): 73–84; "American Family and Demographic Patterns and the Northwest European Model," *Continuity and Change* 8 (December 1993): 389–415; "'The Number and Quality of Children': Education and Marital Fertility in Early Twentieth-Century Iowa," *Journal of Social History* 30 (winter 1996): 367–92.

See also Robert V. Wells, *Revolutions in Americans' Lives: A Demographic Perspective on the History of Americans, Their Families, and Their Society* (Westport, Conn., 1982); *Uncle Sam's Family: Issues in and Perspectives on American Demographic History* (Albany, N.Y., 1985).

6. John Bowlby, *Attachment and Loss,* 3 vols. (New York, 1969–80). Attachment theory is not actually a theory but a conceptual framework based on the principles of evolution and ethology informed by modern biology. Bowlby turned not only to evolution and ethology as explanatory tools but also to cybernetics. Attachment behavior, from the perspective of control systems theory, was modified in response to feedback.

Everyone, says Bowlby, whatever his/her cultural milieu, retains an atavistic awareness of the perils of being unprotected. Thus, a human infant attaches itself to a caregiver (and vice versa), a bonding that begins when the young one is 3–6 months old and is complete in most cultures by 18 months. Any threat to that attachment creates fear in the child, and that fear, unattended to, escalates into what Bowlby terms anxiety, the antithesis of security.

Consistent caregiving promotes greater security and, eventually, tolerance for separation from the caregiver as the child builds confidence. Attachment, far from fostering dependence, nutures autonomy. Prolonged separation has the opposite effect. The quality of infant attachment plays a major—but not the only—role in child *and adult* emotional life.

7. Alison Gopnik, Andrew Meltzoff, and Patricia K. Kuhl, *The Scientist in the Crib: What Early Learning Tells Us About the Mind* (New York, 1999), 18–19, 200.

8. Robert Coles, *Children of Crisis,* 5 vols. (Boston, 1967–77); *Uprooted Children: The Political Life of Children* (Boston, 1986); *The Moral Life of Children* (Boston, 1986); *The Spiritual Life of Children* (Boston, 1990); *The Moral Intelligence of Children* (New York, 1997); (with Joseph Brenner and Dermot Meagher) *Drugs and Youth* (New York, 1971); (with Jerome Kagan), *Twelve to Sixteen: Early Adolescence* (New York, 1972).

9. Frank J. Sulloway, *Born to Rebel: Birth Order, Family Dynamics, and Creative Lives* (New York, 1996); Judith Rich Harris, *The Nurture Assumption: Why Children Turn Out the Way They Do* (New York, 1998).

10. R. O. Humm, *Children in America: A Study of Images and Attitudes* (Atlanta Ga., 1978); M. L. S. Heininger et al., *A Century of Childhood, 1820–1920* (Rochester, N.Y., 1984); *Centuries of Childhood in New York* (New York, 1984); *Young America: Children and Art* (Sandwich, Mass., 1985).

Index

Acknowledgments

Lloyd deMause prompted me to enter the field of childhood history more than a quarter-century ago. He also brought my cousin, the late John Walzer, into the enterprise, which further encouraged me. My colleagues in the Department of History at San Francisco State University enabled me to offer a course in the history of childhood, even though some of them were skeptical. Funding from the National Endowment for the Humanities was helpful in developing a slide show on the history of American childhoods, which I showed at colleges and universities (University of California at Berkeley, Case-Western Reserve University, Lehigh University, University of Nevada at Reno, University of Oregon, San Diego State University, University of Vermont, and Swarthmore College), gatherings of historians (Bay Area Colonial historians, Pacific Coast Branch of the American Historical Association, Philadelphia Center for Early American Studies), and meetings of professionals (Child Assault Prevention Training Center of Northern California, Kaiser Permanente Hospital, WestCoast Children's Center). The responses from these audiences sharpened my thinking about the subject.

Two of my colleagues at San Francisco State, Paul Longmore and Moses Rischin, aided my understanding of disabled children and immigrant children, while Leon Litwack at the University of California, Berkeley, lent insights into African American children, slave and free, in the nineteenth century. Jim Rawls at Diablo Valley College improved my chapter on American Indians, while Jim Axtell at the College of William and Mary led me to visual sources on the same topic. Margo Horn of Stanford University read substantial portions of the manuscript, much to my advantage, as did Philip Greven of Rutgers University, who has been supportive of my efforts in the field of childhood studies for many years. Kriste Lindenmeyer of the University of Maryland, Baltimore, offered me thoughtful suggestions on the reorganization of this book, which I was grateful to receive. Aubrey Metcalf, M.D., taught me attachment theory and rendered provocative psychological judgments on some of the actors in the early chapters of the study. Morris Wessel, M.D. of Yale University provided enlightenment on pediatric developments in twentieth-century America. Joe Hawes of Memphis State University and Ray Hiner of the University of Kansas have served as beacons in the sometimes-treacherous field of the history of childhood. Bob Lockhart at the University of Pennsylvania Press has been a never-failing source of information, good sense, and support; he enormously facilitated the publishing of this book, as did Audra Wolfe and Erica Ginsburg. The shortcomings of the book are, of course, mine.